Smart Governance and Policy

Korean Experience: From E-Government to Smart Governance

도서출판 윤성사 250

Smart Governance and Policy
Korean Experience: From E-Government to Smart Governance

제1판 제1쇄   2024년 8월 30일

지 은 이   Seunghwan Myeong (명승환)
펴 낸 이   정재훈
꾸 민 이   안미숙

펴 낸 곳   도서출판 윤성사
주　　소   서울특별시 용산구 효창원로 64길 10 백오빌딩 지하 1층
전　　화   대표번호_02)313-3814 / 영업부_02)313-3813 / 팩스_02)313-3812
전자우편   yspublish@daum.net
등　　록   2017. 1. 23

ISBN 979-11-93058-53-4 (93350)
값 17,000원

ⓒ Seunghwan Myeong, 2024

지은이와의 협의에 따라 인지를 생략합니다.

이 책의 전부 또는 일부 내용을 재사용하려면 반드시 사전에 저작권자와 도서출판 윤성사의 동의를 받아야 합니다.
All Rights Reserved. Please do not use or cite without permission.

잘못 만들어진 책은 구입하신 서점에서 교환 가능합니다.

For the betterment and future of the global community and society,
Social science research and practice,
I dedicate this book to all of you.

Smart Governance and Policy

Korean Experience: From E-Government to Smart Governance

Seunghwan Myeong

YOONSEONGSA

Preface

In the digital transformation era triggered by the Fourth Industrial Revolution, we need a good government that is open-minded, problem-solving, and satisfying to the people. This is only possible through accumulating and disclosing data that everyone can relate to, a public discussion process, and fair and transparent enforcement. In the era of self-governance, we need an open and smart government that can present seemingly feasible policies based on high expertise and accurate future forecasting, as well as conflict management and support. The government must provide a platform for a hyper-connected, socialized sharing economy that goes beyond simply being an intermediary service that connects surplus resources and services through social media. The government, businesses, and people of Korea should be able to access the country's human and material resources anytime, anywhere, and through various access methods, where breakthrough ideas and concrete commoditization and servitization are discussed and traded daily. Such a strategy is an appropriate alternative for a country like Korea, which has a successful track record in the information society and e-government. However, the centralized approach of the past should not be repeated. In the future, the government should play the role of catalyst, enabler, and mediator between public and private markets based on expertise and communication. It should seek to create a better environment for successful domestic companies to enter the larger global market and a truly public role for small and medium-sized enterprises, youth, and vulnerable groups frustrated by repeated failures, giving them a second chance and a platform for hope. We need open policies and smart government for 21st-century coexistence, and this is the basic foundation for government innovation based on digital platforms that people can relate to.

Future societies share a common goal of reconciling ideals and reality, a citizen-centered state, ubiquitous digitalization, artificial intelligence (AI) as water, data-driven work and policies, and open, community-oriented societies. In recent years, "agile" business management strategies have emerged as a keyword for the organizations of the future. Quick decisions and consensus building summarize agile management, rapid planning and experimentation of ideas, correction through failure, platform-centered production and consumption sharing networks, and utilization of digital convergence technologies. It emphasizes meeting frequently to make decisions and take action. It prefers simple, clear strategies and tangible rewards that excite and move the organization and its people rather than creating new organizations. Globally, future societies share a common vision of a citizen-centric state, digital ubiquity, easy use of artificial intelligence (AI) across all sectors of society, data-driven practices and policies, and open, community-driven societies. In this regard, "agile" and "nudge" strategies have recently emerged as keywords for future policymaking and organizational operations. Agile techniques are summarized as quick decisions and consensus building, rapid planning and experimentation of ideas, correction through failure, platform-centered production and consumption sharing networks, and utilization of digital convergence technologies. Nudge strategies emphasize that "gentle interventions that guide people's choices" are paramount in actual policy processes and organizational operations and highlight the role of the "choice architect," the person who creates the "context" for people to make decisions. The untact era caused by the Fourth Industrial Revolution and COVID-19 demands talented people who can grasp the big trends of the times based on accurate data analysis and communication skills to make timely decisions and implement them.

To reach the world-class level, Korea's e-government needs to develop by implementing user-oriented or customer-centered e-government services and including all classes and members of society. In the past, efforts have been made to implement e-government. Still, the process of reflecting the needs of the service's customers by building a system centered on the provider has been insufficient. It is because e-government has been focused on quantitative growth, such as infrastructure expansion, salinization of administrative services, and development of new administrative services, and the way to improve the public's awareness and utilization of e-government services has been focused on simply increasing the number of services. Developing and implementing community e-government services must avoid making the same mistakes. To plan and build community e-government services close to residents, it is necessary to provide services by simply converting existing administrative services into platform-type services centered on the cloud. Implementing e-government services in a way that unilaterally provides services that the provider considers important should be avoided without identifying customer demand for the existing administrative services. Therefore, the demand for the quality of services customers want when receiving administrative services should be fully reflected to enable the active use of various digital services. In the future, the service delivery method based on open platforms is expected to be an important strategic project due to the spread of big data, the Internet of Things (IoT), and multi-channel. In particular, it is necessary to innovate the public service delivery system through various forms and channels so that public services can be provided to all citizens, including the vulnerable in the community.

Therefore, to implement and integrate various channels, it is important to establish a stable and continuous digital platform governance (digital platform governance or e-governance) system for establishing and operating a multi-channel service strategy. However, it is also necessary to avoid the centralized distribution method of the past and establish a governance promotion system that includes the private sector, universities, local governments, local-based companies, and local citizens based on big data analysis and consumer-driven demand generation. Research is also needed on data neutrality in the same vein as net neutrality, improving mechanisms and legal systems for data transactions, distinguishing between the roles of the center and the local government, and guidelines and codes of ethics for data management in local communities. In addition, it is necessary to form and issue discourses from various perspectives, such as public management and mutual monitoring, autonomous control, optimization of regulation and deregulation, and development of happiness index, which are emerging in the cooperative partnership between the central, local, university, local industry, and local communities.

This special English-language edition tries to reflect as much theoretical and empirical research on the new changes in the digital transformation era as possible. It consists of 6 chapters and 1 appendix. Chapters have been added to reflect the advances and changes in new IT. Chapter 1 is the emergence and evolution of e-government, Chapter 2 is the foundation and support system of e-government, Chapter 3 is the understanding and direction of e-governance, Chapter 4 is the era of the 4th industrial revolution and future smart government, Chapter 5 is a smart city, Chapter 6 is artificial intelligence and public administration, Chapter 7 introduces the multi-dimensional decision-making model based on the "Quantum Probability Model," and finally, the appendix is meta(bus) government.

Finally, I thank the researchers and practitioners at the Center for Converged Security and Governance at Inha University and the Graduate School of Smart Governance and Policy for their academic and practical contributions to this book. I would also like to thank Jung Jae-hoon, CEO of Yoon Sung-Sa, for carefully reviewing the writing process with new ideas. Once again, I dedicate this book with all my heart to my beloved parents, my wife and son, my academic peers, and the researchers in my lab at Inha University.

July 2024
In the lab at Inha University, room 9-308
Seunghwan Myeong

Contents

Preface 6

Chapter 1
The Rise and Evolution of E-Government
15

1. Concept and Development Model of E-government 15
2. The Emergence and Development of E-government 25

Chapter 2
Introducing and Adapting Public Management Information System
45

1. Information Systems Development and Management:
   The Difference Between MIS and PMIS 45
2. Policy-Making Models in E-government 53

Chapter 3
Understanding and Moving toward E-Governance
65

1. Definition and Types of E-governance 65
2. Conditions for Implementing E-government 82

Chapter 4
The Fourth Industrial Revolution and ICT Governance

96

1. Industry 4.0 — 96
2. Advances in Technology and Changes in the Public Sector — 106
3. New Administrative Demands and Shifting Administrative Paradigms — 127
4. Smart Governance (Digital Government) and IT Ecosystems — 133

Chapter 5
Smart Cities

141

1. Smart City — 141
2. Smart City Trends — 147
3. How Smart Cities will Evolve? — 158
4. How to Promote Big Data-based Smart Cities? — 161

Chapter 6
AI for Public Administration and Policy

174

1. The Rise of Artificial Intelligence — 174
2. Concepts and Types of Artificial Intelligence — 175
3. Using AI in the Public Sector — 177
4. AI Decision-Making Perspectives and Examples — 178
5. Adopting AI in Public Sector Policy-Making — 181

6. Direction of AI Administration and Policy 195

Chapter 7
Multi-Dimensional Policy Analysis and Decision-Making Model Based on the Quantum Probability
204

1. Game Changer: Quantum Theory and Government 204
2. Intelligent Government of the Future Toward Convergence 206
3. Limitations and Alternatives to the Deterministic Approach 209
4. Theoretical Foundations: Quantum Probability (QP) Theory 214
5. Quantum Probability Model 216
6. Quantum Approach: Rethinking the Relationship between Government and Transparency in Policy Process 219
7. Example: Empirical Test based on Quantum Probability Model 223
8. Policy Suggestions 228

Appendix
Meta-Government Possibilities and Policy Suggestions 230

References 236
Index 237
About Author 239

Smart Governance and Policy

Korean Experience:
From E-Government to Smart Governance

Smart Governance and Policy

Korean Experience:
From E-Government to Smart Governance

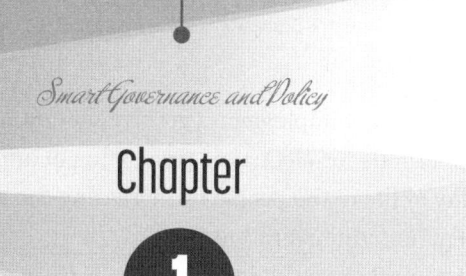

Chapter 1

The Rise and Evolution of E-Government

1. Concept and Development Model of E-government

1) The Concept of E-government

The term electronic government is used in various ways, including e-government, digital government, government online, and cyber government, but they are conceptually similar (Kim et al., 2007: 22). E-government, which began to be mentioned briefly in the U.S. National Performance Review (NPR) in 1993, has since evolved into a concept that crystallizes the relationship between public administration and IT has developed. The term e-government originated from the concept of electronic banking services, which banks developed to serve their customers better. ATMs, credit cards, and nationwide banking connections made banking more efficient and time-saving for customers. The efficiency and convenience of electronic banking led to the expectation that e-government would make communication between the government and the people, between government departments and ministries, and between the government and businesses faster and easier, and e-government evolved into the concept of e-government as we understand it today, to provide more convenient government services to the people.

The concept of e-government is specifically stated in the E-Government Act, which has been in effect since July 2001. Article 1 (Purpose) of the E-Government Act states,

"This Act aims to efficiently implement e-government by stipulating basic principles, procedures, and methods for electronic processing of administrative affairs and to improve the quality of life of the people by increasing the productivity, transparency, and democracy of public administration."

In addition, Article 2 (Terminology) 1 of the E-Government Act stipulates that "E-government refers to a government that utilizes IT to electronically perform the work of administrative agencies and public institutions (hereinafter referred to as 'administrative agencies, etc.') to efficiently perform administrative work among administrative agencies and administrative work for the public."

Based on Article 1 (Purpose) and Article 2 (Terminology) of the E-Government Act, the concept of e-government is summarized as follows. E-government is a government that improves the quality of life of the people by increasing administrative productivity, transparency, and democracy by utilizing IT to carry out the work of administrative agencies and others efficiently.

2) Six Types of E-government[01]

The six types of e-government are categorized based on two dimensions of how we view the future of information: the first dimension is e-government for whom? Moreover, the second dimension is e-government, for what?

The first dimension, "Who is e-government for?" distinguishes between e-government for the state and e-government for ordinary citizens. E-government for

---

[01] The six types of e-government are summarized and organized in SeongDon Hwang, SeungHeum Hwang and Seunghwan Myeong (2000), "Basic Logic and Legislation of Electronic Government," Ministry of Public Administration and Self-Government: 8 - 18. This e-government model and typology were presented in English at the International Symposium of the Korean Association for Public Administration (December 1999: 1 - 15) under the title "Philosophical Implications of Electronic Government in the Fields of Public Administration and Political Science" at Sookmyung Women's University in 1999. They were subsequently used in various research reports without the mutual approval of the co-authors. At that time, there were no strict ethical regulations and evaluation systems for citation and plagiarism, so there was no controversy. Therefore, the e-government model and typology were the product of joint efforts by scholars who participated in legislating e-government at that time. The initial model was presented in my draft presentation, "Philosophical Values and Policy Implications of Knowledge-Based E-Government," in the lobby of the Hilton Hotel in Seoul, Korea, and was revised and presented at the International Conference of the Sookmyung University Public Administration Society after a heated discussion. How this collaborative work was subsequently published without citation in other service research reports is still being determined. As I explained earlier, this was because, at that time, e-government legislation was being developed very urgently. In competition with each other (e.g., Rep. Lee Sang-hee was preparing an e-government bill in the legislature), it was important to publish it early.

the state refers to e-government for specific groups, such as the state, capitalists, and privileged classes. On the other hand, e-government for citizens refers to e-government for people as general citizens, not specific groups within society.

The second dimension, "What is e-government for?" is divided into three categories: e-government for efficiency and productivity, e-government for transparency, and e-government for empowerment. By intersecting the first and second dimensions, six types of e-government can be derived, as shown in Table 1-1. These six types of e-government are not independent of each other. However, they can appear as overlapping types, and sometimes they are transitional, with overlapping types depending on the degree of IT development and democratization.

<Table 1-1> Six Types of E-government

Dimension		Dimension 1: Who is e-government for?	
		Nation	General Citizen
Dimension 2: E-government for what?	Increase efficiency and productivity	Type 1: Bureaucratic government	Type 2: Efficient, Responsive government
	Increase transparency	Type 3: Surveillance government	Type 4: Transparent government to the public
	Empowerment	Type 5: Despotic government	Type 6: Democratic government

Source: Adapted from Chungsik Chung (2009: 66); Seunghwan Myeong (2011: 56).

(1) Type 1: Technical Bureaucratic Government

The first type, techno-bureaucratic government, refers to e-government that promotes efficiency from the perspective of bureaucrats working within the government. In this case, efficiency is understood as specialized knowledge and skills and the Max Weberian principle of bureaucracy, which focuses on instrumental rationality as emphasized in technocratic bureaucracy theory (Etzioni-Halvey, 1985: 54-62), as the key drivers of efficiency. The first type of e-government concept is found explicitly or implicitly in administrative computerization and office automation projects promoted in the early stages of introducing ICT into government work.

(2) Type 2: Efficient and Responsive Government

The second type of e-government, efficient citizen service government, utilizes

ICT to improve efficiency from the perspective of the average citizen. In this case, the average citizen can conveniently receive services from the government with less cost and effort. This e-government concept is currently widely shared among governments and scholars worldwide.

(3) Type 3: Surveillance Government

The third type of government, a surveillance government, is more transparent on the part of the state (or government). This type of transparency means that the government knows more about its citizens so that they can monitor their lives better, which means that the public is transparent to the government. The higher levels (or superiors) know more about the lower levels (or subordinates) within the government. This type of e-government concept is often found in academic literature (e.g., Lenk, 1997), which discusses the side effects of e-government.

(4) Type 4: Transparent Government to Ordinary Citizens

The fourth type of government, transparent to the public, refers to a transparent government from the public's perspective. This type of transparency refers to a situation where the information held by the government is conveniently disclosed to the public, and the entire process of the government's work is well visible to the public before and after. This type of e-government concept has been promoted as a core project of e-government implementation in Sweden (Statskontoret, 1998: 91-106) and the United States (Gore, 1997), which are countries with a high level of democratization and have made considerable progress in e-government implementation. In countries where e-government implementation projects are in the early stages or where the state-centered operating principle has traditionally been the centerpiece of public administration, this concept has yet to be implemented earnestly.

(5) Type 5: Despotic Government

The fifth type, despotic government, utilizes ICT to strengthen the state (or government) 's power over the people. This type of e-government does not exist in practice, but it can be partially manifested in cases such as inspections of anti-government personnel. Even if e-government is not promoted with this intention, this type of e-government will likely be implemented.

(6) Type 6: Democratic Government

The sixth type, democratic government, refers to e-government that utilizes ICT to approximate democratic ideals. This type of government is at the center of the debate in the field of e-democracy, which recognizes e-government as a key means to realize direct democracy that was previously impossible due to time and space constraints and discusses its potential.

3) E-government Scope

E-government is related to the informatization of the public or government sectors in the national informatization project. The scope of e-government can be divided into back office and front office based on the government.

The back-office dimension focuses on the government-to-government (G2G) dimension to eliminate administrative inefficiencies within the government. Representative examples of the G2G aspect include the On-Nara (Government Portal System) and the Administrative Information Sharing System. These projects focus on improving the way the government works and realizing a more efficient government.

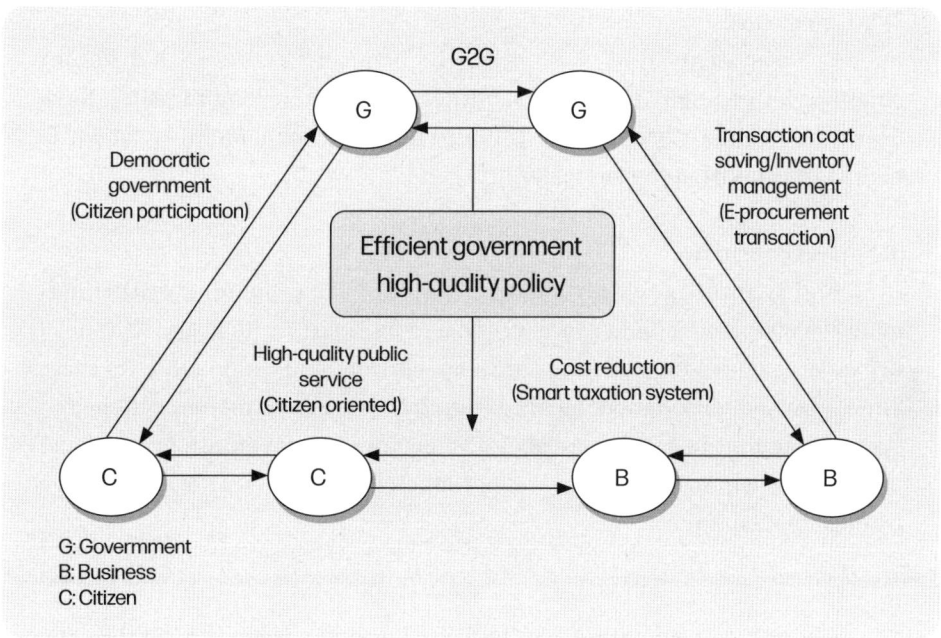

Source: E-Government Task Force (2003), White Paper on E-Government.

[Figure 1-1] E-government Roles and Scope

The front office level focuses on improving the interrelationship between the government and the people and the government and businesses and includes government-to-business (G2B) and government-to-citizen (G2C). Representative examples include 'Government 24' and 'Dasan Call Center'. G2B and G2C-related projects are aimed at improving the convenience of administrative services and the democracy and transparency of public administration by changing the way government services are provided and delivered to businesses and citizens, as well as inducing citizen participation in the national affairs process.

Terms Similar to E-government

1) Digital Government (OECD, 2016)

Governments are pursuing a digitalization strategy to create new public value through more advanced digital technologies for sharing, accessing, and personalizing data between government, businesses, and citizens.

2) E-Governance

Acts, ecosystems, and systems in which various actors with different characteristics, such as countries, corporations, citizens, and NGOs, form networks in the Internet space to build a multidimensional world while maintaining horizontal relationships.

3) Smart Governance

A highly intelligent governance system that redesigns traditional management practices and procedures based on smart technologies and social networks enables governments, businesses, citizens, and communities to share knowledge and information. Smart governance is a governance ecosystem and system that aims to act as a collaborative partner by providing a promotional platform to help social actors create productive and democratic added value through mutual transactions.

The scope of e-government can also be viewed from the perspective of the national government's area of responsibility. Who takes the lead in e-government is ultimately linked to the scope, the framework, and legal and institutional issues.

In terms of the United Nations (UN) evaluation criteria for e-government, the scope of e-government consists of 1) evaluation of e-government services, 2) evaluation of networks (citing ITU measures), and 3) evaluation of education and literacy (citing UNESCO measures). From the perspective of Korean ministries, the roles and scope of e-government are distributed among the Ministry of the Interior and Local Government, the Ministry of Science and ICT, the Ministry of Information and Communication Infrastructure, and the Ministry of Education for Continuing Education. In addition, e-government, which is promoted by each ministry, is not considered the domain of the Ministry of the Interior and Local Government but rather the digitalization business of the ministry in charge, which can lead to conflicts if cooperation between ministries is not smooth. It can be seen as a natural phenomenon caused by the spread and convergence of ICT into all industries, economies, and societies, and is expected to evolve into a platform-type government centered on collaboration and problem-solving rather than the promotion of e-government and informatization centered on disconnected ministries in the current and future hyper-connected and converged societies, which are characterized by the 4th industrial revolution and digital transformation.

<Table 1-2> is a summary comparison of the major legislative contents of the Ministry of the Interior and Safety (formerly the Ministry of the Interior and Self-Government, Ministry of Safety and Security, etc.) and the Ministry of Science and ICT (formerly the Ministry of ICT, Ministry of Information and Communication, Ministry of Science and ICT, Korea Communications Commission, etc.

<Table 1-2> Comparison of Information and Communication Laws and Scope of E-government Policies (as of 2019)

National Informatization Framework Act (Ministry of Science and ICT)	E-Government Act (Ministry of the Interior and Safety)	Information and Communication Industry Promotion Act (Ministry of the Interior and Safety)	Special Act on Promotion of Information and Communication and Convergence Activation (Ministry of the Interior and Safety)
- Establishment and promotion system of national informatization policy (basic plan, implementation plan, CIO, CIO council)	- Provision and utilization of e-Government services: e-complaint handling, e-Government service delivery	- Establishment and Implementation of Information and Communication Industry Promotion Plan	- Establishment of a system for promoting information and communication and convergence activation

- Promotion of national informatization: public informatization, regional informatization, support for private sector informatization, management and utilization of knowledge information resources - Access to information and preventing dysfunction: information culture, internet addiction, bridging the information divide, ICT ethics, etc. - Information and communication infrastructure modernization: high-speed network, Internet address management, etc.	- Electronic administration: e-documents, e-signatures, and paper reduction - Shared use of administrative information - Strengthening the foundation for e-government operations: EA, information resource management (network construction, resource integration management), system stability - Drive e-government implementation initiatives: pilot projects, performance analysis, etc.	- Promotion of ICT: support for commercialization of new technologies, etc. - Promote ICT standardization and certification - Creating a foundation for the promotion of the information and communication industry: cultivating specialized human resources, promoting international cooperation in the information and communication industry, creating an information and communication industry promotion complex, improving distribution structures, and promoting dissemination - Measures to Support IT Companies - Telecommunications Promotion Fund	- Creating a foundation for the promotion of ICT: Development of domestic specialized human resources, upgrading of information and communication network - Promotion of new ICT and services: designation of promising technologies and services, standardization of technologies and services, support for commercialization of technologies and services such as promising information and communication convergence, etc. - Promote digital content, software, and more - Support for enabling information and communication convergence, etc.

* Under the Lee Myung-bak government, the National Information Society Act was under the jurisdiction of the Ministry of Safety and Security Administration due to the dissolution of the Ministry of Information and Communication.

** The National Information Society Act is based on the Basic Act for Promoting Information Society.

4) E-government Development Model

The development model (or stage theory) of e-government has been discussed variously along with its development, including the development models raised by the United Nations (UN), Deloitte, and the Korea Information Society Agency. According to the e-government development model, in the initial introduction stage of e-government, the government focused on providing one-way information. However, interactive information was provided gradually progressing to the development stage. Finally, integrated service provision and information organization transformation occurred.

(1) The United Nations (UN) Five-stage Development Model

The United Nations five-stage e-government development model is categorized as follows: ① emerging stage, ② enhanced stage, ③ interaction stage, ④ transaction stage, and ⑤ networked stage (Choi & Ryu, 2009: 140).

① In the emerging stage, there is an official website and connections to central and local governments through national portals and official government sites.

② In the developmental stage, it starts providing databases online, browsing documents, and providing up-to-date materials such as policies, laws, reports, and newsletters.

③ In the interaction phase, information services are provided through security devices, electronic signatures, public information provision, and regular homepage updates.

④ In the e-transaction stage, fines, taxes, and postage can be paid via credit card, and online bidding for public contracts is possible.

⑤ In the integrated processing stage, G2C construction through integrated networking of public institutions and collecting citizen opinions on government policies through online surveys is actively manifested.

(2) Deloitte's Six-stage Evolution Model

In June 2000, Deloitte Consulting (2000), a global consulting firm, published a report entitled "The Dawn of E-Government," which categorized the stages of e-government development and analyzed the current state of the U.S. government (Lee et al., 2004: 326). The report focuses on implementing customer-oriented government by introducing and utilizing the Internet in the government sector. It divides the e-government development model into six stages based on the degree of utilization of web-based applications and the degree of government transformation.

Deloitte's six-stage e-government evolution model is as follows: ① Stage 1: information publishing/dissemination ⇒ ② Stage 2: 'official' two-way transaction ⇒ ③ Stage 3: multi-purpose portals ⇒ ④ Stage 4: portal personalization: Portal personalization ⇒ ⑤ Stage 5: Clustering of common services ⇒ ⑥ Stage 6: Full integration and enterprise transformation.

① Stage 1: Information Delivery and Dissemination involves government agencies using technology as the foundation for delivering information to their customers.

② Stage 2: The formal two-way communication phase is where government agencies engage in two-way transactions through electronic statements and secure website technologies.

③ Stage 3: The multi-purpose portal involves government agencies providing web portals to customers and businesses to handle cross-agency transactions through a single access point.

④ Stage 4: The customized portal stage is where the government provides customized portals to customers to meet their needs.

⑤ Stage 5: The batching of common services, is where the true transformation of the government structure occurs: the territorial distinctions between government departments and agencies are blurred by integrated customer processing, and the government provides connected, integrated services.

⑥ Stage 6: Full integration and total transformation is when compartmentalization of service delivery disappears, IT is integrated, and frontline and backline (= behind-the-scenes) services are connected. New departments are created, and old ones remain, but a total transformation of the form of government occurs.

(3) Korea Information Society Agency's 4-stage Development Model

In 2000, the Korea Information Society Agency (formerly known as the Korea Computer Center) categorized the development of e-government into four stages. The four-stage e-government development model of the Korea Information Society Agency is divided into the following stages: ① Stage 1: Web construction stage ⇒ ② Stage 2: Interaction stage ⇒ ③ Stage 3: Transaction stage ⇒ ④ Stage 4: Transformation and integration stage (Chung, 2019: 159).

① Stage 1: The web construction stage is where each government organization builds its homepage and unilaterally provides information and services. In the early days of information society, government departments competed to build websites to promote their work, functions, and events. In this stage, there is little interaction or communication with the public via the web or the Internet, and one-way communication by the government dominates.

② Stage 2: The interaction stage involves exchanging information and opinions with the public through the established website. This is where communication and interaction between the public and the government occur through bulletin boards, Q&A, FAQs, chat rooms, etc.

③ Stage 3: The transaction stage is where transactions with citizens and related organizations are processed online based on the web. It is the stage where citizens can receive various public services from the government through the Internet and perform various tasks that need to be submitted to the government (reporting, payment, etc.).

④ Stage 4: Transformation and Integration is the stage of transforming existing tasks, creating new tasks through e-business, and transitioning to a new organizational structure. This stage goes beyond organizational structure and work processing procedures to fundamental changes in the ministry's organization.

2. The Emergence and Development of E-government

1) Background of E-government[02]

(1) A Call of the Times: The Rise of Neoliberalism

The emergence of the neo-liberalism of reinventing government to overcome government failures (NPR, 1993; Osborne & Gaebler, 1992) caused by overcapacity, monopolistic provider positions, bureaucratic inefficiency, and administrative expediency due to the non-market nature of public goods (NPR, 1993; Osborne & Gaebler, 1992) can be seen as the starting point of e-government, moving away from the Keynesian position that government intervention is inevitable due to market failures (Lee et al., 2004: 309-310).

This neoliberal stance is well illustrated by a series of reforms in countries such as the United States, the United Kingdom, and Australia that have centered on downsizing the public sector, performance-based management, and customer-centered service delivery.

Thus, an e-government is a government that actively uses ICT as a catalyst to make these reforms more successful. In the United States, administrative reforms using IT have been quite effective, at least on the surface, since the Clinton administration took

---

02 Adapted from Myeong et al., Introduction to Public Administration (2011: 697-699).

office in 1992 (NPR, 1997).

> **Value Goals for E-government**
>
> 1) Pursue both democracy (openness, transparency, equity) and efficiency (streamlining, effectiveness): kill two birds with one stone.
> 2) Emphasize government-private (business)-citizen cooperative partnerships
> 3) The government's customer is "the people," pursue customer-oriented government
> 4) E-government is a concrete realization of the New Public Administration (which emphasized democracy, equity, and participation in the 1970s), which was followed by the Late New Public Administration (New Public Management Theory, New Governance Theory) through the 1980s with the advent of IT.
> 5) E-government = New Public Administration + New Liberalism + IT + New Public Management + New Governance + New Public Service

(2) Actively promoting e-government in each country: privatization, downsizing, restructuring, workforce reduction, deregulation, etc. in the process of government reform

Stimulated by the success of the U.S. (reform), Commonwealth-centered countries such as the United Kingdom, Canada, and Australia, professional bureaucracy-centered countries such as Singapore and Malaysia, and government-led economic development countries such as South Korea and Japan actively promote e-government. Of course, the methods and processes differ depending on the differences in each country. However, they have in common that they focus on the corporatization of the government and instilling an entrepreneurial mindset from a neoliberal perspective (Lee et al., 2004: 310-311).

Therefore, governments should adhere to the principles of the free market, reduce waste to make the government as small as possible, and adopt private-sector management practices in government operations and management to increase efficiency, decentralization, accountability, efficient resource management, and marketization (Osborne & Gaebler, 1992).

The same position has been taken in government reforms worldwide, including privatization, downsizing, restructuring, workforce reduction, and deregulation. In addition, since citizens are customers like consumers in the marketplace, the key to reform is to introduce a competitive system that allows the government to provide the best services and citizens to choose those services. It will naturally eliminate public organizations that cannot compete.

Background on Creating an E-government Strategy

1) Developing a new environment for digital transformation in the 21st century
① Restructuring government organizations to enable knowledge and information to flow in response to the information society
② Information resources evolve into an integral component of the organization's strategy.

2) Developed countries push for competitive e-government
① United States: Combining administrative reform and IT to promote national competitiveness
② Japan: Leading the way in administrative reform by establishing a government digital transformation plan

3) Adopted the 'E-government Implementation' project in the Roh Moo-hyun government's top 100 national agenda.
① Lack of specificity in improving administrative work procedures using IT in the past
② Promoting the Kim Dae-Jung government's 11 e-government projects and Roh Moo-hyun government's 31 e-government projects.
③ Seek cross-government consensus on the concept and direction of new e-government

4) Lee Myung-bak government's e-government project
① National Informatization Basic Plan (2009)
② Establishment of the Smart Korea Basic Plan (2010)

5) Reach the top of the e-government world
① Korea ranked first in the UN World E-Government Assessment in 2010, 2012, and 2014.
② The UN DESA (Department of Economic and Social Affairs) has been evaluating and publishing e-government biennially since 2001 for 192 member countries. The evaluation indexes are the Development Index (web level, infrastructure level, human capital level) and the Online Participation

Index (online information provision, policy participation, policy-making). Korea has been ranked first in this category for three consecutive years.

2) Evolution of E-government in Korea

(1) The evolution of e-government

From the beginning of e-government to the present, the Korean government has promoted informatization projects focusing on improving efficiency through IT. As a result, it is considered to have achieved many achievements. In particular, the civilian government built unit e-government systems through a catch-up strategy to automate and streamline existing tasks. In contrast, the people's government invested heavily in informatization and the IT industry as an industrialization strategy and used it as a driving force to overcome the IMF. The participatory government promoted qualitative upgrades such as expanding online participation and activating new services based on world-class infrastructure during the growth period of e-government.

<Table 1-3> E-Government Promotion Flow in Korea

Steps	When	Separation	Key takeaways
E-Government Starter	1978-1987	Administrative computerization	The first and second administrative computerization projects (1978-1986)
	1987 to 1996	Administrative Computing	The first and second national computer network projects (1987-1996) - Five networks: administrative, financial, defense, public security, education, and research
E-Government Foundation Builder	1996 to 2000	Promote Informatization	• Building a high-speed telecommunications network (1995-2005) • Public Information Promotion Project - Administrative informatization, economic informatization, social informatization, e·tc. (procurement, passport, patent, customs, etc. informatization)

E-government Startup and Growth Phase	2001-2007	Top 11 E-government Challenges Top 31 E-government Challenges	• Advancing cross-government initiatives (11 priorities) • Expand e-government, including multi-ministry centers (31 tasks) - Government Integrated Computer Center, e-government network, etc.
E-government Maturity	2008 to	Integrate, Connect, and Intelligent	• Promote e-government centered on public use and cross-sector integration • Expanding the number of organizations targeted for e-government promotion (linkage and integration) - Administrative agencies, public institutions, some private organizations, etc. - Modernizing e-government (intelligence, big data, IoT, etc.)

Source: Modified from Seunghwan Myung (2011: 11).

<Table 1-4> Results of the UN's Assessment of E-government Levels in Key Countries

Featured countries	2001	2003		2004		2005		2008		2010-2014	
	A	A	B	A	B	A	B	A	B	A	B
United Kingdom	15	13	12	5	6	5	4	6	2	1	1
United States	1	1	2	1	2	1	3	4	1	2	6
United Kingdom	7	5	1	3	1	4	1	10	25	4	4
France	14	19	7	24	14	23	18	9	3	10	15
Germany	10	9	11	12	12	11	12	22	74	15	14
Japan	27	18	15	18	21	14	16	11	11	17	6

* A = E-Government Development Index, B = Online Engagement Index

Until now, the government's e-government promotion strategy has been characterized by pursuing a public-led, infrastructure-oriented strategy in the early stages of the information society and gradually developing into a private-led, service- and utilization-oriented strategy as it moves into the growth and maturity period. The e-government has utilized informatization as a strategic tool for national growth and has established a basic plan for national informatization to promote directional informatization led by the government.

As a result of these efforts, Korea's e-government ranked first in the world on the E-Government Readiness Index and Online Participation Index in the 2010 UN E-Government Assessment. This achievement improved from sixth place in the E-Government Readiness Index to second place in the Online Participation Index 2008. It is interpreted as Korea gaining momentum to lead global e-government substantially in the future.

(2) Korea's Top-ranked E-government Performance Evaluation

The significance of Korea's e-government's achievement of ranking first in the United Nations e-government evaluation in 2010, 2012, and 2014 is that, first, it can contribute to the revitalization of e-government exports and the enhancement of the country's brand by improving the global image of e-government; second, it can contribute to the revitalization of the economy by supporting online startups and establishing a logistics information network, as well as enhancing the convenience of the public through the provision of customized information due to the maturity of e-government. Third, it can improve administrative efficiency by establishing spatial information and national collaboration systems. It can also strengthen social safety by establishing e-government systems such as disaster response and livestock hygiene management.

Second, industrial information on national knowledge resources has been prepared on the supply side. Through government-led efforts, a vast knowledge information infrastructure has been secured, including the establishment of a database (DB) of about 290 million data in each field, including science and technology, culture, history, and education, and individual economic actors such as citizens and companies have been able to improve their competitiveness more creatively and dynamically through 'utilization of knowledge information' on top of the established infrastructure. It has enabled a virtuous industrial development cycle, including creating new businesses for related companies by establishing support functions to revitalize companies and industries. It is expected to be the key to securing national competitiveness in the future.

(3) Success Factors for E-government Performance

To summarize, the success factors of Korea's e-government performance are due to the policy continuation of investment despite the gap between the investment and the effectiveness of information projects. In particular, a strong centralized strategy led by the government, a strategy to foster the industry, and pioneering investments can be seen as success factors.

The first was the centralized government investment in identifying businesses and fostering industries when the concept of informatization was unknown. It resulted in a strong support system that is rarely seen in the world, with the establishment of the Basic Plan for the Promotion of Informatization, the Ministry of Information & Communication and Informatization Promotion Committee, and the Informatization Promotion Fund.

The second strategy is to promote the linkage between informatization and the IT industry by fostering policies, i.e., promoting e-government and informatization on the demand side while building infrastructure and fostering the IT industry on the supply side. As a result, a virtuous cycle of supply and demand was established, and initial demand for informatization was created through top-down business promotion and 'up-front investment and later settlement'.

The third is a pioneering investment strategy focused on strategic industries. Through selection and focus, this strategy resulted in major investments in the information and communications sector, including semiconductors, CDMA, and high-speed information and communications networks, which helped build the current information infrastructure.

(4) Limitations of existing informatization-focused policies and strategies to address them

With the development of IT, the widespread use of the Internet, and the spread of information across the country, the limitations and problems of existing policies centered on facilitation have been exposed.

First, the continuous promotion of e-government has resulted in the establishment of many information systems in central and local governments. However, data and information systems are operated by agencies, resulting in low compatibility, reduced cost savings, and performance creation through joint utilization.

Second, with the evolution from knowledge to intelligence information, unhealthy cyberculture has continued to develop due to the flood of harmful and false information, increasing public anxiety.

Third, a virtuous value chain from digital transformation to industrialization has

<Table 1-5> Achievements of Korea's E-government and Digitalization Policies

Projects	Civilian Government (1993-1997)	Government of the People (1998-2002)	Participating Governments (2003-2007)
Goals	• Advancing administrative systems through informatization	• Overcoming the IMF and fostering the IT industry through informatization	• Reached $20,000 in national income through informatization
Policy Direction	• DBization of administrative information and establishment of institutional foundation	• Spreading the Internet and fostering the IT industry	• Enabling government innovation and citizen engagement through IT
Policy, Legal & Institutional	• Enactment of the Information Society Act (1995) • Formed the Information Promotion Committee (1996) • Establishment of the Fund (1996) • Plan to build a high-speed information and communication infrastructure (1997)	• Cyber Korea 21 (1999) • Bridging the Information Gap Act (2001) • Information and Communications Network Utilization and Protection Act (2001) • e-Korea 2006 (2002)	• Broadband IT Korea (2003) • BcN Master Plan (2004) • Information Security Mid- to Long-Term Roadmap (2005) • u-Korea (2006)
Public Sector Informatization	• Opened the Public Administration Information Network (1993) • Passport issuance computerized network opened (1994)	• Computerization of real estate registration (2003) • Computerization of online family registers (1999) • G4C, G2G services (2002)	• National Fiscal Information System (2003) • EBS SAT Broadcast (2004) • Full implementation of mobile e-bidding (2005)

	• Launched statistical information service (1995) • Congressional Research Service (1997)	• Opening of 'NEIS' (2002)	• Issued civil documents on the government portal (2006)
Civilian Informatization	• Launched Internet Cyber Market (1996) • Launched Internet banking (1997) • Internet stock exchange introduced (1997)	• Launched Postal Service e-commerce (1999) • Launched B2B e-commerce site (1999) • 10 million information education (2000)	• Launched mobile banking service (1903) • E-commerce tops $300 billion (2004) • 1 Million SME Informationization Plan (2004)
Expand the Information Foundation	• Korea Telecommunications and Internet Service (1994) • High-speed telecommunications network phase 1 project (1995) • Provided Internet WWW services (1995) • Launched high-speed national network service (1997)	• Launched wireless Internet service (1999) • Commercial ATM exchange network opened (2000) • Launch of the third phase of the high-speed telecommunications network (2001) • High-speed Internet reaches 10 million homes (2002)	• Launched home network service (2004) • BcN pilot service launched (2005) • Ranked #1 in the world in the ITU Digital Opportunity Index (2005) • World's first WiBro pilot (2006)
Information Security	• Established the Information and Communication Ethics	• Information Literacy Education for the Disabled (1999)	• Educating the Underserved (2003) • Established the National

Source: Korea Information Society Agency, "Navigating the IT Age" (2010: 11).

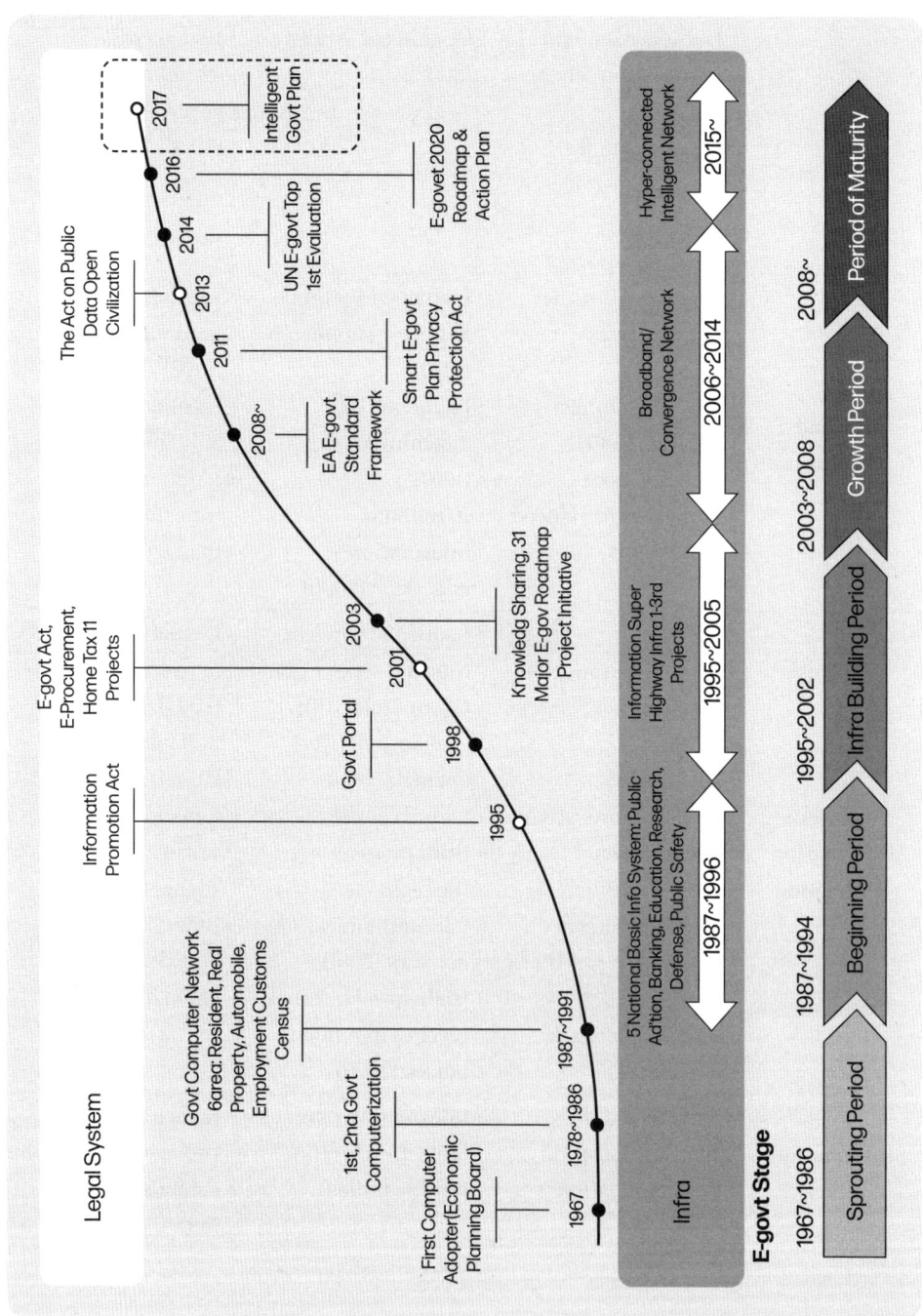

Source: E-Government Division, Korea Information Society Agency (2019).

[Figure 1-2] Changes in E-government in Korea

been formed, and economic growth has been driven, but the long-term slowdown in the growth rate of the IT industry, the lack of revitalization of traditional industries through IT, and the imbalance between IT industries have been raised.

The following are some of the key steps to fundamentally address these challenges and present a new informatization vision and strategy.

First, it is necessary to shift the policy direction from a knowledge society to an intelligence society based on a careful analysis of the problems of the information society drive so far, from 'disconnection and dispersion' to 'communication and convergence' and from 'promotion' to 'utilization'.

Secondly, it is necessary to shift from a government-centered promotion system to a public-private governance collaboration system to address the problems of new information-age dysfunctions such as the shrinking role of humans, dehumanization, and the normalization of distrust and to utilize the expertise of the private sector.

Third, it is necessary to differentiate and specify the new e-government promotion direction and strategy in the digital transformation era in the promotion's background promotion background.

Fourth, the vision and promotion strategy should emphasize the motivation for realizing next-generation e-government (innovation of administrative tasks and systems and realization of volunteer and mediator-type e-government based on public participation).

Fifth, it is necessary to expand the service concept to benefit the people in the administrative service sector and ensure equal access to and delivery of services without marginalization.

Sixth, in the human resources and institutional sectors, it is necessary to establish a dedicated organization, secure informatization experts, improve institutions based on public participation, develop intelligent informatization education programs, and use a specialized team system.

3) Korean-Style E-government

(1) The concept of Korean e-government

Korean e-government refers to a future innovative administrative model that uses IT to improve administrative productivity by electronizing all administrative processes and to make government information and services to the public readily available to anyone, anywhere, anytime (Myeong & Lee, 2011: 704-705).

(2) Vision of E-government: Realizing a people-oriented, efficient, and open government

The e-government vision is to realize an open, people-oriented, and efficient government (Myeong & Choi, 2011: 705).

First, a people-oriented government seeks to maximize people's satisfaction with administrative services by improving their convenience and protecting their privacy.

Second, an efficient government seeks to improve productivity and enhance government competitiveness by streamlining the content and procedures of administrative services.

Third, open government is a transparent government that facilitates two-way communication between the people and the government based on internationally standardized open IT.

Types of Electronic Administrative Services

① Handling electronic complaints
② Disclosure of electronic information
③ Electronic document exchange
④ Joint utilization of administrative information
⑤ Information Resource Management
⑥ Kiosk (KIOSK) refers to an automated civil affairs administrative processor and is used for issuing electronic civil affairs documents, checking civil affairs results, and automating service windows.
⑦ Smart Card: It is usually used in conjunction with a kiosk. Smart cards contain many types of information, such as resident registration and health insurance. They can provide services in healthcare, social security, education, and transportation (Choi, 2006: 215-218).

Targeted Tasks in E-government

1) The scope of e-government is centered on national affairs and gradually linked to local affairs.
2) Overall, state affairs will be divided into six major fields, including

> administrative services, administrative affairs, administrative information, personal affairs of public officials, administrative information base, and laws and institutions, and will be integrated in an interrelated manner.

(3) Goals of E-government

The goals of e-government are as follows (Myeong & Choi, 2011: 706)

First, the convenience and use of public administrative services should be improved. Anyone, anytime, anywhere, should have fair access to the administrative services they want, and administrative services should be delivered to the public through a single window without any functional or organizational restrictions.

Second, administrative digitalization in conjunction with administrative work innovation is required. It is necessary to simplify and standardize the public administrative service delivery system and establish transparent and efficient administrative work processing procedures using electronic and IT.

Third, the strategic integration and systematization of administrative information management. Once collected, information should be electronically converted and archived, shared and reused by authorized users, and all administrative information should be processed as strategic resources and managed regularly.

Fourth, government employees' personal productivity and information literacy should be improved. They need to implement office automation through digitizing paper documents and acquiring the knowledge and skills to meet the changing public needs.

Fifth, develop and build an administrative information base. Open and standard IT should be adopted to interconnect and operate various information resources, and all government PCs should be connected to the administrative ICT network and provide administrative information to authorized users.

Sixth, improve laws and institutions. Continuously improving administrative systems oriented toward e-government and reviewing and introducing advanced systems suitable for new systems and business procedures resulting from establishing e-government are necessary.

4) Examples of E-government Initiatives in Major Countries

Countries around the world are implementing e-government projects from various perspectives according to their specificities and policy directions, and the main contents of e-government implementation in each country are as follows (Kim, Seok-Joon, et al., 2001: 203-265).

(1) United States

① Background of E-government in the United States

The emergence of e-government in the United States can be traced back to the Clinton administration, which announced its intention to "use IT to improve the quality of life for the American people and revitalize our economy." The announcement defined e-government as "a government that uses IT to interact with and serve its people according to the needs of the people who are the government's customers." Since then, countries around the world have competitively pursued e-government as a means to complete administrative reforms successfully.

What countries have in common in their e-government efforts

1) A strong commitment to e-government from top leaders
2) Promote comprehensive administrative reform using IT
3) Efforts by government officials with expertise
4) Pioneering pilots with a strong drive structure

---

② Selecting and Promoting Targeted Redesign of Administrative Work through IT since 1993

Since 1993, 13 projects have been selected and implemented, including the implementation of Electronic Benefit Transfer (EBT), integrated and electronic access to administrative information and services, and the development of methods for redesigning administrative work through IT. As a result, the Documentation Work Reduction Act was enacted to reduce the documentation burden on the public, and the Information Resource Management Reform Act was enacted to provide legal support for information support and to streamline information resource management.

In 1997, the government proposed a 21st-century reform plan to "provide services under the conditions that people want," based on evaluating government innovation activities and utilizing new IT such as the Internet.

(2) Japan

In 1995, influenced by the U.S. e-government initiative, the government established the Basic Plan for Promoting Administrative Information and has since developed an electronic document exchange system, an administrative information location guidance system, and an authorization system.

The Institute of Administrative Information Systems in Japan has systematized the idea of realizing e-government as an administrative reform measure through seven recommendations and five basic strategies (Chung, 2009: 52).

① Seven suggestions for making e-government a reality
② Realization of one-stop administrative services
③ Realization of non-stop administrative services
③ Overcoming geographical limitations in providing administrative services
④ Electronic disclosure of administrative information
⑤ Electronic delivery of information
⑥ Electronification of legal hold documents
⑦ Electronic Document Interchange (EDI)

　Five fundamental strategies to enable e-government
① Establishment of a public-private information network
② Introduce personalized identification codes
③ Establish a privacy policy
④ Revision of various procedural regulations
⑤ Alignment with administrative reform

In 1997, the Basic Plan was revised to make e-commerce practical and reduce the burden on citizens in government applications and reports.

(3) United Kingdom

In 1996, the government announced its e-government policy, a form of government that uses IT to provide new services to the public and businesses. It launched seven pilot projects, including an electronic joint complaint room and electronic forms.

Open Data Policy Trends in Major Countries

1. United States
① The Obama Administration announced the implementation of Transparency and Open Government on January 21, 2009, as a national policy.
② Government ministries and public institutions promoted strategies and action plans to promote "information transparency, citizen participation, and collaborative systems." The Open Government Initiative (OGI), which is related to Government 3.0, was launched on December 8, 2012, when the Office of Management and Budget (OMB) released the Open Government Directive (OGD).
③ Specifically, in March 2009, the federal government announced a plan to build a government-wide federal data repository. In May of the same year, the U.S. Department of the Interior (DOI) and the Environmental Protection Agency (EPA), led by the General Services Administration (GSA) and the Office of Management and Budget (OMB), launched the "Data.gov" site, which is open to the public.

2. United Kingdom
① The United Kingdom enacted the Reuse of Public Sector Information Regulation 2005 in June 2005.
② In January 2010, we launched Data.gov.uk, a pan-government open data portal, to expand access to government data, enhance government transparency, and provide valuable public information to make the government and related industries function more efficiently.
③ In June 2012, the government released the Open Data White Paper, which outlined steps the public sector is taking to improve data accessibility and usability and government policies to enable the public to benefit from open data.

3. Japan
① The Japanese government established the "Open Data Strategy for Electronic Administration" in July 2012 as a basic strategy for promoting the utilization of open data. It established the following basic principles: ▲ actively disclose open data directly by the government, ▲ use machine-readable formats,

▲ promote utilization regardless of profit or non-profit purposes, and ▲ promptly disclose public data that can be disclosed.

② The Japanese government is promoting policies to utilize and revitalize big data considering private sector use and is also preparing plans for data openness, basic technology R&D, human resource acquisition, and standardization. The Cabinet Chief Cabinet Secretary is in charge of the national open data strategy, and based on this, each ministry, including the Ministry of Internal Affairs and Communications and the Ministry of Economy, Trade and Industry, will prepare ministry-specific strategies.

③ The Japanese Ministry of Economy, Trade and Industry is planning DATA METI, a policy that aims to revitalize the economy by opening up data held by the Ministry of Economy, Trade and Industry to be utilized by companies, and the Public Data Working Group, established by the Ministry of Economy, Trade and Industry at the end of August 2012, has prepared the necessary regulations to open up public data.

④ Providing public data in a form that businesses can use through 'DATA METI' enables businesses to use the data to provide more convenient services to users, thereby contributing to the efficiency of economic activities and revitalizing the economy (Ministry of Science, ICT and Future Planning, 2013; Lee, 2014).

Summary

Smart Governance and Policy

Electronic government refers to a government that utilizes IT to efficiently carry out the work of administrative agencies, etc. to improve the quality of life of the people by increasing the productivity, transparency, and democracy of administration. Six types of e-government can be categorized based on two dimensions (1st dimension: Who is e-government for?, 2nd dimension: What is e-government for?). The six types are: Type 1 (technical-bureaucratic government), Type 2 (efficient public service government), Type 3 (surveillance government), Type 4 (transparent government to the public), Type 5 (despotic government), and Type 6 (democratic government).

The development model (or stage theory) of e-government has been discussed variously along with the development of e-government, and among them, the United Nations (UN)'s five-stage development model, Deloitte's six-stage development model, and the four-stage development model proposed by the Korea Information Society Agency are representative. According to the e-government development model, in the initial introduction stage of e-government, the government focused on providing one-way information, but as it gradually progressed to the development stage, interactive information was provided, and finally, integrated service provision and information organization transformation occurred.

The reasons behind the emergence of e-government include (1) the call of the times (the emergence of neoliberalism), (2) the active promotion of e-government by governments (privatization, downsizing, restructuring, workforce reduction, deregulation, etc. in the process of government reform), and (3) the attributes of ICT (speed, accuracy, interactivity, sharing, equity, etc.).

Looking at the evolution of e-government in Korea, from the beginning of e-government to the present, the Korean government has focused on improving efficiency through IT. It has achieved many achievements as a result of promoting informatization projects. In particular, the civilian government used a catch-up strategy to automate and streamline existing tasks by building unit e-government systems. In contrast, the people's government invested heavily in informatization and the IT industry through an industrialization strategy and used it as a driving force to overcome the IMF. During the participatory government, the government promoted qualitative upgrades such as expanding online participation and activating new services based on world-class infrastructure during e-government growth. Through these efforts, Korea's E-government ranked first in the world in the E-government Readiness Index and Online Participation Index in three consecutive UN E-government Assessments in 2010, 2012, and 2014. This achievement is a significant improvement from sixth place in the e-government readiness index and second place in the online participation index in 2008, and it is interpreted as securing the momentum for Korea to lead global e-government substantially in the future.

Countries worldwide are implementing e-government programs from various perspectives, depending on their particular circumstances and policy directions. The emergence of e-government in the United States can be traced back to the Clinton administration, which announced its intention to "use IT to improve the quality of life of the American people and revitalize the economy." In addition, since 1993, the United States has selected and promoted 13 tasks (targeted for redesigning administrative work through IT), including implementing electronic benefit transfer (EBT) and developing an integrated and electronic approach to administrative information and services. As a result, the Paperwork Reduction Act was enacted to reduce the paperwork burden on citizens, and the Information Resource Management Reform Act was enacted to provide legal support for information support and to streamline information resource management. In 1997, the government proposed a 21st-century reform plan for "providing services under the conditions desired by the people" based on evaluating government innovation activities while utilizing new IT such as the Internet.

Inspired by the U.S. e-government initiative, Japan established the Basic Plan for the Promotion of Administrative Informatization in 1995 and has since developed an electronic official document exchange system, an administrative information location guidance system, and an authorization system. In 1997, the Basic Plan was revised to practicalize e-commerce and reduce the burden on citizens in filing government applications.

Korea has been focusing on e-government projects to improve efficiency and public service, from the computer network-centered projects in the 1980s to the 11 core Projects of e-government in 2001 and the 31 Projects of the e-government roadmap in 2003 to the five major tasks of the 'New IT Policy' of the Lee Myung-bak administration in 2008, to intelligent e-government and digital government innovation. While the previous e-government has been promoted with the characteristics of Web 1.0, which is one-way and provider-centered, and Web 2.0, which is focused on delivering information and providing online services, the next generation of e-government will be promoted with the characteristics of Web 3.0, which is based on intelligent convergence technologies such as artificial intelligence, big data, cloud, and Internet of Things to develop a production and consumption ecosystem in which suppliers and consumers who value participation, sharing, cooperation, and openness simultaneously. It is analyzed that the problems of e-government in the past are due to the lack of personalized services and integrated channels, lack of open data management system, accessibility problems, and security issues. Intelligent e-government will overcome the existing limitations of e-government and pursue change and innovation at a more fundamental level. The driving force for this change and innovation is the development of artificial intelligence technology. Intelligent e-government can also be defined as a government that gains the trust and support of the people by first finding and proposing services that individuals need and by transparently and securely opening and sharing all state operation information. Intelligent e-government is more advanced than traditional e-government in various fields by utilizing the latest technologies, such as artificial intelligence and big data analysis.

Research Questions

1. Based on the six types of e-government, categorize and discuss the paradigm shift in administration and types of e-government in Korea by era.
2. Explain the emergence of e-government and the values it promotes.
3. Discuss the origins of the E-Government Act and how it will be revised.
4. Discuss the differences and similarities between e-government in the Web 1.0 and Web 2.0 eras and e-government in the Web 3.0 era.
5. Explain the limitations of traditional e-government and the direction of intelligent e-government.

Chapter 2

Introducing and Adapting Public Management Information System

1. Information Systems Development and Management: The Difference Between MIS and PMIS

1) Management Information System (MIS)[01]

(1) Concept of management information system

Public Management Information System (PMIS) has its roots in Management Information System (MIS) in business administration. The term MIS is commonly used to refer to management information systems. Therefore, MIS will be used hereafter.

MIS refers to an integrated human-machine system that provides information to support an organization's management, analysis, and decision-making functions (Ahn, 1995: 193). The elements comprising an MIS include hardware, software, manual processing procedures, models for analysis, planning, control, and decision-making databases.

MIS is categorized into broad MIS and consultative MIS. A broad MIS consists

---

[01] The 'Management Information System (MIS)' section is organized by referring to the contents of Ahn Moon-seok's (1995) "Information System Theory" (3rd edition) Chapter 6 and Lee Yoon-sik's "New Administrative Information System Theory" Chapter 3.

of a Decision Support System (DSS), an Information Processing System (IPS), and a Data Processing System (DPS). The Information Processing System (IPS) is called the consultation MIS.

If we relate MIS to the organizational system, the Decision Support System (DSS) corresponds to the upper organizational system, the Information Processing System (IPS) corresponds to the middle organizational system, and the Data Processing System (DPS) corresponds to the lower organizational system. In other words, DPS corresponds to a word-processing system with repetitive and clear processes in the lower organization, IPS corresponds to a word-processing system that converts data into information in the middle organization, and DSS corresponds to a word-processing system that analyzes and completes information for decision-making in the upper organization. A simple representation of this is shown in Figure 4-1.

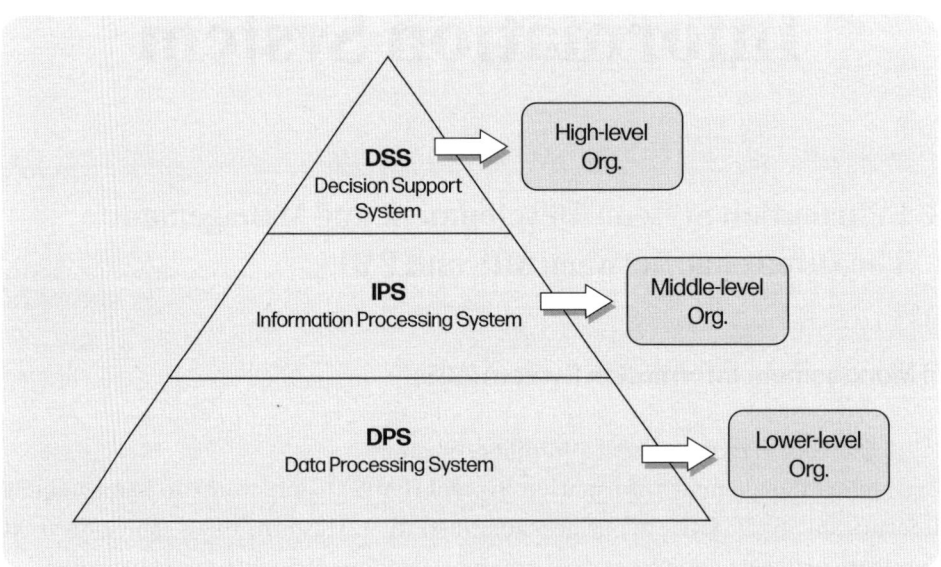

[Figure 2-1] Relationship between MIS and the Organization

(2) Characteristics of the management information system

The characteristics of MIS are as follows (Ahn, 2009: 196-198).

First, an MIS is an integrated system in which humans and machines are interconnected, i.e., it is a decentralized system in which humans handle the tasks that humans can handle, and machines (computers) handle the tasks that machines can handle. In an MIS, humans perform tasks such as entering data, analyzing tasks, and using results. Contact between humans and machines (computers) occurs in many ways, but the main contact is through terminals. When "computer-based" is used in information systems, it implies that humans and computers interactively process information through terminals. Since MIS is an integrated system that presupposes an organic relationship between humans and computers, MIS designers must recognize the information processing behavior of human users and the information processing limitations of computers. Only then can smooth information processing be realized.

Second, because MIS is an organization-wide system, measures must be taken to integrate piecemeal developments. This integration can be achieved through standardization, guidelines, and networking, but essentially, the system's design system must take this into account during the design phase. In other words, the MIS must have a holistic view of the system in whatever form it takes.

Third, MIS has a database as an essential component. Database refers to the maintenance and management of data in a state that users can easily use. Deciding what data to collect, process, and preserve in what state is a very important factor for the successful design and operation of an MIS.

Fourth, MIS must have decision mathematical models and continue to develop these models for new decisions because MIS involves more than just repetitive tasks; it also involves the ability to support decision-makers in their decisions.

2) Administrative Information System

(1) Concept of administrative information system

Public Management Information System (PMIS) has its roots in the Management Information System (MIS) of business administration. The term PMIS is commonly used to refer to public management information systems. Therefore, we will refer to it as PMIS.

The concept of administrative information system refers to the administrative system for national information management as a man-machine system that collects, retrieves, processes, and provides various information to support the provision of administrative services, the formation, execution, and evaluation of policies, and the operation and management of administrative organizations, and the main contents are as follows (Choi, 1999: 374-376; Park et al., 2005: 23-27; Lee et al., 2004: 38-40).

The administrative information system can be called a public management information system.[02] . The structure of the administrative information system is

---

[02] A Management Information System (MIS) is a part of an information management system that provides managers with the information they need to plan for the organization's future and make other

shown in Figure 2-1.

(2) Difference between PMIS and MIS

While MIS is conceptualized at the micro-level of the organization, PMIS, on the other hand, is conceptualized and used not only at the micro-level of the organization but also at the macro to super-macro-level of the country.

The difference between PMIS and MIS centers on information processing in public and private sector organizations. The information processing process of an environment-related system goes through four stages, "① Monitoring, ② Interpretation of information and exploration of alternatives, ③ Goal setting and plan formulation, ④ Evaluation," and the main differences between PMIS and MIS are as follows (Ahn, 1995: 212-217).

① **Data collection phase: passive**

The private sector actively collects information. On the other hand, the public sector relies heavily on passive methods of information gathering, primarily through reporting, which requires a high degree of coercion and, therefore, low costs to collect information. Organizations in the public sector are willing to rely on compulsory reporting, such as reports from environmental constituents, without expending any energy (and without incurring any costs) because of the public sector's ability to mobilize public power in data collection.

② **Interpret information and explore alternatives: Heuristics techniques**

The private sector tends to apply rational models that seek the optimal solution according to an algorithmic[03] Interpretation. On the other hand, the public sector prefers incremental and satisfying models, which are "easier to adapt to the environment and realistic interests," according to heuristics techniques.

③ **Goal setting and planning: abstract and inchoate**

The private sector aims to make a profit, so its goals and long-term planning horizon are concrete. The public sector, on the other hand, has multiple abstract

---

management decisions. The management information provided by an MIS is necessary for routine managerial decision-making.

03 An algorithm is a method that is solved in a certain order and leads to an exact answer. On the other hand, a heuristic is a method of solving a problem or making a judgment about an uncertain situation, but without a clear cle, and can be translated into English as a "quick fix" or "quick estimation".

and intangible goals and a short planning horizon. Moreover, frequent changes in policymakers and the accompanying goal shifts result in the "property of no memory" of goals.

In public sector organizations, setting a long-term planning horizon of 5 to 10 years is difficult because agency heads serve relatively short periods (1-2 years) before rotating to other positions or retiring.

④ **Step 4: Evaluation: Democracy, Responsiveness, and Equity**

The pursuit of profit drives the private sector, which has clear evaluation criteria, such as economics and efficiency. The public sector, on the other hand, has unclear and variable evaluation criteria, with a focus on democracy, responsiveness, and equity. In addition, public sector organizations are often inert when setting goals, making feedback more difficult than in the private sector.

A change in policymakers can turn a highly desirable initiative targeted by a predecessor into a "useless, budget-draining project". Private sector organizations, on the other hand, have clear objectives, and their predecessors' goals stay the same with personnel changes, making it easier to evaluate business performance than in the public sector.

(3) Necessity of administrative information system

The reasons or purposes for PMIS include rationalizing the policy process, increasing the efficiency of administrative work, improving the quality of administrative services, and improving administrative work (Lee et al. et al., 2004: 40-44; Choi et al., 2006: 365-376; Kim et al., 2001: 195-198; Choi, 1999: 372-377).

① **Rationalization of the policy process**

As information socialization progresses, the government's openness to disclose information is increasing, and public awareness is improving, which requires rapid informatization of administrative and policy processes. Therefore, digitalization is necessary to improve participation and responsiveness in the policy process.

The administrative information system collects and analyzes information on people's needs, making them the object of the policy agenda. It rationally conducts the process of setting specific policy goals, exploring and creating alternatives, analyzing alternatives, and evaluating and selecting alternatives. To rationally execute policies, it uses analytical techniques from management science.[04] Such as Operational Research (OR), Planning Evaluation Research Model (PERT), and Cost Process Method (CPM) to improve the efficiency of execution.

② **Streamline administrative tasks**

An administrative information system can reduce the cost of workforce, budget, time, and space by mechanizing repetitive tasks and collaboratively utilizing administrative information. It can also reduce manual labor, increase the time available for professional work, and automate structured and repetitive managerial decisions.

③ **Improve the quality of administrative services**

Administrative information systems can speed up the processing of administrative affairs, enhance equity, eradicate corruption, increase friendly public service, improve the accuracy of civil service processing, and develop various public services.

④ **Improve administrative tasks**

PMIS makes it possible to (1) consolidate and unify teller services, (2) provide administrative services in adjacent areas, (3) simplify administrative documents and forms, and (4) systematize administrative decision-making authority.

(4) Features and functions of administrative information systems

① **Features of PMIS**

The features of PMIS can be categorized into two types: general features and design-operational features. The general characteristics of PMIS are as follows (Ahn, 1988: 7-8; Lee, 2009: 137-138).

First, it supports the administrative activities of administrative officials and the general public. PMIS is primarily a support system for administrative officials working in national organizations and public institutions. PMIS is also a system that supports the general public in accessing and utilizing administrative information more easily.

Second, it controls administrative and policy activities. PMIS makes it easier for the public to provide feedback to the administration; through this feedback, it is possible

---

04 Management science refers to scientific and quantitative analytical methods to explore optimal alternatives in problem-solving and decision-making. The types of analytical techniques in management science include (1) Operation Research (OR), (2) Liner Programming (LP), (3) Game Theory, (4) Simulation, (5) PERT, and (6) Critical Process Method (CPM).

to control administrative and policy activities.

Third, it is an artificially designed and manufactured management system. PMIS is designed to develop and apply various software corresponding to artificial intelligence (AI) necessary to streamline administrative activities and increase effectiveness.

Fourth, it is a system of human-machine interaction. PMIS is a system formed based on the mutually organic relationship between human and mechanical elements. This means that the use of mechanical enzymes, including computers, is required to streamline administrative information activities, and people must be able to understand and apply the principles of such mechanical operations. These characteristics also imply that PMIS controls and manages the people involved in information activities and the machines.

PMIS is designed and operated based on the above general characteristics. These design and operational features are derived from the fact that many stakeholders have different interests in the administrative organization, so its goals may become uncertain (Ahn, 1995: 243-244), and the design and operational features are as follows.

First, it is linked to the organization's planning process. PMIS has a long-term goal of determining the organization's "desired" future direction and discovering how to get there, and a short-term goal of solving the organization's problems. As such, it is linked to the organization's planning process.

Second, it is based on using computers and communication technologies for information processing. As one of the computer application fields, PMIS is designed and operated using developed computer and communication technology.

Third, it revolves around a content-centered theory. There are two main theories of information systems: procedural theory and substantive theory. Procedural theory holds that there is a best process for building and operating information systems; information systems theory is about discovering and applying this process. On the other hand, the content-centered theory is that no process leads to a good information system in principle, and information system theory is about discovering what the information system processes, what the impact is, and what factors affect the content. If MIS is generally a process-centered theory, PMIS is a content-centered theory.

Fourth, we design and operate information systems for organizations in the public sector. An information system is a theory about information management in an organization, and its contents vary depending on the environment in which the organization is located. MIS is a system that designs and operates information systems for organizations in the private sector, and PMIS is a system that designs and operates information systems for organizations in the public sector.

② **Features of PMIS**

An administrative information system performs vertical, horizontal, and integrative functions, and the main contents are as follows (Davis & Olsen, 1985, ch.2; Lee, 2009: 140-144).

First, the vertical function of PMIS. PMIS is responsible for supporting various administrative and policy activities within an administrative organization. It is responsible for different functions depending on the hierarchy of the organizational structure. These functions are called the vertical functions of PMIS. The vertical functions of PMIS are as follows.

- A strategic planning function that supports strategic policy planning and decision-making at the highest levels of management (or top policymakers).
- It is a management function that supports tactical policy planning and decision-making at the middle management level.
- It is an operational control function that supports operational planning, decision-making, and control at lower management levels.
- Routine processing functions that support the day-to-day operations of lower-level administrative organization members.

An easy-to-understand representation of the vertical functions of PMIS is shown in Figure 2-2.

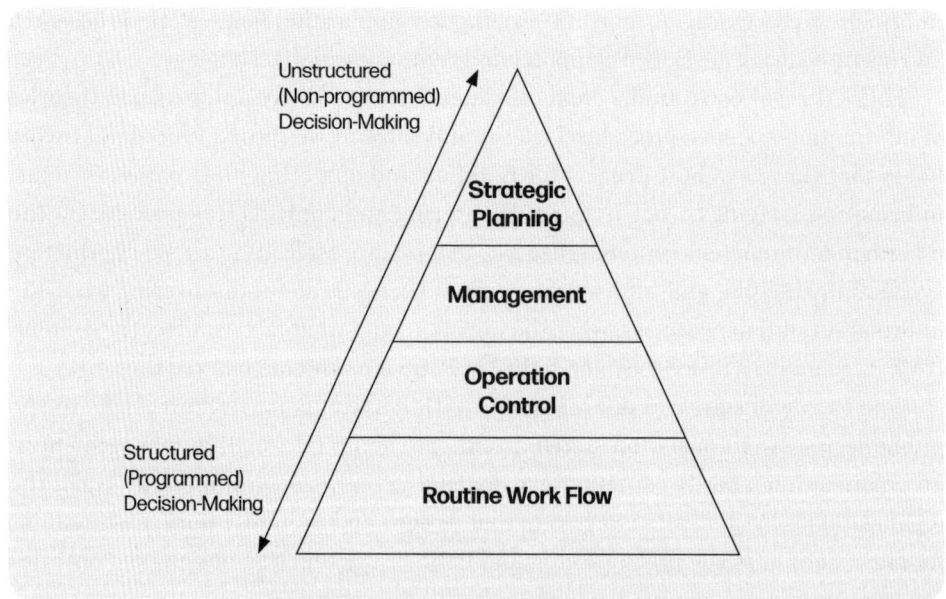

[Figure 2-2] Vertical Functions in PMIS

Second, the horizontal function of PMIS. PMIS performs information management functions differently, and it is supported by subordinate administrative organizations depending on their business areas. These functions of PMIS are called horizontal functions. An example of a PMIS's horizontal functions is the PMIS's ability to support general administration, financial accounting, human resource management, etc. As these functions become more diverse and complex as administrative tasks are subdivided, it is necessary to add functions that coordinate these functions to the PMIS in order to perform these horizontal functions efficiently and effectively. In addition, for PMIS to perform horizontal functions efficiently, it is necessary to fully consider the influence of non-economic political factors and other factors in the immediate environment of the administrative organization rather than managing and controlling information from an exclusively economic perspective, as in MIS.

Third, the integration of the PMIS. Since PMIS performs vertical and horizontal functions almost simultaneously rather than separately, the function of PMIS should be considered in terms of integrating these two functions. The ability to perform both vertical and horizontal functions of a PMIS together is called the integrated function of a PMIS. This integrated function does not mean that both functions are performed simultaneously in the same proportion but rather that they are performed simultaneously to achieve a specific purpose. In the case of managing the information required to perform various tasks at the lower levels of the administrative organization, information management enables the members of the lower levels to provide the information required by the upper levels of the organization. Eventually, the entire organization performs the information function together organically, and this integrated administrative information management function is performed throughout the administrative organization.

2. Policy-Making Models in E-government[05]

1) Policy-Making Process and Information and Communication Technology

The policy-making process refers to setting policy goals to solve a policy problem,

---

05   The "Policy-making model in e-government" section is based on Myeong (2001). "Limitations of rational policy-making and information systems in e-government and the possibility of knowledge-based administration," Informationization Policy, 8(3): 9-23.

exploring, comparing, and evaluating alternatives to achieve the set goals, and adopting the preferred alternative as a policy (Heo, 1988: 91). Information utilization is essential in two ways to explore, develop, and select alternatives (Lee, 1990: 699).

First, in the policy-making process, a thorough analysis of the situation in which the policy problem and goals are placed is necessary to correctly recognize the problem and set policy goals to solve it. For this analysis, information on the social environment, institutional structure, human resources, and the availability of material resources is essential.

Second, information is essential for exploring and analyzing alternatives to achieve set policy goals.

The role of ICT as a tool for producing information for policy-making has been proposed in various ways (Choi et al., 2007: 142). Computers enhance the technical performance of policymakers and help them act rationally by compensating for weaknesses in information selection and memory (Simon, 1973). ICTs also contribute to the decision-making process by helping to review and determine when and under what circumstances communication is necessary. ICTs enhance communication and access to information, and enhanced communication and access to information further develops the core knowledge of an organization (as a professional services firm, such as a law firm, tax and accounting firm, or consulting firm) through the discovery and combination of knowledge (Martin, 1994). Improved access to information allows decision-making processes to be more formalized (Hurber, 1984), and it provides organizational members with easy and timely access to the common information they need to do their jobs.

In other words, depending on the stage of the policy-making process and the content of the main activities at each stage, the policymaker may choose different information sources and means of acquisition to make decisions (Saunders & Jones, 1990). In addition, contextual factors such as the time to arrive at a decision, the importance of the decision to the manager, and the interpersonal relationships already established between the manager and the policymaker determine the mix of "source → acquisition (means of delivery) and time" of individual information in the policy-making process.

2) Significance and Constraints of Rational Policy Making

(1) The significance of rational policy making

Rational policy-making is a policy theory based on rational models. A rational model is a theory that consists of theoretical assumptions about how individual preferences determine individual behavior. The core of the rational model is that individuals explore all available information (or alternatives). Through systematic information analysis, they choose the action that optimizes or maximizes their expected utility and profit. Therefore, rational policy-making based on the rational model is also a theory that when a specific problem occurs or is predicted, the policymaker accurately recognizes the problem, grasps all relevant information, and makes a rational policy decision every time without interruption in the process of setting policy goals, collecting information, analyzing and interpreting alternatives, and selecting alternatives.

Six factors must be satisfied for rational policy-making based on a rational model to be possible (Allison, 1972; Jung, 1998).

① Know all of society's value preferences and their relative weights.
② Know all available policy alternatives.
③ Know all the consequences of each policy alternative.
④ Each individual's preferences are stable and consistent, allowing for accurate interpretation and use of information.
⑤ Calculate the ratio between the social value realized and the value sacrificed by each policy alternative.
⑥ Determine the most optimal policy alternative among the alternatives.

In order to make such rational policy decisions, it is necessary to introduce information systems with advanced ICT to enable decision-making systems. The reason is that the utilization of information is essential for rational policy-making. From an information system perspective, introducing and utilizing information systems are essential for rationalizing the policy-making process because information systems are designed on the premise of rationality. In the case of private management information systems (MIS), the possibility of rational decision-making is higher than in public organizations because they use algorithmic and rational modeling approaches in the analysis and interpretation of information and operate mainly on relatively targeted and quantifiable information (Ahn, 1997). Therefore, the emergence of sophisticated information systems in policy-making has increased the possibility of rational policy-making compared to the past (Choi et al., 2007: 146).

However, no matter how advanced ICT and information systems are, it is difficult to identify all possible alternatives from a rational modeling perspective, weigh them, and select the best cost/benefit ratio.

(2) Factors that Constrain Rational Policy-Making

There are five main limitations to rational policy-making based on rational models. First, not all alternatives can be identified during policy-making. Second, the values of all alternatives cannot be compared in an accurate weighted manner. Third, the information used in practice is limited by the nature of the organization and the environment, and the information obtained is also limited. Fourth, policy-making and policy implementation should be seamlessly linked in theory, but in practice, most policy implementation often develops differently from the initial policy goals. Fifth, internal and external variables, such as organizational structure, role relationships among organizational members, and stakeholder conflict and negotiation processes, often lead to the selection of compromise alternatives that are satisfactory in practice rather than rational choices.

Empirical research on information collection and actual use in the policy-making process (Oh, 1996; Oh, 1998) suggests that the "collection → distribution → use" of information assumed by the rational policy-making model is not automatically linked. Policymakers may collect information without intending to distribute it or distribute it to other people or organizations without using it. By not considering these different stages of the information process, the rational model's assumptions about the flow of information in the policy process are significantly out of step with the real world (Oh, 1998: 201). An analysis of the policy-making process in the U.S. public mental health sector shows that policymakers rely primarily on internal sources of information at the information-gathering stage and do not share information with others at the information-allocation stage (Oh, Chulho et al., 2002: 95). An analysis of the determinants of information sharing among U.S. state governments found that information sharing is influenced more by organizational proximity, especially functional proximity, than by the technical factors of a well-designed information sharing system (Hinnant & Bretschneider, 1997). In other words, information sharing is more likely to occur with organizations and agencies with similar functions than with organizations with significant functional differences. These findings empirically demonstrate that the rational policy-making assumption that the "collection → distribution → use" of information automatically leads to selecting the optimal alternative does not hold in practice.

Rational policy-making is limited because it does not reflect the real world, where many variables are at play. Even with the introduction of information systems, rational policy-making cannot be achieved if policymakers or policy participants intentionally conceal or withhold information while analyzing or communicating information. Therefore, contextualized policy-making based on limited rationality that can pursue realistic and satisfactory choices rather than perfectly rational policy-making is an alternative to correct policy-making.

(3) Root Cause of Difficulty in Making Rational Policy-making: The Gap Between Theory and Practice

The fundamental problem with rational policy-making based on rational models is that we need to close the gap between theory and reality, knowing that rational models cannot fully account for many variables in our reality. The way to close the gap between theory and reality is to reform (or innovate) within the organization deliberately. In particular, since ICT play a merely instrumental role, if human will, organizational culture, and institutional improvement are not preceded, the introduction of ICT (information systems) into administrative organizations can only be at the level of 'administrative computerization' or 'office automation.'

As information systems are information and management systems based on the interaction of people and systems, strategies must be applied to organizations by the proportion of rational, irrational, and supra-rational areas. Therefore, the Rationalization of the policy-making process in the information society is more appropriate to apply the concept of 'flexible rationality' that adjusts the level of rationality to the organizational situation rather than the perfect rationality of the pure rational model. Assuming that the application of ICT and information management systems helps to rationalize the policy-making process, the gap between theory and reality can also be referred to as the gap between perfect rationality and reality (Choi, 2007: 149), so efforts should be made to narrow the gap between theory and reality.

As shown above, there is a gap between the collection, actual use, and distribution of information in public institutions, which is not sequentially linked to theory and practice. As a result, introducing ICT and information systems only sometimes leads to rationalizing the policy-making process. The gap between theory and practice is manifested as follows.

First, compared to private companies, public organizations have lower funding levels, specialized staff, and information literacy.

Second, most systems rely on top-down, rationalized information management systems of the past.

Third, the abolition of the Ministry of Information and Communication after the previous Lee Myung-bak government (2008-2013) resulted in a workforce shortage and low morale for the computer department and digital transformation.

Fourth, an attempt must be made to narrow the gap between theory and reality due to the lack of a promotion system, such as a digitalization officer based on the concept of information resource management.

For the above reasons, the gap between theory and practice is not closing, and it is not easy to rationalize policy decisions and processes at this level.

In addition, while managers mainly do decision-making in the private sector (corporations) and tend to focus on solving problems related to profit, decision-making in the public sector involves more people, including social organizations and interest groups in addition to politicians and bureaucrats, and problem-solving is also related to various ideologies such as social efficiency and equality. In other words, the public sector involves more people in the policy-making process than the private sector, so the gap between theory and reality of rational policy-making is bound to be larger than in the private sector. In the public sector, the positions of various stakeholders must be considered, and the policy-making process is subject to conflict and negotiation with them to make satisfactory policy decisions that can form mutual consensus.

An alternative to narrowing the gap between theory and reality and making policy decisions that do not cut off the flow of information is to abandon rational policy-making based on rational models and choose contextual policy-making models that fit real-world situations.

3) Policy-making Models in E-government: Contextualized Policy-Making Models

(1) The need for contextualized policy-making

In the process of rational policy-making (including information systems based on the rational model), there is a large gap between the actual information flow and the policy-making process, so the simple application of information systems based on the rational model may result in policy decisions that do not help solve real problems. The problem with the existing information system is that the flow of information needs to be connected. In other words, if rational policy-making is to explore and analyze all possible alternatives, the process of collecting, accumulating, transmitting, and using information must be interconnected. However, the gap between theory and reality limits existing rational information systems. Therefore, the information system designed on the premise of rationality hinders rational policy-making.

Bounded rationality favors policy decisions that are realistically appropriate by placing information in context. From the perspective of bounded rationality, applying knowledge management systems that focus on sharing knowledge and know-how among organizational members may be more effective in information sharing.

As we have seen in the previous section on the theory-practice gap, in real-world organizations, too much information can be confusing for rational policy-making, and the information needed for rational policy-making is not much-fragmented information but useful information that can provide clues to the organization's goals and solve problems in a given situation. Such information is knowledge based on the experience and know-how acquired by the organization's members during their work. Therefore, mutual knowledge-sharing among organizational members must abandon the passive attitude of relying on the automatic linkage of information processes and build a foundation for reducing trial and error by actively sharing experiences of success and failure in work performance (Choi, et al., 2007: 153). The foundation, in this case, is not a foundation from a systemic perspective but rather a foundation that is formed based on organization, work, people, and culture, which is more like an open system that can predict the changing environment in advance and respond appropriately.

Contextualized policy-making refers to policy-making that is based on knowledge derived from the experiences of the organization's members and sublimated, preferably through a form.[06] It can be said that contextual policy-making is an administration that selects or takes action on alternatives that have formed mutual consensus through a systematic knowledge management system that enables mutual experience and opinion exchange among organizational members in recognizing problems and selecting alternatives when making policy decisions (Oh, Chulho, et al., 2002: 102). Therefore, to implement contextual policy-making, it is necessary to clarify cause and effect relationships at the problem recognition stage through a learning process that can expand individual knowledge into organizational knowledge and ICT

06　　Knowledge can be divided into formal and tacit knowledge according to its form and organizational and personal knowledge according to the degree of sharing, and the main characteristics are as follows (Oh et al., 2002: 103).
① Formal knowledge: Objective knowledge that can be expressed in language. It is transmitted and acquired through language and is easily transferable.
Example) Research reports, books, databases, computer manuals, work procedures, etc.
② Tacit knowledge: Subjective knowledge that is difficult to express in language. It is conveyed through metaphors and is difficult to transmit as knowledge acquired through experience.
Example) Organizational culture, craftsmanship, etc.
③ Organizational knowledge: Organizational knowledge. It is mainly formalized in language.
Example) Organizational culture, systems, institutions, business processes, etc.
④ Personal knowledge: Knowledge at the individual level. It refers to the conceptual knowledge contained in an individual's brain.
Example) Knowledge embodied in individuals, etc.)

such as intranets, data warehouses, and data mining that can systematically support knowledge creation, sharing, and utilization by organizational members are required. In addition, in terms of organizational structure and culture, leadership, incentive provision, institutionalization, organic flat structure, and emphasis on process and results (rather than inputs) are required (Choi, et al., 2007: 155).

(2) Prerequisites for contextualized policy-making: administrative reforms

Administrative organizations are perceived as organizations that produce rigidity and numerous procedures and regulations due to their bureaucratic (hierarchical) structure. Administrative reform can be seen as the opposite of this perception of administrative organizations, i.e., administrative reform is a concept that aims for an organization that is more flexible, non-bureaucratic, and with fewer unnecessary procedures and regulations (Choi et al., 2007: 155). Reform has two meanings (Bozeman & Straussman, 1991).

First, reforms are tangible and intangible "things" that exist, such as new ideas, outputs, programs, and technical capabilities. In addition to technological reforms, administrative reforms include management and policy reforms. Management reforms include new ways of hiring people, reallocation of resources, and redesign of work (Daft, 1978), while policy reforms can be defined as "changes in the core strategy of an organization to achieve its major goals" (Zaltman et al., 1973: 16). Reforms in management and policy are context-appropriate, and different management methods and strategies are needed in response to the new administrative environment.

Second, reform is processual in the sense of 'the act of reforming.' Administrative reform as a process is a concept that focuses on the process of adaptation and implementation rather than the invention itself, such as scientific and technological inventions or new ideas (Mohr, 1969; Zaltman et al., 1973). Therefore, it refers to the reform linking policy-making and policy implementation, such as seamless administration (Han, 1998) (Oh, Chulho et al., 2002: 104).

Based on the two aspects of reform, we can define it as "new ideas, management methods, strategies, and (technological) solutions that allow the members of an administrative organization to adapt to the environment and induce change in interacting with it."

(3) Deriving a contextualized policy-making model

To summarize the process of overcoming the limitations of rational policy making (gap between theory and reality) and deriving a contextual policy making model through administrative reform, ① the assumptions of policy making based on the rational model have limitations, ② the information system is designed based on rationality, but there is a gap between theory and reality in the actual distribution and use of information, ③ As an alternative to overcome these information system limitations, contextual policy-making is pursued, which has the potential to make comprehensive and rational policy-making by linking the flow of (organizational) knowledge through mutual sharing of knowledge based on work experience among organizational members, and ④ In order to implement contextual policy-making, administrative reforms such as unified purpose shared by organizational members,

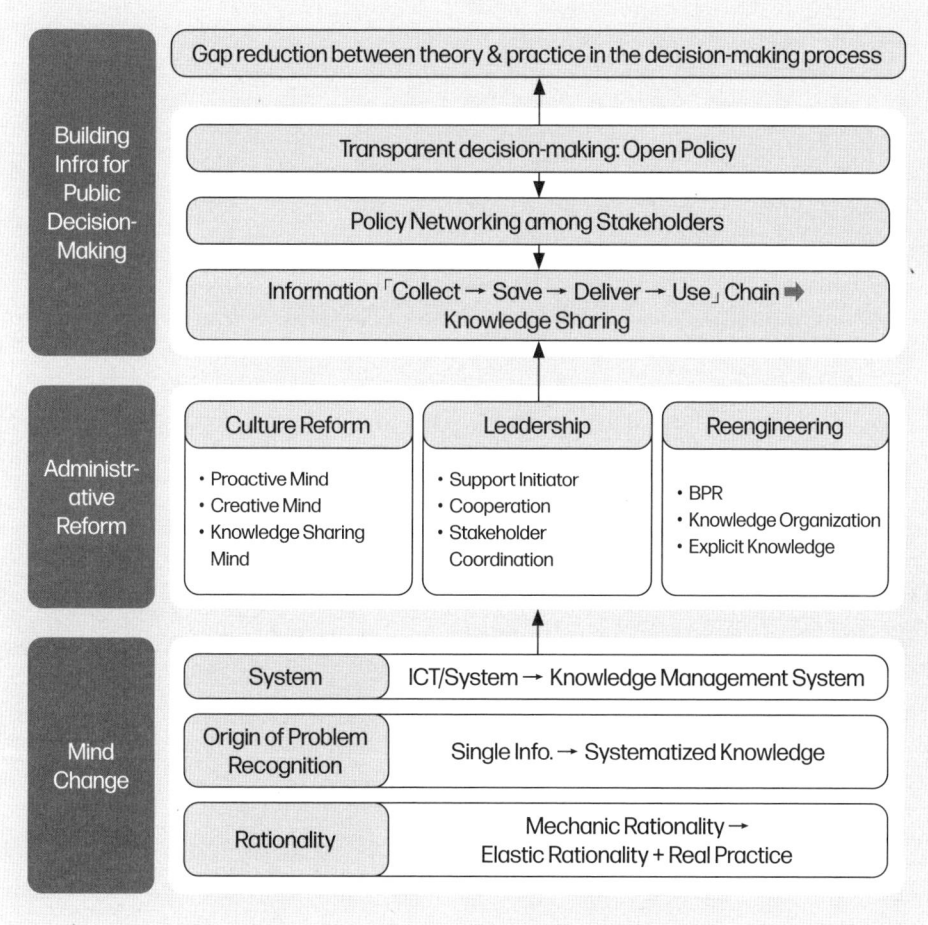

Source: Seunghwan Myung (2001: 20) Theorem.

[Figure 2-3] Contextualized Policy-Making Models to Overcome the Limitations of Rational Models

overcoming the expectation-performance gap between organizational members and stakeholders, and harmonization among organizational members centered on the top management level are necessary for correct policy-making (Choi et al: 158-159).

Combining the above discussion, we can derive a contextualized policy-making model, as shown in Figures 3.

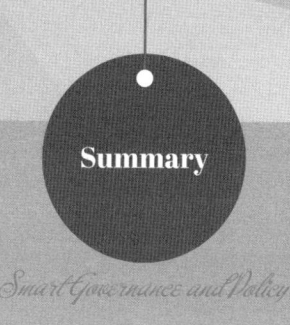

Summary

Public Management Information Systems (PMIS) have their roots in Management Information Systems (MIS) in business administration. The term MIS is commonly used to refer to management information systems, and PMIS refers to public management information systems.

An MIS is an integrated human-machine system that provides information to support an organization's management, analysis, and decision-making functions. The components of an MIS include hardware, software, manual processing procedures, models, and databases for analysis, planning, control, and decision-making. A broad MIS consists of a Decision Support System (DSS), an Information Processing System (IPS), and a Data Processing System (DPS). The Information Processing System (IPS) is called the MIS of the consultation. The components of the MIS include hardware, software, database (database), procedures, and operators. The activities performed by the MIS can be categorized as ① processing of variable data, ② management of basic files, ③ preparation of reports, ④ handling of questions, and ⑤ other support functions.

A Public Management Information System (PMIS) is a man-machine system that collects, retrieves, processes, and provides various information to support the provision of administrative services, the formation, execution, and evaluation of policies, and the operation and management of administrative organizations, and is an administrative system for national information management.

The difference between PMIS and MIS centers on information processing in public and private sector organizations. In the data collection stage, ① MIS actively collects information, while PMIS relies heavily on the passive method of reporting. In the information interpretation and alternative exploration stage, MIS applies a rational model that pursues the optimal solution based on algorithmic analysis, ② but PMIS prefers an incremental model and a satisfaction model based on the heuristics technique (which is easy to adapt to the environment and adjust realistic interests). ③ In the goal setting and planning stage, MIS aims to pursue profits and has a long-term planning period, while PMIS has a short-term planning period with multiple, abstract, and intangible goals. ④ In the evaluation stage, MIS aims to pursue profit and has clear evaluation criteria such as economy and efficiency. However, PMIS has unclear evaluation criteria, is prone to change, and focuses on democracy, responsiveness, and equity.

In policy-making, information is essential for making the right policy decisions. Policymakers may use different ICTs to acquire information from various sources depending on the policy-making process. Even if ICT and information systems are advanced, it is only possible to identify some possible alternatives from a rational model perspective, weigh them, and select the best cost/benefit ratio, as there are many difficulties in practice. To summarize the process of deriving a contextual policy-making model through administrative reform by overcoming the limitations of rational policy-making (gap between theory and reality), ① the assumptions of policy-making based on rational models have limitations, ② information systems are designed based on rationality, but there is a gap between theory and reality in the actual distribution and use of information, ③ As an alternative to overcome these information system limitations, contextual policy-making is pursued, which has the potential to make comprehensive and rational policy-making by linking the flow of (organizational) knowledge through mutual sharing of knowledge based on work experience among organizational members, and ④ In order to implement contextual policy-making, administrative reforms such as unified purpose shared by organizational members, overcoming the gap in performance expectations between organizational members and stakeholders, and harmony among organizational members centered on the top management level are necessary for correct policy-making.

Research Questions

1. Explain the relationship between the council's management information system (MIS) and the broader management information system.
2. Describe the components of a management information system (MIS).
3. Explain the concept of a management information system (MIS).
4. Explain why utilizing information in the policy-making process is necessary.
5. Discuss the limitations of rational policy-making and how they can be overcome.

Chapter 3

Understanding and Moving toward E-Governance

1. Definition and Types of E-governance

1) Definition of E-governance

Scholars have variously defined the debate on what e-Governance is out of a clearly defined concept. It has been described as "a new way of public administration that utilizes communication methods in virtual space such as the Internet" (Kim, 2000: 134) or public policy that maintains order in the Internet space for competition, order, and development in virtual space in an institutional sense (Coyle, 1998). In a broader sense, e-governance is defined as "dealing with the relationship between the Internet and government, the relationship between government and democracy, and the relationship between democracy and communication." In general, it is defined variously as a form in which the operating principles, such as the decision-making structure and communication process of an organization or group, are not centralized and top-down by one or a few people but are carried out through the participation of multiple actors in a decentralized and horizontal way (Song, 2004).

E-Governance itself can be defined as a socio-technical system in which IT elements called 'e' (technical subsystem) and political-social elements called 'governance' (social subsystem) interact (Myeong, 2000). In general, the development direction of IT, which constitutes 'e,' has evolved from analog to digital, from one-way to two-way, and from decentralized to integrated processing. Politics and society, which constitute "governance," have evolved from a monolithic ruler, the government, dominating its subjects, the citizens, by force, to a multinuclearized government, the market, and civil society working together to solve problems through a horizontal consultation network. Therefore, e-governance is "a network of various actors, such as states, companies, citizens, and NGOs, with different characteristics in the Internet space, building a multidimensional world while maintaining horizontal relationships."[01] E-Governance is also referred to as digital governance or cyber governance.

If e-governance is seen as the implementation of governance through cyberspace, it is necessary to understand the concept of 'cyberspace' and the concept of 'governance.' Kim et al. (1997) define cyber as 'information flow and control' and space as 'visualization and realization,' therefore, cyberspace is "the reproduction of actions in real space by enabling real-time sharing through smooth flow and control of multimedia information." In addition, Ha and Choi (1999: 170) explain cyberspace as "a network of networks with strong openness and interconnectedness, and a space or place that has specific functions and activities through the application of IT (Ha et al., 1999).[02]

On the other hand, the concept of governance has also been defined in various ways. Some view governance as a substitute for government, as a mechanism for government operation that can overcome the limitations of government (Kim, 2000; Kim, 2000), while others view it as a process or procedure that is pursued to achieve desirable public goals regardless of who is in charge (Lynn & Hill, 1999). However, both perspectives agree that pursuing the public purpose or good should be democratic, transparent, equitable, and legitimate.[03] In general, governance refers to the decision-making structure and process of an organization or group using IT that involves

---

01   This e-governance is distinct from Internet governance, defined as "the management of domains or the maintenance of order in Internet space with the goal of competition, order, and progress in virtual space."

02   It raises the question of how cyberspace behavior differs from physical behavior. This issue needs to be clarified at the legal level. However, since various transactions are already established in cyberspace, they should have the same effect as transactions or acts in physical space. However, cyberspace should not be viewed as a complete replacement for physical space but rather as a complementary space where transactions and social behaviors can occur under temporal and spatial constraints. For example, electronic commerce is already spreading, and e-mail, electronic benefit transfer (EBT), electronic tax payment, and home banking are effective in a form that compensates for the unnecessary time and space limitations of physical space.

03   Another governance concept is an alternative pattern of state management encompassing the dimensions of management, policy, and organization (Kim, 2000).

multiple actors in a decentralized and horizontal manner rather than centralized and top-down by one person or a few.

The discussion of e-governance is based on the idea that advances in ICT have enabled citizens to directly participate in the policy-making process by enabling interactive communication and information sharing across time and space. The discussion on e-governance aims for small government. It acknowledges the emergence of citizens as new participants in terms of spatial location and virtual space and seeks to expand their participation in content. IT's expansion of governance mechanisms in cyberspace is recognized as one of the means to enable more governance and is being used as a new model to revitalize democracy compared to traditional models (Peters, 1998; Kim, 2000).

<Table 3-1> Highlights of E-governance

Issues	Contents
Focus	'Less Government, More Governance'
Spaces	Mediate through cyberspace
Participants	Governments, citizens, NGOs, interest groups
Contents	Increase engagement with non-governmental actors

<Table 3-2> Types of Participation in Traditional Model and E-governance

Engagement Metrics	Traditional Model	E-governance
Engagement Form	Cause (Representative)	Private/Collective (Individual/Collective)
Engagement Areas	Inside the rafting	Inside and Outside the System
Types of Engagement	Passive/Reactive (Passive/Reactive)	Active/Interactive (Pro-active/Interactive)
The Impact of Engagement	Indirect/Delayed (Indirect/Delayed)	Direct/Immediate

Suppose the implementation of e-government in the past aimed to increase the efficiency and accessibility of government administrative service functions by combining them with IT. In that case, e-governance extends participation in major policy-making and implementation. In other words, governance means increasing the number of governed people. In particular, the development of the Internet and ICT has significantly lowered the cost of political participation and information acquisition for ordinary people while increasing their accessibility. These changes in the material foundations favor interactive political participation, continuous mutual feedback, and a more open system of governance. In this sense, e-governance emphasizes achieving the common good through actual consensus among members of society rather than personal gain.

2) The Rise of the E-governance Discussion

(1) Technical Aspects

The development of IT has made it possible to actively utilize these technologies to pursue autonomous participation and interactive communication with members of society anytime, anywhere. In general, the development of IT is credited with enabling the rapid and accurate processing of large amounts of data and the interactive sharing of information and access to information.

First, the speed of IT allows for rapid communication across time and space, from individual to individual, individual to organization, and organization to organization. The proliferation of the Internet can deliver a wealth of information in terms of volume and speed compared to other media, which can expedite decision-making by reducing the number of intermediate nodes through which information flows up and down the organization.

Second, interactive communication has been made possible by developing networks based on the Internet and integrated systems. With the development of IT, individuals and organizations can share information across time and space without the effort of repeatedly entering information. For governments, the interactivity of the Internet has allowed them to get immediate responses to their policies from the public and reduce the burden of unnecessary work. At the same time, it has allowed citizens to get the services they want quickly.

Third, the development of IT has changed how information is distributed, leading to the institutionalization of information disclosure in the information society. The development of IT has increased the ability to process huge amounts of information without errors. It has allowed it to open and share information the government previously monopolized with the public. Public scrutiny of government and information transparency has become possible. In Korea, the electronic disclosure of government information has been promoted since 1994 with the passage of the Act on the Disclosure of Information by Public Authorities.

Fourth, the development of IT has provided users with low-cost mechanisms to involve members of society in each stage of decision-making actively.

These characteristics of IT are manifested in the efforts to build an e-government that actively utilizes IT in the administrative work of the government by taking full advantage of the advantages of IT. An electronic government is a government that seeks to actively utilize IT, especially the Internet, in government affairs to achieve efficient government. E-government is designed to actively utilize the government and the people in conducting national administrative affairs to improve administrative productivity and to provide citizens with the information or services they want whenever and wherever they want them. IT is generally recognized as having brought about the following changes in government operations.

- Technical role: Digitalization of government operations and the resulting efficiencies (automated filing of tax forms, e-voting, periodic information reporting)
- Supportive role: Promote transparency through the disclosure of government information and increase citizen participation in government services
- Innovative role: IT as a tool for government service delivery that provides the same information to each member of society through e-mail and websites.

On the other hand, the development of ICT was expected to elevate citizens to direct participants in policy-making by enabling them to access more information, seek new information from political institutions and organizations, and express direct political demands.

With the help of technological advances, it was expected that all citizens would be able to participate directly in the public policy-making process and that democratic ideals could be achieved by utilizing new media in the political process to provide a variety of opportunities for discussion and participation between citizens and political leaders (Arterton, 1994). Alvin Toffler also believed that in the 21st century, with ICT enabling widespread political participation by the general public, a semi-direct democracy could be possible, in which the general public participates in the policy-making process rather than being governed by a small elite (Toffler, 1990).

(2) Ideological Background

The development of IT was expected to offer governments the possibility to overcome Keynesian government's failures. Keynesian government's non-monopolistic provision of public goods, inefficient bureaucracy, and administrative cronyism led to government failure, and reinventing entrepreneurial government was required to overcome it (Osborne & Gaebler, 1992). The rise of neo-liberalism, especially in the international community, led to active attempts to utilize IT in state administration. Countries such as the United States, the United Kingdom, and Australia, which began actively utilizing IT in public affairs in the 1990s, sought to overcome public sector inefficiencies and achieve performance-oriented government management through e-government.

This move parallels the new public government's emphasis on introducing private management techniques, performance-based management, and customer-centered administration. Korea has also attempted to utilize IT to improve administrative work processes and enhance administrative processing and policy-making support capabilities through joint use of administrative information.

On the other hand, as the existing system of representative democracy, which is an 'agent system' that converges, integrates, and coordinates various interests through political parties and parliaments, has shown practical limitations, the possibility of 'e-governance' has emerged as a complement to the existing system, as it is no longer able to resolve various conflicts effectively. The use of cyberspace by citizens based on portal sites or communities is spreading as they expand their relationships with the real world or form new ones through cell phones, messengers, and mini-homepages. In the virtual space built through the Internet, a group exchanging communications through a computer network forms a virtual community, establishing a new governance situation.

From the citizen's perspective, using IT has led to greater civic engagement by reducing transaction costs, reducing harvesting congestion, and increasing opportunities for rational choice. The active adoption of IT has been sought to create new relationships and manage the destiny of communities through active communication between citizens, governments, and businesses.

3) Nature and Characteristics of E-governance

It is necessary to derive the nature and characteristics of e-governance in connection with the existing concept of governance. The concept of governance can be seen as an alternative cognitive framework to the existing nation-state-centered governance system in a situation where the state's ability to govern is weakening, and the demand for governance is increasing (Kwak, 2000). Therefore, it is necessary to carefully consider whether E-governance refers to the part of the concept of governance that applies 'e' technology or whether it means the emergence of new governance in another sense.

The emergence of governance has been associated with establishing a new order of liberal democratization, decentralization, and autonomy in the political, economic, and social fields due to changes in deindustrialization and postmodernization. Of course, it is indisputable that ICT has played a role in these changes.

However, the potential of ICT to change a new society needs to be carefully diagnosed once again. It should be understood that along with the development of ICTs, new forms of management will emerge, and the authority and role of the state will be reoriented to meet the new changes.

Because e-governance is still in a stage of incremental development, there needs to be more effort to approach its substance as a distinct concept from governance, and the prevailing view has been to apply the concept of governance broadly to include e-governance. However, if offline and online forms of governance are expressed differently, and if the goals of the two concepts are fundamentally different, efforts to understand e-governance as a distinct concept from governance will be necessary.

The online participation form will be an upgraded implementation of the traditional offline participation form based on technological advances. Currently, e-participation is mainly realized at the level of participation in the policy process through information provision, direct complaint handling, and policy discussion boards using websites. As the development of e-government begins with internal government efficiency as a starting point and gradually expands outward, citizen participation is still in its infancy. However, it is likely to undergo very rapid changes and progress in the future.

E-governance has the potential to be very different from traditional governance dynamics and pathways because it requires simultaneous strategy selection and foundation building, depending on the degree of cumulative social consensus on how to engage. To date, e-governance is mainly manifested in exploratory applications of IT in governance, making it difficult to distinguish it from governance. In other words, governance and e-governance focus on increasing the input of non-governmental actors in the policy-making process by facilitating community and communication. However, this aspect of increased participation through ICT is extended to e-voting, where the final decision is made. In that case, e-governance may develop differently from the governance elements.

The basic e-government framework will be completed when e-voting is actively adopted, and various technical and institutional foundations need to be established before entering this stage. These foundations include technical foundations such as authentication and information protection, the willingness of citizens to voluntarily participate in the adoption and application of such technologies, cultural foundations, and legal and institutional support for such a system to become a reality.

There are several obstacles to making e-voting a reality. First, it will be very important to ensure that the fundamental voting elements, such as authentication and data protection, can be operated democratically, technically, and institutionally. Only when e-voting systems are proven reliable and efficient in helping democracy be achieved will e-voting be enabled.

<Table 3-3> Election Principles in E-voting

Principles	Existing Polls	Applying Election Principles in E-voting
General Election	To recognize the right to vote in principle to all citizens who have reached a certain age, without limitation of eligibility requirements based on social status, education, property, race, faith, and gender.	Ensure all voters have the right to vote without discrimination (free terminal access for all voters via account password cards)
Equal Elections	Granting all voters the equal right to one person, one vote	To ensure one person, one vote, you need to prevent duplicate voting, which you can do by distributing password cards to each voter with a separate authentication key.
Direct Elections	Electors directly elect electors instead of selecting a midterm elector	Restrict the ability of proxies to vote on behalf of voters (using biometrics such as fingerprint and iris)
Secret Elections	A counterpart to open elections. It prevents the electorate from knowing which candidate they have chosen, often ensured by using blank ballots.	Separate voter information-related data from vote value data, blocking roots that can track individual voters' voting history

Source: http://www.goodvoting.com/present/present02.htm의 Content edit cleanup.

In modern democracies, there are four basic principles of elections (voting): universal, equal, direct, and secret. As with traditional offline elections (voting), these principles should be observed in e-voting, conducted online or via wireless communication (see Table 3-3).

For normal elections to occur under e-voting, all voters must be granted voting rights (password cards) without discrimination. All voting processes must be simplified and use human-centered interfaces so that people with disabilities and other technologically disadvantaged groups can vote without problems. In order to ensure that all voters have one person, one vote, it is necessary to prevent duplicate voting, for example, by distributing a password card with a separate authentication key to each voter. Direct elections require special technical considerations to limit the ability of proxies to vote on behalf of voters, including using biometric technologies such as fingerprinting and iris recognition, which are becoming more common, to prevent proxies from voting.

Because voters' choices of candidates must be kept strictly confidential, the technology must be able to separate data about voter information from data about vote values, blocking the path to an individual voter's vote.

Most formal studies of existing e-voting systems have emphasized the importance of certain requirements or criteria that the system must eventually fulfill, i.e., the need to eliminate all or part of the process of showing up in person at a polling place, showing one's face and ID, and casting a ballot, and replace it online. Different institutional arrangements must be implemented to meet these requirements, with corresponding economic, political, and social effects.

E-voting will have a very positive effect on voting efficiency and democratization. With its ease of use and accessibility, e-voting will engage voters and increase representation by boosting declining voter turnout. It will significantly reduce the incidence of invalid votes due to all kinds of mistakes in traditional voting methods and dramatically reduce the time required for casting and counting. From a cost perspective, it will also reduce the cost of printing ballots and participation in voting, as well as the cost of human resources to manage the vote count.

Voting in the traditional sense is often understood as a very passive form of participation that allows people to minimally express their wishes by electing representatives to govern on their behalf in situations where direct democracy is not possible. However, it is difficult to engage further after voting, as there are few mechanisms and appropriate institutional arrangements to oversee and monitor whether the elected representatives represent and reflect their wishes.

However, the development of ICT has made it possible for isolated individuals

<Table 3-4> Effects of E-voting

Separation	Effects of e-voting	Description.
Economic Aspects	Rapid Vote-Counting	The time spent counting will be dramatically reduced. Rapid vote counting will eliminate wasteful voting elements, such as exit polls.
	Reduce Costs	Reduce the cost of printing ballots, fees to participate in the election, and staffing to manage the vote count.
Political and Social Aspects	Increase Turnout	E-voting, with its ease of use and accessibility, will engage voters and increase representation by boosting declining voter turnout.
	Reduce Invalid Votes	It will significantly reduce the incidence of invalid votes due to all kinds of mistakes in the marking method.
	Changing the Decision-Making Process	By making it easier to vote, we will see a shift from a system in which a few people make decisions based on past polls to a system in which citizens make decisions themselves.

Source: http://www.goodvoting.com/present/present02.htm에서 Modification cleanup.

to easily communicate with each other, which has led to a significant change in the traditional concept of centralized governance. In the end, the emergence of new governance is very significant in that it has changed the centralized decision-making system of a few people within the existing state system to a network system in which many people can participate.

Whether the development of 'e' technologies will stop at maintaining the current governance situation, it is difficult to elicit a very positive answer. The production of cheap hardware, the availability of easy-to-use software and interfaces, and the development of mobile technology will make the e-space ubiquitous and popular. The development of ICTs will dramatically improve intercommunication, which will dramatically change decision-making: Whereas voting in the past was limited to electing representatives, e-voting will return not only the election of representatives but also the final policy-making power to the hands of citizens, who will be able to make decisions directly.

It can be said that conventional governance has made up for the shortcomings of representative democracy, which is characterized by centralized decision-making by a small number of people and has set the stage for a change to pluralistic democracy. In response, it can be predicted that e-governance will create a fully integrated network that can resolve asymmetries and inequalities in the expression of various interests that may exist even within a pluralistic democracy, causing a return to direct democracy in which the majority participates in decision-making. In this sense, e-governance needs to be discussed as a future social management system different from governance.

<Table 3-5> Characteristics of E-governance

	Traditional governance	Governance	e-Governance
Decision Making	• Fewer Centralized Decisions	• Decentralized and Distributed Decision-Making	• Multi-disciplinary Decision Making
Directionality	• Adversarial Indirect Democracy	• Pluralistic Consultative Democracy	• Majoritarian Direct Democracy
Value	• Efficiency • Responsiveness	• Efficiency • Democracy • Responsiveness	• Democracy, Efficiency • Democratic Management
Subject	• Government	• Network	• Citizen • Markets

4) Types of E-governance by Stage of Development

E-citizen participation, as envisioned by e-government, can be understood as the participation of e-citizens in networked cyberspace in e-government built for e-politics and e-administration. E-public participation can occur in various ways, such as citizens demanding the provision or disclosure of information, handling complaints directly, conducting e-surveys to gather public opinion, or e-voting to make policy judgments or decisions.

Citizen participation in government is often presented very broadly, such as in Arnstein's (1969) and OECD's (2001) typology of citizen participation, which considers the simple provision of information by government to citizens as a form of participation. In addition, citizen participation typically evolves from initial passive access to information to increasingly active participation (Zimmerman, 1986), and citizens visiting e-government to access simple and straightforward information they need can be seen as a form of electronic citizen participation.

<Table 3-6> Eight-stage Model of Civic Engagement

Engagement Steps	Engagement Highlights	Nature of Engagement
Step 8	Citizen Control	Citizen Power Tiers
Step 7	Delegated Power	
Step 6	Partnership	
Step 5	Placation	Formal-Purposeful Engagement Phase
Step 4	consultation	
Step 3	Unilateral Informing	
Step 2	Citizen Clinical Therapy (therapy)	Non-engagement Phase
Step 1	Citizen Manipulation	

Source: Arnstein (1969). Applied theorem in Institute for E-government (2004a).

Electronic citizen participation in e-government is expected to be an excellent alternative to revitalize low offline citizen participation by creating a cyber information space that transcends the time and space constraints in citizen participation in government. ICT have been shown to have positive effects on citizen participation, such as "facilitating participation," "broadening the scope of participation," and "increasing the quality of participation" (Office of the e-Envoy, 2002).

First, "facilitating participation" means making it easier for citizens to exercise their democratic rights. In this respect, ICTs have positively impacted by making it easier to access information, engage in collective debate, participate in policy formation, and review government functions.

Second, "broadening participation" refers to the participation of diverse and broad-based groups of people in policy-making processes. The Internet space can facilitate the participation of people and groups traditionally excluded from participation because it is non-exclusive, inclusive, inexpensive, and can remove many time and space constraints.

Third, "expanding the quality of participation" means enabling more sustained and in-depth interaction rather than one-off engagement to build strong, active, and lasting relationships between citizens, social institutions, and government agencies (Institute for E-Government, 2004a).

The OECD (2001) categorizes citizen participation into three main types: information, consultation, and active participation, and points out that not only is citizen participation and influence in public administration increasing as it progresses, but the way government and citizens communicate is also shifting from one-way to two-way to more active and engaged participation.

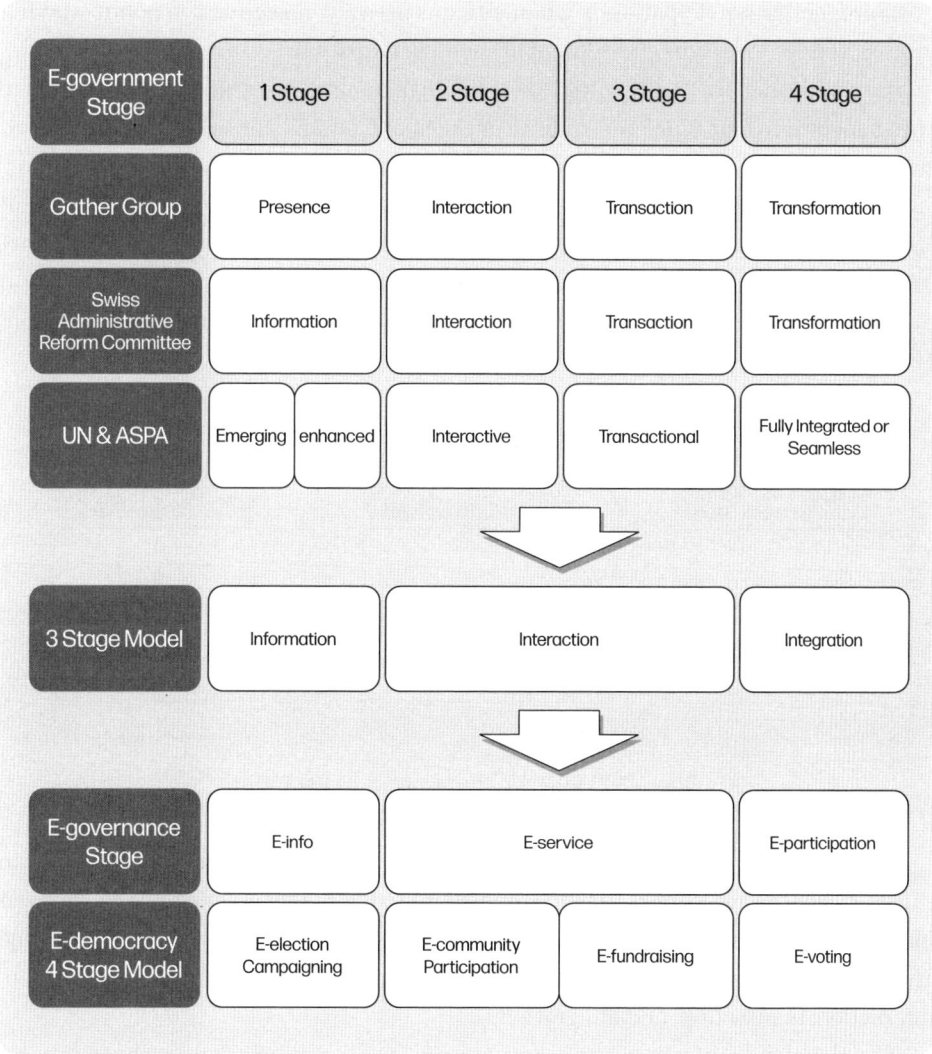

Source : Adapted from the Institute for E-government 2004a.

[Figure 3-1] Model of the Developmental Stages of E-government and E-governance

First, informational participation involves providing citizens with information unilaterally produced by the government, where the government actively reaches out to citizens while citizens remain passive.

Second, in a consultative system, there is two-way communication between citizens and the government. However, the government unilaterally determines the way of communication, and it is limited to the rules and channels specified by the government.

Third, active participation is when citizens actively engage in the policy-making process and set the terms and content of their participation.

Based on the OECD's typology of civic engagement, we can categorize e-civic engagement into four types: informative engagement, passive consultative engagement, active consultative engagement, and active participation.

The most important factor in developing e-government services is the level of communication and activity between the government and the citizen: one-way communication is simply the transfer of information, while two-way communication can be categorized as interaction or transaction, which is the exchange of information. The final stage integrates communication and activity (Figure 3-1).

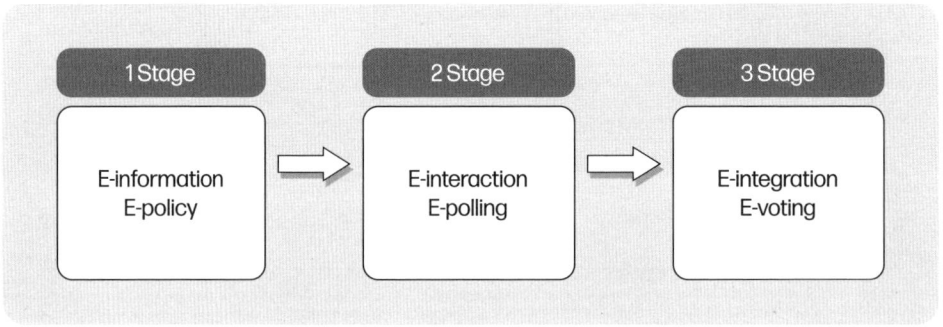

[Figure 3-2] Stages of E-governance Evolution

Using the stages of e-government to illuminate the stages of civic engagement, the stages of civic engagement as the most important tool for democracy can be categorized into four phases: e-election campaigning, e-community participation, e-fundraising, and e-voting, which closely align with the four stages of eGovernment: information, interaction, transaction, and integration.

The development stages of e-governance can be expressed in three stages: e-information, e-complaint, and e-participation. In the stage of e-information, the government provides information unilaterally; in the stage of e-complaint, citizens demand specific services from the government, and the government responds; and in the stage of e-participation, citizens actively participate in and influence the government's policy-making process and make final decisions by voting on major decisions.

As such, the implementation of e-governance is likely to be achieved in stages, similar to the growth of e-government, rather than in one fell swoop. Phase 1 is the electronic information delivery phase, which provides citizens with the information they need to participate online, including information on government policies, initiatives, bills, projects, candidates, and elections-related campaigns. By providing information on the participation information that citizens want to receive from time to time, citizens will be able to acquire more in-depth information on government operations, enabling more advanced forms of participation.

<Table 3-7> Developmental Stages and Characteristics of E-governance

Stages of UPP Evolution	Attributes
Stage 1 e-information	Providing citizens with the information they need to participate online (e.g., materials on government policies, initiatives, bills, projects, and candidates and campaigns related to elections)
Stage 2 e-interaction	Collect opinions through bulletin boards and e-communities created on the network, and collect public opinion through e-polling.
Stage 3 e-integration	A stage where citizens directly participate in government policies and decision-making, expressing their opinions and making decisions jointly between citizens and the government, where all decisions are made online, including policy decisions and elections for elected officials (e-voting)

The second stage is policy convergence, where citizens' opinions are actively funneled into the government through e-policy proposals or e-policy surveys, creating an interaction between the government and citizens. With the achievement of e-interactions, citizens will have an avenue to participate in policy online. The government-citizen interaction will produce a very positive effect as the evaluation of the current policy, what is going wrong, and complaints are injected into the policy process in real-time.

Stage 3 is the stage of e-integration, where citizens directly participate in government policies and decisions, express their opinions, and jointly make decisions between citizens and the government. All decisions can be made online, including policy decisions and elections for elected officials. E-integration is only achieved when it is fully possible for citizens' final decisions to be finalized through e-voting. Electronic voting has been a constant in e-government, but mobile technology will allow for more efficient and proactive vote management in the future.

The interest of citizens as participants in the realization of e-democracy can be seen as information disclosure and participation. By providing citizens with the information and channels for participation anytime and anywhere, the rationality of policy decisions will be enhanced, and e-democracy will be realized. Citizens, as rational actors, will give up participation if the opportunity cost is greater than the cost of participation, so it is necessary to provide easy and inexpensive means to participate anytime, anywhere. In addition, e-government should activate the formation of e-community by providing various policy discussion rooms, public hearings, bulletin boards, and opinion-gathering spaces on the network and actively promote and implement e-polling and e-voting to expand the channels of participation so that citizens can voluntarily participate in and form public opinion.

5) Types of Relationships Between Actors in E-governance

E-Governance can be categorized based on the relationships between the primary actors: government, business, and citizens. Heterogeneous actor relationships between government and business, government and citizen, and business and citizen form one axis of the taxonomy, while homogeneous actor relationships between government and government, business and business, and citizen and citizen form the other axis.

Among the various relationships between the three actors that exist as ideological types, the importance of government in governance has focused on the relationships between government-government, government-citizen, and government-business. In e-government, government-to-government relationships are represented by e-intergovernmental Relationships (e-IGR) and have been understood as G2G in existing studies. Government-business relationships are represented by e-Government-Business Relationships (e-GBRs), which have often been conceptualized as G2B in the literature. Government-citizen relationships have been primarily understood as G2C or G4C and can be represented by e-government-citizen Relationships (e-GCR) (Holmes, 2001; Reddick, 2004).

e-IGR is primarily concerned with the relationships between governments at different levels within the government. In contrast, e-GBR and e-GCR are concerned with the relationships between governments and those outside the government. Research on e-IGR can be divided into two categories: research on the relationship between government departments and the relationship between central and local governments. Much e-IGR research focuses on the relationship between government departments (e.g., KITA 2002; Park, 2003; Performance Institute, 2002). For the implementation of desirable e-Governance, more discussion is needed not only on the relationship between government departments but also on the relationship between the central government and local governments (KITA, 2002b; E-Government Institute, 2004a; E-Government Institute, 2004b).

The e-GBR has only been partially researched, and the achievements are small. The main aspects of e-GBR include building and implementing e-government public service projects through outsourcing between the government and companies, providing standardization and networking to public ministries and organizations, and providing information system and service management education to public servants. Discussions on investment evaluation of informatization projects, the introduction of IT and systems, and government procurement and contracting are taking place at a rudimentary level (Im, 2002; E-Government Institute, 2004a).

Various studies have been conducted on e-GCR so far, mainly focusing on the provision and improvement of public services or citizen participation in public services (Jung, 1998; Park, 2003; E-Government Institute 2004a; 2004c; Shi & Carmine, 2000; Accenture, 2003a, and many others).

In addition, citizen-corporate relations (e-CBR), business-business relations (e-IBR), and citizen-citizen relations (e-ICR) under e-Governance can also be major factors affecting e-Governance. However, they have yet to be specifically approached. e-CBR is the relationship between citizens and companies, an asymmetric governance structure favoring companies. However, with the development of ICT, it is highly likely to change to a structure in favor of citizens. Citizens as consumers and customers will be able to form strong communities under e-Governance, enabling them to exchange useful information and actively voice their opinions to companies.

e-IBR refers to the relationships between businesses and organizations that create e-governance to help businesses make optimal decisions. It will focus on joint marketing, resource-sharing, and standardization strategies to increase productivity and elicit favorable attitudes from governments and citizens. e-ICR refers to the relationship between citizens and citizens under e-government. The formation of communities among citizens with similar interests will be very active, and competition among groups to gain control of decision-making is also likely to intensify.

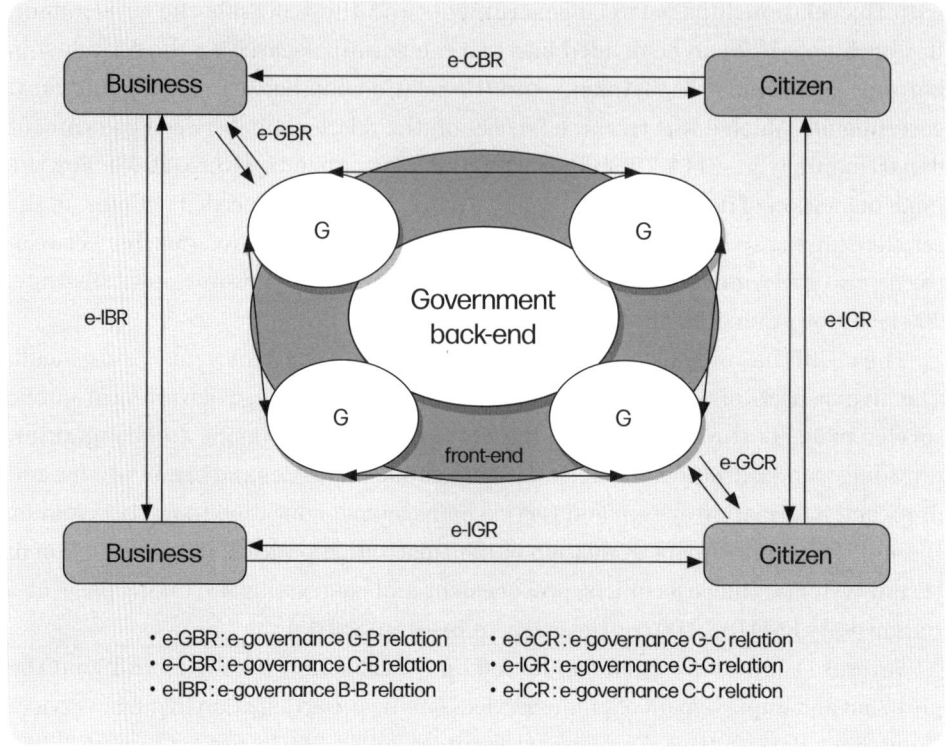

[Figure 3-3] Types of Relationships between Actors in E-governance

2. Conditions for Implementing E-government

1) Effective E-governance: Efficiency and Democracy

The greatest contribution of ICT today is the promotion of mutual understanding between members of society. Since John Locke's social contract theory, the debate and conflict over the priority of the individual or the group in the maintenance of social order and the operation of the state have persisted to this day. The government, as an agent representing the interests of the group rather than the human rights and rights of the individual, is still recognized as the only system of social and state operation. However, developing ICTs enables us to overcome these limitations and foresee the possibility of Jürgen Habermas's public dialogue. This argument becomes even more compelling when we look at the properties of ICTs.

The most important attribute of ICT is the ability to process complex and large amounts of information and data accurately and quickly. Other attributes of ICT include speeding up, accuracy, interactive sharing, and easy access.

First, using ICT (e.g., e-mail, video conferencing) facilitates communication across time and space between individuals and organizations. In other words, it reduces opportunity costs by eliminating the need for physical travel and gathering. Decision-making is also expedited by reducing the number of intermediary nodes through which information flows up and down the organization (Huber, 1990). It is especially effective for matters that require immediate action, as it eliminates the need for intermediate steps by networking the information flow between the lower levels that sense information and the higher levels that make decisions. It is especially effective for issues that require immediate action. In addition, the decision-making process requires collecting and analyzing a wide variety of information, and the search engines and database-connected application software provided by Internet technology make this faster. It can improve the ability to respond quickly to a rapidly changing environment. In the private sector, where organizational change is relatively easy, there are many success stories of rapid work processing and decision-making through the strategic use of ICT.

Second, accuracy is one of the most important attributes of IT, which refers to the ability to process huge amounts of information without error computationally (Taylor, 1986). It is especially important to reduce the uncertainty required when individuals are exploring and analyzing different alternatives, and real-time, accurate information and indicators provided by various institutions help individuals make accurate judgments about specific issues and policies. It is especially true on the supply and demand side of the relationship between producers and consumers, where accurate information enables rational choices and affordable prices at various levels. The case of Amazon in the US is a prime example of this.

Third, interactive sharing is an attribute of ICT that is becoming increasingly important with the development of Internet-based networks and open, integrated systems, which reduces unnecessary work burdens by sharing information as input to a single meeting, enabling citizens to receive the services they want without visiting the government, and enabling interactive communication between the government and citizens and between individuals and individuals at the same time. ICT is a key attribute that opens the door to government and creates a forum for public discussion between government, businesses, and citizens.

Fourth, ease of access has the effect of improving organizational flexibility and transparentizing and formalizing the decision-making process by enabling members of the organization to easily access each other's information at the decision-making stage, facilitating the exchange of opinions and providing easy access to common information needed to perform their work.

Let us analyze the attributes of ICTs concerning ideological and institutional aspects. First of all, the attributes of speed and accuracy may be more positive from the neoliberal perspective, and the attributes of interactive sharing and ease of access may be more positive from the participatory governance and NGO advocacy perspective (Rhodes, 1996; Thorson & Han, 1998), which emphasize consensus through interaction among social communities. It is because the speed and accuracy of ICTs produce the values of efficiency and effectiveness, and the interactive sharing and accessibility of ICTs produce the values of openness, transparency, and equity. In other words, speed and accuracy can be subject to performance evaluation that measures the ratio of benefits to costs and the achievement of goals, provided that there are precise criteria and indicators that can be quantified.

<Table 3-8> Attributes of ICT, Neoliberal reforms, E-governance, and their Relationship to E-government

Properties of ICT	Neoliberal Reforms	Governance	E-governance	E-government
Quickness, accuracy (efficiency, effectiveness)	• Adopt private-sector management practices (competitive principles) • Decentralized organization • Quantified performance Evaluations	• Market model	• A system that enables efficient access to and acquisition of information and error-free consultation of citizens in the policy-making process of government agencies.	• Streamlining governance with ICT • Electronic business processing (e-payments, e-document distribution) • Quantified performance evaluations • Online budgeting/accounting

Interactive Sharing (Openness, Transparency)		• Engagement Models • New model	• Citizen engagement • Engage lower levels of the organization • Actual public good • Administration across time and space	• Activate cyber organizations such as cyber committees • DB and online publication of HR management • Online open forums and policy real names • Establishing a 24-hour one-stop/non-stop service system • Establish an information-sharing system • Open government homepage
Ease of Access (Equity)		• Engagement Models	• Equal access to information • Provide affordable universal service	• Equal access to information • Delivering affordable universal services (such as low-cost PCs) • Set up an e-complaint center
Other Factors not related to ICT Attributes	• Deregulation Model	• Deregulation Model	• Applicants for corporate and civic roles • Pursuing a knowledge government that values individual creativity	• Applicants for corporate and civic roles • Pursuing a knowledge government that values individual creativity

Chapter 3 Understanding and Moving toward E-Governance

The latter is linked to one of the pillars of e-governance, democratic government, which goes beyond efficient state management and service delivery to recognize the autonomy of civil society and seek the decentralization and sharing of power to pursue open and transparent public debate in the policy-making process; to respect the fundamental rights of citizens and promote the welfare of the underprivileged; and to emphasize ethical responsibility in the mutual exchange of information and the production of content. It is made possible by the openness and accessibility of ICTs, among other things.[04]

In other words, e-governance has elements of governance. It is based on the openness and accessibility of ICTs. It seeks to achieve the real public good through autonomous participation and interactive communication between members of society at any time, anywhere. It is mainly discussed in the literature on electronic democracy (Baddeley, 1997; Budge, 1996; Hill & Hughes, 1998; Rash, 1997), which discusses various positive possibilities but has not yet been institutionalized due to problems such as[05][06]

Based on the above discussion, e-government is a comprehensive and innovative future government that includes neoliberal reform elements based on market principles and various governance models' participatory and new governance orientation. It also enables governance in cyberspace based on the properties of ICTs, represented by the Internet.

---

04   In Korea, there are currently 13 million Internet users. The reasons for this are as follows (Kyu & Choi, 1999). First, the emergence of the WWW and browsers that made it possible to view various information has made it possible for anyone to use information scattered around the world; second, the Internet is not a centralized and unified network but an autonomous network of individuals that make up the whole, expanding like the division and multiplication of cells. Third, it can be used regardless of the type or speed of the network, such as the general public network, ISDN, LAN, or dedicated line, by using the transmission protocol called TCP/IP.

05   Real-world examples include the Minnesota Electronic Democracy Project, which has been operating in the United States since 1994 (Hwang et al., 1999), the 1999 "Cyber Yugo" (http://www.juga.com), and the electronic town hall" attempted by Ross Perot during the 1992 US presidential election (London, 1994).

06   They point out that cyberspace behavior, transactions, and information exchange are still dominated by a small group of young people, professionals, computer enthusiasts, and netizens and criticize their lack of responsibility for social and policy issues. They argue that the adverse effects of deviation and differentiation caused by such instantaneous and fragmentary cyberspace behavior and expression of opinions will continue to increase. Social responsibility, personal morality, and ensuring access to people with low incomes will become more important issues.

2) Possible Changes in Government Organization[07]

Civil society in South Korea has tended to prioritize 'political participation' by focusing on criticism and checks on the abuse of power by the representative government. However, after the democratization of society to a certain extent after 1987, the focus has gradually shifted to 'policy participation,' which involves not only unconditional criticism of the government but also participation in the policy-making and implementation process more maturely and suggesting policy alternatives. In that sense, the relationship between civil society and the government in Korea has moved from a spectrum of 'confrontation' and 'support' to a 'collaborative' relationship that maintains mutual tension while promoting consensus, which is the framework for governance.

Many examples of successful collaborative governance exist between civil society and governments abroad. If we look at the characteristics of these cases, we can see that in addition to the elements of 'checks and balances' and 'public service provision' between civil society and the government, creating a public forum is very important in establishing a cooperative relationship. In South Korea, on the other hand, while social capital has been built to some extent, the public debate process still needs to be stronger, and there are few examples of good governance. However, after conflicts between the government and citizens, the importance of public forums is gradually being recognized.

However, it is important to note that the need for governance with civil society does not imply a so-called "decline of the state." Rather, governments are "restructuring or transforming the state" through governance (Pierre & Guy Peters, 2000; 196). While the modern state used to exercise its 'power of domination' unilaterally over its citizens, the state under governance has a 'power of consultation' that enhances its legitimacy and policy effectiveness through communication with its citizens. Therefore, the process of restructuring the state requires a change in the concept of the government's ability to govern. Instead of being considered a powerful government based on its legal and institutional strength, governments with contextual and entrepreneurial capabilities should be recognized as competent. In short, "political capacities" are more important for governments than "formal power." Therefore, governments should rely on good governance outcomes rather than coercive policy tools or governance techniques, as in

---

[07] Sections 2 through 4 below are excerpts from Lee, Dongsoo, "Discussion Democracy in the Digital Age," Philosophical Studies, Vol. 64, Supplement: Democracy and Populism in the Digital Age (2004)," which the author presented for discussion in a small group.

the past. Only in this way can governments be both legitimate and effective.

Therefore, the government is still the most important political actor under governance. If governance refers to an alternative form of governance other than government, then the question arises of who is responsible for governance. There is also a difference between the complexity of modern society and the actual policy-making processes surrounding government and what the role of government should be. If the government does not lead governance, the power relations of existing organizations will determine policy, which may have unintended consequences. Therefore, 'governance without government' can be considered dangerous, and governance by government and civil society is basically 'state-centric governance.' In this sense, government and governance should be complementary, not opposing each other.

3) The Potential for E-democracy: Ensuring Procedural Rationality in the Policy Formation Process

One of the secrets of modern democracy's rise and evolution is its use of popular sovereignty and representative government as two pillars. Democracy is based on the principle of 'rule by the people.' However, to realize this ideal in practice, modern democracies have adopted a system of representative government in which sovereignty or rights reside in the people on the one hand. However, power, as the specific authority to protect and guarantee those rights, is delegated to agents of the sovereign. In short, the power source comes from the people, but the direct exercise of that power is vested in the government and parliament, which the people mandate through elections.

However, as societies entered the postmodern and postindustrial era in the late 20th century and beyond, with more diverse preferences, interests, and opinions, representative democracy gradually lost its authority because it no longer represented a wide range of needs and wishes. It led to increased citizen dissatisfaction, and governments could no longer effectively govern with dissatisfied citizens. Therefore, representative democracy today has reached its limits in terms of both legitimacy and efficiency.

To solve the problem of representation, elements of direct democracy must be introduced. However, it is impossible to recreate the direct democracy of ancient Athens in an already large and complex modern society. Therefore, a more realistic solution is to establish participatory democracy, an alternative to representative democracy that complements it rather than replaces it. Participatory democracy aims to revitalize democracy through the interest and participation of citizens in the political process, even if they do not directly hold public office.[08]

However, representative government and civil society define the nature of participation differently depending on their positions. First, civil society views participation as a political function of "checks and balances" to prevent the government, delegated authority by its citizens, from abusing its power. On the other hand, representative governments want to engage civil society to fulfill government functions to the extent that they are beyond their capacity. In the former, citizens seek to form groups and form an organized anti-power to check and criticize government abuses of power. In this case, the relationship between the government and civil society is 'adversarial.' In the latter case, the government wants organized civil society to be pragmatic rather than political and to share the role of providing public services. In this case, the relationship between government and civil society is supportive.

Both of these characteristics are important in their own right. However, if CSOs focus too much on 'checking and criticizing,' the government's ability to formulate policies will be stronger, and even if policies are implemented, they will be less effective. On the other hand, if the role of civil society organizations is limited to providing public services, it may make it easier to implement policies. However, it will no longer be able to challenge the validity of the policies themselves or the legitimacy of the government's abuse of power, which will hinder social development in the long run. Therefore, civil society organizations have limits in terms of both legitimacy and efficiency

Therefore, participation in "governance shaping" is a new requirement to enhance the legitimacy and effectiveness of policies and form a collaborative partnership between government and civil society. Participation is not just about checking and criticizing the government or providing public services; it is more conducive to democracy when it is governance-oriented in the policy process.

4) Social Capital and Public Discourse

For governance to be possible, two conditions must be met: social capital and the formation of a public sphere. Social capital is an intangible asset that increases productive activity and refers to norms, trust, and networks that facilitate coordination and cooperation for mutual benefit. Whereas physical capital is capital

---

08   For a detailed discussion of the limitations of representative democracy and participatory democracy, see Dongsoo Lee, "Discussion Democracy in the Digital Age," Philosophical Studies, Vol. 64, Special Issue: Democracy and Populism in the Digital Age (2004: 72-74).

within materials, such as tools, and human capital is capital within people, such as skills and abilities, social capital is capital within the social interactions that occur between people, including respect for each other, a shared system of representation, interpretation, and meaning, and the promotion of relationships and ties among members (Coleman, 1988: 100-101).

Robert D. Putnam argues that for this social capital to be formed, citizens must join social organizations and participate voluntarily (Putnam, 1995: 65). As a prerequisite, Putnam considers civil society's historical and cultural context and the existence of horizontal, voluntary civil society organizations independent of government influence. In particular, membership in social organizations has a positive impact on the accumulation of social capital because internally, they socialize members within a democratic culture, educate them on the need for trust and cooperation, and externally, they connect citizens to political systems and institutions, provide a collective expression of interests, and offer a variety of competing or cooperative groups that constitute a pluralistic policy.

However, not all social organization membership is positive for social capital formation. First, social capital and political capital are not the same thing, and the latter harms social capital formation, even though it can lead to vertical or political trust between leaders and citizens. In addition, religious affiliation is inversely related to citizenship. It is because civil society is based on secular trust, not on religious beliefs. Political party membership is only sometimes positive for social capital accumulation because it is an act of group self-interest, and membership in closed unions, bar associations, and medical associations is not helpful because it is compulsory.

On the other hand, the nature of social organizations that will be conducive to social capital formation should be voluntary, horizontal, formal, and rely on secondary relationships (Park, 2001: 8-9). Only voluntary organizations can produce trust and interaction of social capital and be bottom-up. In contrast, vertical organizations with hierarchical relationships, such as families, religious groups, and authoritarian political groups, are negative for social capital formation. In addition, familial organizations based on tribes or small communities are homogeneous and exclusive because they are based only on primary trust (thick trust), such as the same tribe, class, race, and region. In contrast, members of a social organization must be impersonal and have thin trust, which is only possible when the organization is formal and secondary.

Second, forming a public forum means expressing and discussing citizens' opinions in the public sphere, leading to a consensus among the participants. Jügen Habermas considers a public forum a "network for communication" (Habermas, 1996: 360). In other words, a public forum creates a communication structure that aims to achieve social integration through the act of dialoguing, debating, and deliberating together in a process of discussion in which individuals continuously change their opinions and preferences and build a collective consensus.

When a public forum is formed, citizens not only have the right to speak and deliberate, but they also have the power to check and monitor the power of the government through the process of discussion, and the policies decided through discussion in the public forum can satisfy both legitimacy and efficiency. It is because citizens who participate in the discussion process accept the decisions made through the process as legitimate self-decisions and voluntarily submit them, and such submission helps implement the policy efficiently. Therefore, for a policy to be both legitimate and efficient, the validity and rationality of the policy-making process are more important than the logical consistency of the policy itself. No matter how good a policy is, it cannot be properly implemented if the society in which it is to be implemented and the beneficiaries of the policy are opposed to it.

Decisions made behind closed doors without such a public forum can easily degenerate into 'power politics.' Even if policy decisions are made through institutional politics or party politics, it is difficult to properly reflect the opinions and desires of citizens because, as mentioned earlier, the representative capacity of institutions and political parties in modern society is limited. In contrast, 'public debate politics', which is carried out through the process of discussion in the public forum, does not replace power politics or institutional politics but rather complements them and aims to make whatever policy decisions are made through the process of exposing various opinions in society and reaching consensus through discussion so that it can become a decision with social unifying power.

State power, interest groups, and the media can mislead public opinion without a public forum. If the state is too powerful, it can suffocate public debate, and if interest groups dominate and take over civil society, public debate can disappear. Media outlets can be tempted to control public opinion. Therefore, it is difficult to form a proper public debate when the power of the state, interest groups, and media is excessive. For public opinion to be properly shaped, the participation of citizens living in the everyday world is of utmost importance because the beneficiaries of any policy are ordinary citizens, and policies that are disconnected from their daily lives are ineffective. In that sense, a "forum for experts" disconnected from the real world is useless. It is a 'technocratic bureaucratic ban on the public forum' enforced at citizens' expense (Habermas, 1996: 351). However, the role of the government is crucial for the formation of a public forum and the realization of public politics because in order for decisions to be accepted as legitimate, there must be norms of debate, a liberal political culture, and democratic procedures, which the government can secure through legal and institutional procedures.

5) E-governance Failures and Dysfunctions

Since the 1980s, "accountability" has become a dominant value in the public sector, including governments and parliaments, as well as in business and civil society. However, Internet governance is ecologically fragile and constrained by the ambiguity of the responsibility center, which is a multi-participant system without proprietary ownership. As a result, the principle of imposing accountability is disconnected from normative systems such as laws in the real world due to issues such as anonymous transactions and piracy.

On the other hand, transparency is essential for realizing democratic values by opening up decision-making structures, processes, and policy outputs. The right to know through disclosing necessary information must be balanced with protecting values or personal information. Therefore, social capital, such as trust, is essential to e-governance for economic, political, and social development. However, suppose e-Governance loses trust due to network dysfunctions such as hacking and cyber terrorism or free-riding on the Internet discourse space. In that case, it will undermine social capital, essential for economic and social development.

Thus, in Albert Hirschman's three alternatives of exit, voice, and disloyalty, e-Governance is characterized by its fragile nature, as "exit," let alone "voice" or "disloyalty," is as easy as a click on the Internet. In this respect, healthy e-governance requires a sense of shared mission and norms to continue to protect and develop public forums for communication and exchange. It is within this shared sense of purpose that e-democracy, e-government, e-commerce, and other sectoral applications can be enabled.

6) Other Considerations in Building E-governance

First, a dilemma that may arise in building e-governance is the issue of privacy and the scope of information acquisition. As the opportunities for participation in the future policy-making process become wider, it is necessary to thoroughly prepare for privacy protection in identifying the characteristics of participants and groups. On the other hand, if the public forum is to be organized according to certain rules, the details of participants must be consistently identified to prevent dysfunctions such as negligence or exodus. Because of these ambivalences, the scope of privacy protection and information acquisition can only be found through various pilot projects or cases.

In a similar vein, the design of e-governance interfaces needs to consider two things at the same time: consistency and simplicity in interface design are required to emphasize the ease of access aspect, but on the other hand, a variety of presentation styles and languages are needed to embrace the interests and concerns of different communities. Also, in the case of consultation or active participation, a simple design is desirable because the process should be straightforward. However, participants and moderators will need a rich and varied menu and procedure-specific confirmation process, even if the process is somewhat complex, to have a more in-depth discussion.

On the other hand, the legal basis needs to be considered for the current E-Government Act. Suppose e-governance is considered a more evolved state management system than e-government. In that case, it is possible to consider amending and supplementing the cyber participation section of the E-Government Act, i.e., expanding the provision for collecting opinions through information and communication networks in Article 28 of the E-Government Act to meet the purpose of E-governance.

However, the "E-Government Act" is limited in scope to administrative agencies and contains mostly provisions related to systems and business promotion, so it is not enough to fully realize the vision and meaning of E-governance. In this case, there may be a way to enact a higher law with a basic legal character encompassing legislation, judiciary, and administration, i.e., a tentative 'E-governance Act.' However, even if an e-governance law is enacted, there is a burden to fundamentally revise the Administrative Procedure Act itself because all administrative procedures must be changed.

Summary

Smart Governance and Policy

E-governance is a socio-technical system in which the IT element of 'e' (technical subsystem) and the political and social element of 'governance' (social subsystem) interact. The emergence of e-governance has been driven by technological (advances in IT) and ideological (reinvention of entrepreneurial government to overcome the failures of Keynesian government in providing non-monopolistic public goods, inefficient bureaucracy, and cronyism). E-governance requires simultaneous strategy selection and infrastructure building, depending on the degree of cumulative social consensus on how participation should work. Suppose e-governance is extended to e-voting, where the final decision is made through increased citizen participation through ICTs. In that case, it may take a different form from the traditional elements of governance.

Electronic citizen participation in e-government is expected to be an excellent alternative to revitalize low offline citizen participation by creating a cyber information space that transcends the time and space constraints for citizens to participate in government. ICT positively affect citizen participation, such as 'facilitating participation,' 'expanding the scope of participation,' and 'improving the quality of participation.' In e-government, government-to-government relationships are represented by e-intergovernmental Relationships (e-IGR), which has been understood as the concept of G2G in previous studies. Government-business relationships are represented by E-government-Business Relationships (e-GBRs), commonly utilized in the literature as G2B. Government-citizen relationships have been mainly understood as G2C or G4C and can be expressed as e-government-citizen Relationships (e-GCR).

There are four main conditions for e-government implementation. The first is the expansion of efficiency and democracy for effective e-Governance implementation. Second is the possibility of change in the government organization; third is procedural rationality in the policy formation process for e-democracy. The fourth is the formation of social capital and public debate. In addition, obstacles and dysfunctions of e-Governance should also be considered when implementing E-government.

In addition to the study of governance in public administration since the 2000s, the development of e-government has also seen a shift toward e-governance that emphasizes citizen participation. In terms of the overall development of the Internet, the term Web 2.0, or Internet 2.0, was coined by Tim O'Reilly in 2004. Moreover, it has become easier to use the Internet, and users from all walks of life have evaluated that a revolutionary change is occurring in information sharing, communication, and socialization. While previous e-government studies have focused on providing electronic services to citizens and building and reforming efficient government and administrative systems, e-governance extends the concept to democratic processes such as policy proposals and strengthening relationships with residents, civil society, and businesses. Advances in IT have moved beyond Web 2.0 to Web 3.0, mobile and cloud computing technologies, and convergence technologies, which are emerging issues affecting the information society and E-government.

Research Questions

1. Discuss the similarities and differences between traditional democracy and e-governance from a citizen participation perspective.
2. Describe the context in which e-Governance emerged and describe the nature and characteristics of E-governance.
3. Describe a model of the developmental stages of E-government and e-governance.
4. Discuss the different types of relationships between actors in E-governance.
5. Discuss the contributions of social capital and public forums to E-governance.

Chapter 4

The Fourth Industrial Revolution and ICT Governance

1. Industry 4.0

The Fourth Industrial Revolution was first mentioned in early 2018 at the World Economic Forum (WEF) on January 20, 2018, in Davos, Switzerland. The WEF brings together thousands of business leaders, politicians, economists, and other experts worldwide to discuss solutions to current and future economic challenges. When the Fourth Industrial Revolution was first mentioned, it was the first time in the Forum's history that the field of science and technology was chosen as a major agenda item.

Experts differ on the concept of the Fourth Industrial Revolution. The fourth industrial revolution builds on the digital revolution, representing a new way technology is embedded in society and the human body (Nicholas, 2016). However, the popular concept of the Fourth Industrial Revolution refers to a revolutionary era brought about by the convergence of ICT (ICTs), and at the core of the revolution are new technological innovations in six areas: big data analytics, artificial intelligence, robotics, the Internet of Things, crewless transportation (drones, driverless cars), three-dimensional printing, and nanotechnology (Wikipedia, 2018).

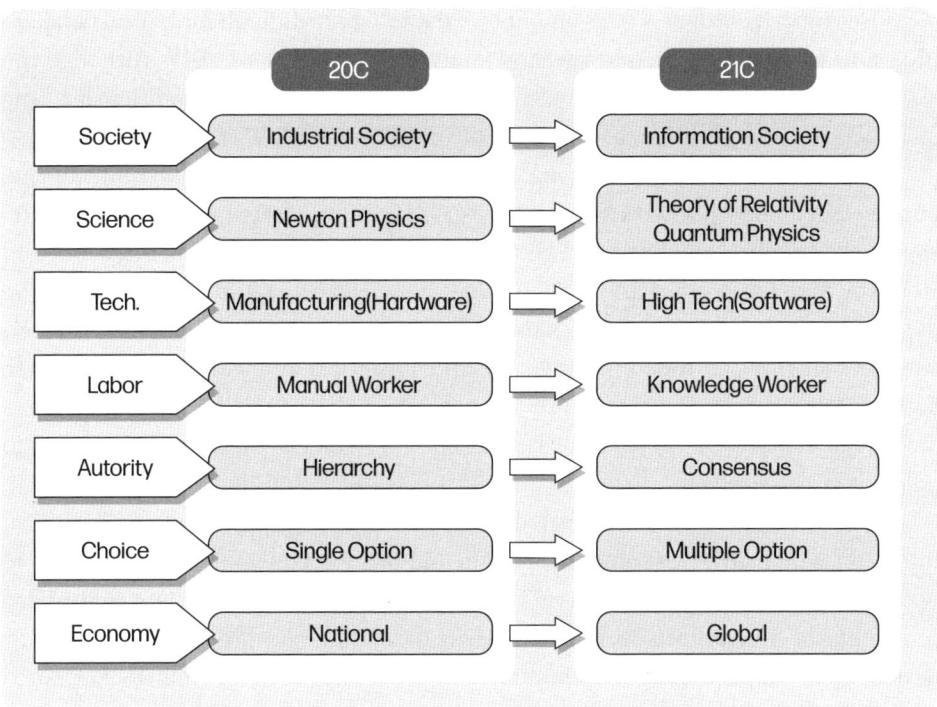

[Figure 4-1] Changing the Future Landscape: A 21st Century Paradigm Shift

Since the 21st century, the industrial structure has shifted toward high-value-added industries. Just like the shift from the primary or secondary industry to the tertiary sector, the service industry, in the past, the Fourth Industrial Revolution will enter a different industrial era. The demographic structure is also changing. In the past, society was centered on large families, and it has changed to a nuclear family. However, it is now shifting from atomic families to single-person households, and we are entering society for the elderly and an aging service society as we enter the age of 100. In addition, the population pyramid will change rapidly due to low fertility rates. We are facing new challenges in the 21st century as we enter a low economic growth rate, high unemployment, unstable and uncertain society, and changes in industrial structure and demographics.

1) The Rise of Big Data

Big data is data and data collection, storage, analysis, and utilization technologies characterized by vast amounts, variety, and high data processing speed. As stated in a

McKinsey report, big data is large amounts of data that are difficult for typical database programs to collect, store, manage, and analyze (Manyika et al., 2011). Although the quantitative aspect of big data tends to be emphasized due to the modifier "big," the qualitative meaning is closer to the essence of big data (Kim, 2017).

Big data is obtained by acquiring databases. These can be internal and external or structured and unstructured databases. Once you've started collecting big data, you'll need to collect the types and kinds of data for your purposes. Then, cleanse and store the data (structured and unstructured data, cleansing and storage). Once the data is collected and organized, it is time to process and analyze it. Analytical models such as real-time, artificial intelligence, and statistical analysis can be applied to data processing. Once the big data results are obtained, they can be used for business or policy purposes, or the analysis results can be visualized and used in reports to enhance persuasiveness.

While there has always been much data, it is now possible for computers or artificial intelligence to analyze vast amounts of data and make predictions. The movement to open public data is expanding based on expanding access to public data centralized in one place, companies accumulating their data, and data processing technology development. In particular, this movement is occurring in the US and the EU. Korea has enacted the "De-identification Measures Guideline (June 2016)," a guideline for protecting and freeing big data containing personal information after de-identifying. A representative example is the Owl Bus, a night bus in Seoul. In addition, various other studies are underway, including personal information protection (Lee, 2016: 509-559), public data utilization (Lee, 2011: 47-64), social media analysis (Lee et al., 2013: 211-219), cultural industry (Yoon, 2013: 157-179), and public services (Lee, 2013: 121-123). As big data evolves, various fields attempt to converge and the ripple effects will be enormous.

2) Artificial Intelligence

Artificial intelligence (AI) is a field of computer science that focuses on solving cognitive problems primarily related to human intelligence, such as learning, problem-solving, and pattern recognition (Amazon, 2018). While generalized AI is easy to develop, it is deep learning that we, as a species, are critically interested in. The human brain was able to create because of the accumulation of knowledge and continuous learning through experience. Through the learning process, we have adapted to our environment and survived. AI also makes judgments or learns according to the situation, and 'AI's learning' is deep. Deep learning is a branch of machine learning that involves layering algorithms to gain a deeper understanding of data and identifying relationships that humans may be unable to recognize. After sufficient training, algorithmic networks can make predictions or interpret highly complex data (Amazon, 2018).

Artificial intelligence, the main subject of science fiction movies that modern society has been imagining, is no longer just a movie. Through continuous research since the past, AI technology, a technology that mimics human thinking, has been developing through the recent convergence with big data technology. In the recent Go match between Lee Sedol 9 and AI AlphaGo, AlphaGo raised awareness of the opportunities and dangers of AI development. Recently, AI has been revisited along with the Fourth Industrial Revolution. AI has been recognized as a new growth engine by governments, industries, the financial sector, and countries worldwide that have announced plans to foster AI. In particular, the IT industry has been expanding investments in AI-related R&D, and M&A. AI has recently been established in the banking, securities, insurance, media, and medical fields, and other industries will quickly adopt AI.

AI has five skill elements: learning and reasoning, contextual understanding, language understanding, visual understanding, and perception and cognition (Korea Institute of Property Research, 2016).

<Table 4-1> Five Technical Elements of AI

Technical Elements	Subject	Content
Learning and Inference	Knowledge Expression	Express analyzed knowledge in a language computers can understand
	Knowledge Base	Build a database of expertise, troubleshooting methods, and more
Understand the Situation	Understand Emotions	Recognize and distinguish human moods and emotions
	Understanding Space	Accurate perception of space and time
	Collaborative Intelligence	Interact with, understand, interpret, and respond to other entities
	Self-Understanding	Recognize and understand your personality and psychological traits

Understanding Language	Natural Language Processing	Morphological, object recognition, and semantic analysis of human language
	Question and Answer	Provide contextually appropriate answers to questions.
	Speech Processing	Translate digital speech into a language that computers can process.
	Automatic Translation:	Automatic translation and interpretation from one language to another
Understanding Visuals	Content-based Video Search	Extract features from video data for indexing and searching
	Behavioral Recognition	Recognize the behavior of moving objects in videos.
	Visual Knowledge	Extract and generate knowledge from video data.
Perception and Cognition	Understanding Human Life	Understand human life and intelligently help you in your daily life
	Cognitive architecture Computer modeling of human mind structure from a cognitive psychology perspective	

3) Cloud

Different IT organizations have slightly different definitions of cloud computing. Wikipedia defines cloud computing as a web-based software service that places programs on utility data servers online, allowing them to be loaded and used on demand on computers and mobile phones (Lee, 2013). Cloud computing is a type of Internet-based computing that refers to the technology of processing information on other computers connected to the internet rather than on one's computer, and is a model that enables shared computer processing resources and on-demand, anywhere-accessible access to data and computing resources (e.g., computer networks, servers, storage, applications, and services), enabling rapid access and system operation with minimal administrative effort (Hassan, 2011; Mell, 2011; Wikipedia, 2018).

In the Fourth Industrial Revolution context, the cloud is a broader concept. The cloud refers to data gathered on servers on a network and technology that uses computing infrastructure to store data and process information. It is a concept in which computers and information devices act as network access terminals, and

ICT functions are borrowed through the network rather than owned. It has various strengths, such as flexibility, economy, and efficiency. The cloud is emerging as an infrastructure that can realize new ICT technologies such as artificial intelligence (AI), big data, and the Internet of Things (IoT). The world's leading IT companies (Amazon et al.), SW companies, mobile operators, and equipment manufacturers are actively investing in the cloud and competing for leadership, centering on the US market, where leading companies are located. In Korea, the "Cloud Development Act" (March 2015) was enacted to promote the development of the cloud industry by providing government support to foster the cloud industry, improving existing regulations that are obstacles to industry development, and creating a safe service use environment by establishing grounds for user protection.

The cloud's technology elements include:
- virtualization (using one resource as if it were many),
- distributed processing,
- security and privacy, and
- open interfaces (allowing users to extend and change program functionality).

4) Blockchain

In early 2018, Korea became interested in 'blockchain' or 'blockchain technology'

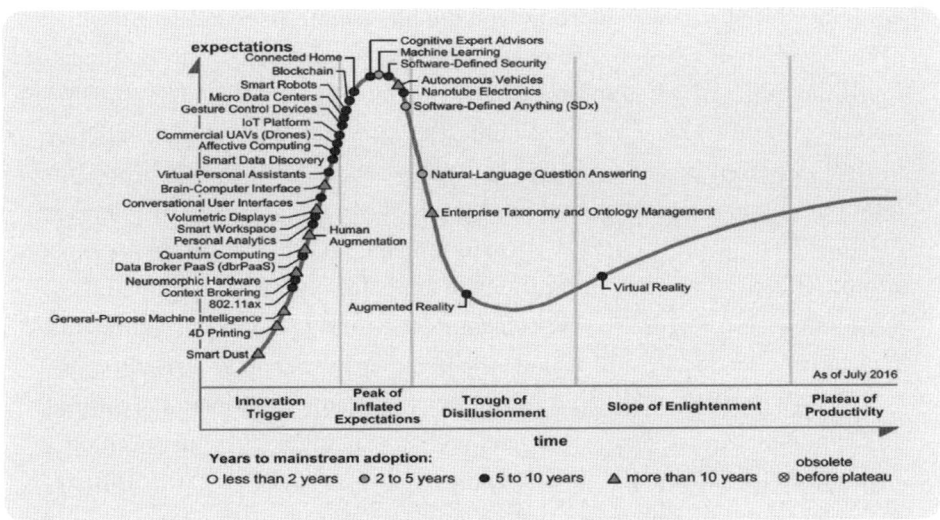

Source: Gartner, "Hyper Cycle for Emerging Technology 2016" (2016).

[Figure 4-2] Predicting Future ICT Developments

through media reports on virtual currency and economic news. According to a survey by Gartner, a world-renowned IT advisory organization, blockchain is evaluated as a technology with unlimited potential for development, as shown in Figure 4-2.

Blockchain refers to a technology that records and manages ledger data by participants rather than a centralized server. Unlike storing data on a specific central server, blockchain is a technology that distributes transaction information to all users of a peer-to-peer (P2P) network and records and manages it jointly (Moon, 2017). Because blockchain does not store data information on a centralized server but records and manages it collaboratively among participants, it is much less prone to hacking than existing technologies, even if hackers threaten the centralized server. Blockchain uses distributed processing and cryptography to ensure high security, speed, and transaction transparency. Because of these advantages, the fastest application of blockchain is the cryptocurrency market, and many cryptocurrencies are traded on cryptocurrency exchanges based on blockchain. Some popular examples include Bitcoin, Ethereum, Ripple, and Ada.

Case: Blockchain Application Plans and Possibilities

Governments and local governments have also recently become keenly interested in this research trend. Recently, the Seoul Metropolitan Government announced that it is considering applying blockchain to eco-mileage, which provides economic benefits to citizens who save electricity, water, and gas; youth allowance, which supports young people looking for jobs; public employee welfare points; and the payment eBar system, which pays for construction projects ordered by the city. The central government also announced its intention to build a blockchain-based e-certificate issuance and distribution platform. The promotion of e-government has made it possible for most administrative and public institutions to apply for online civil complaints or issue online certificates. However, documents resulting from civil complaints, such as certificates, are still issued only in paper form, and as a result, paper certificates must be submitted by mail or in person. Financial institutions and companies must keep paper documents, causing a lot of inconvenience and social costs to the public and companies. To reduce this, the Ministry of the Interior and Safety established an electronic certificate issuance and distribution platform in 2019. They issued electronic certificates in 2020 after a pilot service at the end of 2019. To this end, in 2020, it plans to present a blueprint for the issuance and distribution of e-certificates, including a blockchain-based e-certificate issuance and distribution center, an electronic document wallet, and an information strategy plan for the authenticity verification and user authentication system of e-certificates. Currently, citizens apply online, print out paper documents, and submit them by mail or in person. However, when the service is introduced, citizens can submit certificates to administrative and public institutions, private institutions, and organizations anytime via smartphone or online, dramatically improving public convenience. With the need for higher security levels, lower costs of building systems and managing data, and lower economic costs, blockchain technology is making tremendous strides, and its expected value will be enormous.

5) Internet of Things

The Internet of Things (IoT) is a technology that connects various objects to the Internet by embedding sensors and communication functions into them, i.e., connecting different objects through wireless communication (Wikipedia, 2018). It is an artificial intelligence technology that enables objects connected to the internet to exchange data, analyze themselves, provide learned information to users, or remotely control them. It is a technology that refers to the spatial connection network between objects (object to object, object to person). Implementing two-way communication between objects with ICT provides users with high-value-added complex services related to objects (linking data collected by sensors). IoT is an essential technology for smart homes, factories, and cities. Countries like the United States, Japan, Germany, and South Korea are building factory automation systems utilizing the Internet of Things to reduce production costs.

The Internet of Things is a key enabler of the Fourth Industrial Revolution, helping to reduce costs, increase production efficiency, eliminate blind spots, and transform smart processes, smart logistics, and transportation. In the future, as 5G enters the commercialization phase, data communication speeds will become even faster, increasing the possibility of converging and utilizing the IoT in various fields. The technological elements of the Internet of Things include wireless technology, big data, cloud technology, and multiple devices and objects.

6) 4th Industrial Revolution and Public Administration

The advent of the Fourth Industrial Revolution brought about major changes in many areas of society. The active introduction of the 4th Industrial Revolution technology is predicted in the industrial sector, especially. In December 2015, Amazon, the world's leading logistics company, registered a patent titled "Automated inventory management system (9,216,857, December 22, 2015)" for efficient warehousing and shipping using ground and airborne crewless aerial vehicles, heralding the era of the Fourth Industrial Revolution in earnest. In the case of Amazon, the company specializes in using drones on the ground (Kiva) and in the air for delivery and inventory management. Kiva are co-bots that can collaborate with humans. Kiva's role in logistics automation has resulted in dramatic cost savings that are unparalleled in the past. In addition to the logistics industry, IBM's AI, Watson, has been applied to the healthcare industry, where it is used as a medical assistant to check patients' conditions, recommend surgical procedures, and consult with doctors. Watson's cancer diagnosis accuracy rate is 96%, higher than human doctors.

These two examples are just the beginning of the Fourth Industrial Revolution. Converging technologies is expected to create various new services. IBM's Watson is also a convergence of big data and AI technologies.

In the era of the Fourth Industrial Revolution, changes in the public administration sector are particularly noteworthy. Before the Fourth Industrial Revolution, Korea successfully promoted national informatization and e-government with the advent of the information age and the rapid development of ICT. The services we can easily access today, such as Government 24 and the National Tax Service's online year-end settlement, are the result. We do not have to go to the government office to get the necessary administrative documents in person. E-government in the 4th Industrial Revolution era is expected to change the administrative paradigm beyond this convenience fundamentally. In the Fourth Industrial Revolution era, we need a wise and good government that can solve problems beyond improving administrative efficiency and transparency through automation (Myeong, 2017). For example, suppose AI in charge of administrative complaints can immediately resolve complaints on behalf of existing administrative personnel by utilizing big data, analyzing them, and eliminating the room for conflict in advance. In that case, unnecessary procedures and transaction costs will not occur. The evaluation criteria for future administration will be how much people can trust administrative agencies based on predictive administration and evidence-based verification. A government centered on speed, trust, consensus-building, and competent problem-solving will be good.

Article: The Premise of "Smart Government" is Trust and Empathy.

In 1999, before the turn of the 21st century, Microsoft (MS) founder Bill Gates took the world by storm with his book Speed of Thought, which clearly and easily explained the business revolution that the Internet revolution would bring in the 21st century. Now, nearly 20 years later, we're in the midst of another major change: the Fourth Industrial Revolution. The problem is that this change is similar to the early 21st century Bill Gates predicted 20 years ago.

He emphasized paperless offices, e-commerce, personalized service, the importance of numerical information, strategic information management, a spirit of adventure, digital learning communities, convergent thinking, integrated platforms, and government for the people.

The only thing that has yet to change in the Fourth Industrial Revolution is the advancement of technology, including the emergence of the Internet of Things, quantum leaps in data processing and mobile, and the rise of artificial intelligence. We have entered a more connected, instantaneous, and highly intelligent society. Therefore, it is more common to refer to it as a hyper-connected society, a smart society, a digital society, or an intelligent information society rather than the Fourth Industrial Revolution.

At some point, we have fallen into the trap of the Fourth Industrial Revolution, and we are disrupting our present and future, repeating the ideological conflicts of the pre-information society, and continuing the unnecessary war of attrition between the center and the provinces, government, and government, and city and city. Although everyone shouts that the people and citizens are the masters, decentralization and balanced development, the power struggle to share power and money is the essence of the current chaos. Sharing what is concentrated is a call that everyone can agree on. However, fundamental reflection and consideration of the times beyond power distribution should be prioritized.

We must ask ourselves why we are still repeating the ills of the industrial and bureaucratic era. It may be a fundamental problem that we all have, but the so-called red waste liquidation cannot solve that. Is the authoritarianism, closure, and exclusivity that pervades our society the root cause? It is difficult to form a consensus, and there is constant communication, but policies without empathy and reactive exhibitions are repeated. As we move toward a smart or highly intelligent information society, we need a tentative "Smart Society Promotion Committee" and specialized support organizations to plan the future society and coordinate ministry projects and conflicts. Smart government, smart city, smart community, and the Fourth Industrial Revolution should be promoted. In addition, in the era of decentralization, institutions and councils representing local governments should be formed to consider regional development and balanced development, avoiding the existing centrally-driven promotion method.

The difference between now and when Bill Gates talked about the speed of thought is that, in addition to technological advances, there is an even more important "speed of consensus" that must follow. It is about more than just the speed of thought. It is about who can win the hearts and minds of citizens and individuals first to gain their trust and empathy. The government and public institutions that are faster, more accurate, predictable, and more communicative will win. Whether it is the National Assembly, the government, or the Blue House, if it repeats the slow, back-and-forth policies and the fight for their rice bowls, it will be rejected by the entire nation, not to mention 20-30 generations. It's time for a "smart government that can handle the speed of empathy," with warmth and emotional intelligence, to read people's minds in a timely manner and at the speed of light.

(Source: Culture Daily article, February 7, 2018., Seunghwan Myeong (President, Korean Association for Policy Studies, Professor, Inha University)).

2. Advances in Technology and Changes in the Public Sector

1) Advances in IT Technology

(1) Top 10 strategic technologies and user-centered computing that have shaped the IT industry

In 2019, market research firm Gartner Group released its Top 10 strategic Technologies that will drive the IT industry. The top 10 strategic IT trends for 2020 are hyper-automation, multi-experience, democratization of expertise, human augmentation, transparency and traceability, autonomous edge, distributed cloud, autonomous things, blockchain for action, and artificial intelligence security. Gartner's strategic technology trends consist of two types of technologies. The first are new technologies with transformative potential emerging from their nascent state and showing broader impact and use cases. The second group is those experiencing rapid growth, expected to peak in the next five years. Gartner's top 10 strategic technology trends for 2020 include the following

① **Hyper-Automation**

Hyperautomation combines multiple machine learning, packaged SW, and automation tools to accomplish a task. Hyperautomation is a concept that encompasses not only a wide range of tools but all phases of automation itself. It includes sensing, analyzing, designing, automating, measuring, monitoring, and reevaluating. Hyperautomation primarily focuses on understanding the range of automation mechanisms, their relationships, and how they are combined and organized. The beginning of hyperautomation is robotic process automation (RPA). However, RPA itself does not mean hyperautomation. Hyperautomation requires combining different tools to replicate human involvement in a task.

② **Multiple Experiences**

By 2028, the multi-experience will dramatically change how users perceive and interact with the digital world. Interactive platforms are changing the way people interact with the digital world. Virtual, augmented, and mixed reality also change how people perceive the digital world. These shifts in perception and interaction models are driving the multi-sensory, multi-modal experiences of the future. "We're going to move from a model where people have to understand technology to a model where technology understands people," said Brian Burke, research vice president at Gartner, "so the role of understanding intent will shift from the user to the computer."

③ **Democratize Expertise**

The democratization of expertise focuses on providing people with technical expertise, such as machine learning and app development, or business domain expertise, such as sales processes and economic analysis, through highly simplified experiences that do not require additional and expensive training. Citizen development and no-code models, as well as the rise of "citizen access" roles such as citizen data scientists and citizen integrators, are examples of the democratization of expertise. Gartner expects four key elements of democratization to accelerate through 2023. These are the democratization of data and analytics, the democratization of development, the democratization of design, and the democratization of knowledge. The democratization of data and analytics refers to tools aimed at the professional developer community and data scientists. In contrast, the democratization of development refers to AI tools that can be leveraged in custom applications. The democratization of design is the proliferation of low-code and no-code, along with the automation of additional app development functions that empower citizen developers, and the democratization of knowledge is the access of non-IT professionals to tools and expert systems that enable them to leverage and apply specialized skills without requiring their original expertise or training.

④ **Human Augmentation**

Human augmentation explores how technology can enhance human perception and the body as an integral part of the human experience. Physical augmentation enhances humans by implanting technological elements, such as wearable devices, into the human body to alter innate physical capabilities. Cognitive augmentation can be achieved by evaluating information and utilizing applications on traditional computer systems and new multi-experience interfaces within smart spaces. Increasing levels of augmentation of the human body and perception will become commonplace over the next decade as individuals seek personal enhancement. It will create a new "consumerization" effect, enabling employees to leverage and extend their enhancements to enhance their work environments.

⑤ **Transparency and Traceability**

Consumers increasingly recognize the value of their personal information and demand control over it. Businesses recognize the growing risks of protecting and managing personal data, and governments are implementing strong regulations to ensure that they do. Transparency and traceability are critical to meeting these demands of digital ethics and privacy. Transparency and traceability refer to attitudes, behaviors, enabling technologies, and practices designed to meet regulatory requirements, preserve an ethical approach to using artificial intelligence and advanced technologies, and rebuild vanishing trust within companies. As organizations build transparency and trust practices, they should focus on areas such as AI and machine learning, personal data protection, ownership and control, and ethical design.

⑥ **Autonomous Edge**

Edge computing is a computing topology where information processing, content collection, and delivery are handled close to the information's source, storage, and consumer. Edge computing seeks to handle traffic and processing locally to reduce latency, leverage the capabilities of the edge, and enable greater autonomy at the edge. "Edge computing has received much attention due to the need for IoT systems that can provide disconnected or distributed capabilities in an embedded IoT world for specific industries, such as manufacturing and retail," said Burke, research vice president at Gartner. "However, as the edge becomes increasingly sophisticated and autonomous with specialized computing resources and richer data storage, edge computing will become a dominant factor across virtually all industries and use cases."

⑦ **Distributed Cloud**

A distributed cloud is when a public cloud service is deployed in multiple locations. The original provider is responsible for the service's operation, governance, updates, and development. Distributed clouds represent a significant change to the centralized model of most public cloud services and will drive a new era of cloud computing.

⑧ **Autonomous Things**

Autonomous things are real-world devices that utilize AI to automate functions that used to be performed by humans. Autonomous things are often implemented in robots, drones, self-driving cars, autonomous ships, and home appliances. The automation of these devices goes beyond the automation provided by strict programming models, leveraging AI to create advanced behaviors that interact more naturally with their environment and people. As technology improves, regulations allow, and social acceptance grows, more and more autonomous objects will be deployed in uncontrolled public spaces.

⑨ **Practical Blockchain**

Practical blockchain is a technology that has the potential to reshape industries by building trust, providing transparency, enabling value exchange between business ecosystems, potentially reducing costs, speeding up transaction settlement times, and improving cash flow. Asset tracking also provides value in various other areas, such as tracking food throughout the supply chain to make it easier to find the source of contamination or monitoring individual parts to support product recalls. Another area where blockchain has potential is in identity management. Smart contracts can be programmed into the blockchain, where events can trigger specific actions. For example, a payment is made when a product is received. "Blockchain is still immature for enterprise implementations due to several technical challenges, including low scalability and interoperability," says Burke. Despite these challenges, blockchain has significant innovation and monetization potential, so organizations should start looking at it, even if they don't actively adopt it anytime soon."

⑩ AI Security

Artificial intelligence and machine learning will continue to enhance human decision-making across various use cases. While this creates countless opportunities to implement hyper automation and leverage autonomous things to transform business, it presents significant new challenges for security teams and risk leaders. The IoT, cloud computing, microservices, and highly connected systems within the smart space create various possible attack points. Security and risk leaders must focus on three key areas: protecting AI-powered systems, improving AI security defenses, and anticipating attackers' use of AI for criminal purposes.

Meanwhile, the "human-centric smart space" is the structure used to organize and assess the key impacts of Gartner's 2020 Strategic Technology Trends. Putting people at the center of technology strategy is paramount for technology. It reflects how technology impacts consumers, employees, business partners, society, and others.

"Smart spaces are based on a human-centric concept," said David Cearley, vice president of Gartner. "Smart spaces are physical environments where people and technology systems can interact within an increasingly open, connected, organized, and intelligent ecosystem," said David Cearley, vice president of Gartner. "People, processes, services, and things come together in smart spaces to create more immersive, interactive, and automated experiences. "Everything an organization does is driven by how technology directly and indirectly impacts individuals and groups. It is a human-centered approach."

Since 2010, the strategic importance of mobile devices has increased significantly across industries as ICT technologies have accelerated trends such as mobilization, networking, convergence, and complexity. With the advent of smartphones due to changes and advancements in mobile technology, convergence services with various services have begun to emerge. In other words, mobile technology and convergence technology are evolving from simple hardware technologies to application services that can create demand according to market needs. The continuous development of mobile technology has evolved into an intelligent and integrated system by converging with other industries, breaking down the boundaries between sectors such as voice, data, telecommunications, broadcasting, and finance, and spreading to the public and private sectors. These changes and developments in IT technology are converging with various social systems to revolutionize the entire country and society, including the economy, people, lifestyle, labor, and public administration systems. They are evolving into services such as smart business, smart life, smart work, and smart government. In recent years, intelligent, concurrent, and shared IT that connect the virtual and physical worlds, such as artificial intelligence, machine learning, digital twins, interactive platforms, and blockchain, have emerged, requiring a fundamental and comprehensive transformation of the existing bureaucracy-centered government operations and work methods. The IT technologies underlying the development of various IT services include Web 2.0, Web 3.0, mobile and cloud computing technologies, and convergence technologies, and the main characteristics of these technologies are as follows (Myeong et al., 2011: 67-70).

(2) Web 2.0 vs. Web 3.0

Web 2.0 was first raised during a meeting between O'Reilly Media and Media Live in 2003. At the time, O'Reilly executive vice president Dale Doherty suggested that Yahoo, Amazon, Google, and others that remained dominant after the dot-com bubble burst shared distinctive strengths and could be grouped under a new concept called Web 2.0. Although there are many definitions of Web 2.0, Web 2.0 is a next-generation web that has evolved from the existing portal-centric Web 1.0 to an open Internet where users actively produce, share, and consume information and knowledge. Web 2.0 refers to a new environment in which Internet users can freely post and share various contents with others and actively engage users through social networking services such as Cyworld.

Web 2.0 has four main forms of service, including the following:

First, the decisive factor distinguishing Web 1.0 from Web 2.0 is the change in the platform. Whereas the original web was a window for sharing information through a browser, the Web in Web 2.0 is the web as a platform responsible for the development and dissemination of new information and services;

Second, there is collective intelligence, as represented by Wikipedia. Wikipedia, an encyclopedia on the web, allows anyone to be an author. When someone writes a description of a word, its meaning, or a neologism, others can view, rate, comment on, and edit it. It is an important example of collective intelligence that transcends the limits of individual intelligence, which is what happens in Web 2.0;

Third, there is the concept of the long tail. The long tail contrasts the traditional 80:20 rule, meaning it is not the top 20% that makes money but the long tail. For example, in the case of Amazon, a large part of the overall revenue structure is not the top 20% of bestsellers but the bottom 80% of books;

Fourth, combinatorial services are called mash-ups. Mash-ups are the most common and easy-to-use service method for Web 2.0 companies.

As we move through the 2010s, IT is moving beyond the Web 2.0 era and entering the Web 3.0 era. Although the definition of Web 3.0 still needs to be clarified, it is abbreviated as Web 3.0, which stands for sharing, participation, openness, personalization, and intelligence. The technology behind Web 3.0 is the semantic web, a next-generation intelligent web that allows computers to understand the meaning of information resources and make logical inferences. For example, whereas Web 2.0 was all about listing much information in a highly linked order, Web 3.0 is about recognizing the current situation and rearranging the necessary content to provide context. As information accumulation continues to accelerate, there will be a glut of information, so the powerhouses of the future web era will be those that can sift and process information. Web 3.0 refers to the intelligent web as a platform that controls and manages the physical and logical space of the web, and it is evolving into a personalized web tailored to individual thoughts and ideas.

(3) Cloud Computing Technology

Cloud computing creates an environment where you can work on your documents anytime, anywhere, on any device, as long as you have an internet connection. It allows programs to be stored on a main computer connected to the internet and used collaboratively. It enables a system where computers are grouped independently, and certain programs scrape the information on these computers to answer the user's questions. It eliminates the need for each individual to install separate software and allows computers to work together to perform complex tasks that no single computer can do. The cloud, currently the biggest topic in the computing market, is developing into 'mobile cloud computing' by combining with the mobile craze led by smartphones. As a result, domestic portal companies such as Naver and Daum and telecommunication companies such as SKT and KT are launching cloud services to support mobile.

(4) Convergence Technologies

Convergence occurs when concepts or things, usually from different contexts, come together to provide synergies greater than the arithmetic sum of their parts. In recent years, convergence has been commonly called digital convergence, primarily within the IT domain.

Digital convergence is defined as "the provision of the same (or similar) services over different network platforms or the performance of similar functions by different devices" or "the phenomenon of different networks delivering similar kinds of services, different kinds of devices receiving similar kinds of services, or the emergence of new services." Convergence in the IT sector has focused primarily on the convergence of wired and wireless, voice and data, broadcasting and telecommunications, and terminal convergence.

However, as IT has begun to permeate society and intimately impact our lives, it has become a catalyst for convergence across industries, transforming existing industries, enabling connections between disparate industries, and creating new ones.

2) Changes in Government as Technology Advances

The rapid development of IT technology has led to rapid changes in government functions and roles. In particular, the leap in the public informatization sector has been particularly dramatic. This change in public information is manifested in three main areas: first, user-centered public information through the Web 3.0 era; second, public information through public-private-public cooperation; and third, public information that maximizes accessibility through convergence, and the main contents are as follows (Myeong, 2011: 70-72).

(1) User (people) centered open government

IT technology has constantly evolved to become more user-centered. Society has evolved from an industrial society of mass production and consumption to an information society, a paradigm shift that emphasizes individuality and creates demand accordingly. Since the internet was widely applied to industries around 1993, Korea's public informatization has made remarkable progress, becoming one of the world's most advanced e-government countries. Let us look at the development of e-government in Korea from 2002 to 2012. We can see that IT technology is no longer used in a provider-centered but rather in a user-centered manner that fully recognizes individuality. Especially now that we have moved beyond Web 2.0 and entered the Web 3.0 era, these technologies are evolving toward pursuing a new form of government that pursues interactive sharing, openness, and transparency.

Public informatization is predicted to create public services in the direction of respecting individual human beings, realizing voluntary participation of citizens, involvement of lower levels in organizations, the pursuit of actual public good, and administrative perspectives that transcend time and space. IT will strengthen user (people) centered administrative services and develop into a new form of government governance. The progress of user-centered public information through IT technologies such as Web 2.0 and Web 3.0 can be expected, as shown in Table 4-3.

<Table 4-3> Public digitalization of government centered on users (people)

Technology	Open Government	
	Current Government	User-centered Government of the Future (Predictions)
Web2.0, Web3.0, Mobile Technologies, etc.	• Activate a cyber organization, such as a cyber committee • DB and online publication of HR management • Online open forums and policy real names • Establish a 24-hour one-stop/non-stop service system • Establish information sharing systems • Open government homepage	• Citizen engagement • Engage lower levels of the organization • Actual public good • Administration across time and space

Source: Myeong et al., (2011: 71).

(2) Public Digitalization of public-private-public partnerships

Early IT technologies were adopted based on their promise and utility. The focus was on how effectively the provider could deliver the unit's expected tasks or services. Therefore, in the public digitalization sector, these technologies were focused on fulfilling only a few functions required for the unit's work.

However, as the scope of a unit task or service expands and the work evolves to more complex levels, it is not only the technology's effectiveness, but also how quickly and accurately it can support the task or service. It creates a dual challenge: maximizing efficiency and effectiveness simultaneously. These challenges for IT are related to the fact that, in the context of neoliberal reforms, private-sector management practices have been introduced into public-sector administration, introducing the principle of competition. This perspective emphasizes decentralized organization and quantified performance evaluation, and, more recently, it has been argued that this perspective can create a framework for efficient access to and acquisition of information and for the undistorted input of citizens into the policy-making process of government agencies.

In light of the above, the future government is called upon to pursue a knowledge government that emphasizes individual creativity and the government's role as a supporter of business and civic activities. Based on the current IT technology and public informatization, the public informatization of the future government in public-private-public cooperation can be predicted, as shown in Table 4-4.

<Table 4-4> Public digitalization of public-private-people partnerships

IT and Neoliberal Reforms, etc.	Open Government	
	Current Government	Converged Future Government (Predictions)
• IT Technology - Web 2.0 - Web 3.0 and more • Neoliberal reforms - Adopt private-sector management practices (competitive principles) - Decentralized organization - Quantified performance evaluations • Governance - Markets and Deregulation Models	• Streamlining governance with IT • Emphasize efficiency in electronic business processing (e-payments, e-document distribution) • Government-centric public services	• Applicants for corporate and civic roles • Pursuing a knowledge government that values individual creativity

Source: Myeong et al., (2011: 72).

(3) Public information maximized for accessibility through convergence

So far, open government has been built around users having easy access to information services provided by the government. This biased user perspective of information services means the system has been built from the provider's perspective.

However, as the evolution of IT technology has progressed to the acceptance of integration and convergence technologies, users who need to become more familiar with traditional digitalization can naturally receive information services in their surroundings. This convergence creates new services and maximizes the ease of access to information services tailored to the individual user.

Based on the above, we can predict that the future government will evolve into a form that maximizes user accessibility. This transformation will require equal access to information and information services and a universal service delivery system with little or no cost to access these services. The future government's public digitalization that maximizes accessibility through the convergence of IT technologies is shown in

Table 4-5.

<Table 4-5> Public digitalization of future government maximizing accessibility through convergence

Technology and Governance	Open Government	
	Current Government	Future Government Maximizes Accessibility through Convergence (Prediction)
• IT Technology - Convergence technologies - Cloud computing - Client computing and more • Governance - Engagement Models	• Information and technology-savvy users (people) • Provide affordable universal service	• Equal access to information • Service provider-centric

Source: Myeong et al., (2011: 72)

3) Emergence of Platform-type Government as IT Technology Advances

(1) Future government roles and platform capabilities

With the development of IT technology, e-government is evolving into a form of people-centered public digitalization, public digitalization of public-private-public cooperation, and public digitalization that maximizes accessibility through convergence. The government of the future (e-government) will be transformed into a new paradigm of government roles rather than the traditional form of government interference while strengthening the linkages between government, people, and businesses. The functions of the government that can realize such a change in the future can be defined as platform functions, which can be conceptualized in three ways (Myeong et al., 2011: 74-77).

First, Interconnectivity. It is because once the future government has configured the platform functionality, it will naturally connect users to exchange information assets they own. The values owned by each other can be expressed through information or economic means. Here, this linkage function refers to strengthening the linkage between mutual users who have formed a linkage before the existence of the platform or are sufficiently connected. Therefore, the entities that comprise the platform are not involved in creating these connections but only in organizing the infrastructure to facilitate them.

Second, it attempts to create and strengthen connections between previously unconnected entities. Entities not interconnected without a platform that exists independently and operates within separate mechanisms become newly connected through the platform. It also serves as a platform mechanism for creating new value-added.

Third, it is the function of creating added value through the platform. By going through the platform, costs are reduced, or new value is added that could not be generated before it is created, increasing the wealth of the entire society. In this case, added value means not only economic added value but also social added value.

(2) Define a conceptual model of future platform government

The functions of the government that can realize the changed appearance of the future government can be defined as platform functions, and based on the three functions conceptualized by these platform functions, three types of future platform governments can be defined as follows (Myeong, 2011: 46-55; Myeong et al., 2011: 77-79).

First, the collaborative government is a future platform government that functions based on the interconnection capabilities of the platform and centers on factors that strengthen government-private cooperation. Collaborative government is a type of relationship that increases the added value of the government by utilizing various resources generated when people and businesses access the platform and join the platform mechanism to reprocess services and increase social value.

Second, an intelligent (= smart) government is a future platform government that strengthens administrative services to accommodate people's needs based on enhancing the linkages between previously unconnected entities. The smart government will have a relationship in which the people and enterprises access the platform, and the resources owned by the people are reprocessed (value enhancement) through the platform to increase the added value of the users (people and enterprises).

Third, a transparent government is a future platform centered on communication, participation, and trust factors based on creating added value through the platform. A transparent government will have a relationship form in which the government accumulates resources on the platform and recycles them into resources that increase the added value of each user by recycling them among the government, citizens, and companies.

4) The Nature of Platform Government

(1) Characteristics of collaborative government (platform government)

Productivity in a smart society is characterized by information production generated through sharing and self-generation. New added value is produced through cooperation, unlike the traditional way of creating and distributing information.

It means that new value-added resources are created by the mutual sharing of resources between social actors for the creation of new value-added resources by the government and the creation of new value-added resources by the private sector. Therefore, an overlapping sharing area is formed in each location, and a cooperative relationship for creating new value-added is formed and strengthened within it. This area of sharing is the platform of platform-type government. Since cooperation is conducted through the platform formed in a smart society, information sharing and movement are directed toward the platform.

Based on the functional look of the platform, which is shaped by the productivity attributes of these smart societies, the characteristics of a collaborative future government include

First, the occurrence of collaborative government is interrelated with economic regime change. The government cannot create the socially relevant value-added that the public sphere must produce unilaterally. Therefore, it creates value through cooperation with other social actors, namely the private sector. In the traditional public sphere, the government has led and implemented many policies to resolve social conflicts and regional balances. However, recruiting the private sector in local communities and strengthening civil society's influence in the public sphere requires a partnership with the government, which will likely be isolated if it ignores it and maintains the old ways.

Second, platform-based collaborative government will settle into a mechanism that repeats a virtuous co-evolution by accumulating information shared and self-generated on the platform through mutual sharing and distribution.

Third, by collecting information and opinions from private partners (citizens, companies), the collaborative government will strengthen public services suitable for each individual's needs.

(2) Characteristics of intelligent government (platform government)

A smart society requires the government to provide an intelligent service foundation. It is because private sector actors (people and companies) and consumers want new services that the government takes care of for them. In other words, the government should provide various devices to accommodate the needs of these service consumers and intelligentize them. In other words, it should shift from providing unilateral services to users through legislated policy projects to an intelligent government that can predict and manage transaction mechanisms so that private sector actors (people and companies) can actively interact with each other and produce and consume through various channels. The characteristics of such an intelligent government are as follows.

First, in a smart society, the center of gravity of transactions shifts to the private sector and individuals, so government services must be intelligent, proactive, personalized, and customized.

Second, the most characteristic feature of intelligent government is strengthening administrative services to accommodate people's needs. The strengthening of administrative services to meet the needs of the people is caused by the government's acceptance of the diversity of the people. This acceptance of diversity has its roots in changes in people's lifestyles. First, as people's way of life becomes more diverse due to globalization and the influx of foreigners, the government must accept diversity to resolve it and strengthen intelligent administrative services for diversity management. In addition, social conflicts become a major issue in a weakly diverse society, so the government should always be able to predict conflicts caused by diversity and resolve them in advance or on time.

Third, a platform-based intelligent government means that people and enterprises can access the platform. The resources owned by the people are reprocessed through the platform (value enhancement including servitization) to create added value for users (people and enterprises), or the government provides intelligent and active customized services to users according to the needs of users stored on the platform through the platform. It means a service delivery mechanism in which the government's functions are enhanced through the platform, and the improved government services' benefits (added value) are delivered to users (citizens and businesses). The services provided by the government at this time are intelligent services, which means building an active service system that visits each citizen and customized services that accommodate the diversity of the people. This proactivity, acceptance of diversity, and conflict resolution are possible because the platform is accessible to both providers and consumers at the same time.

Fourth, improving the reliability of the government's information (database) is a prerequisite for implementing an intelligent government.

(3) Characteristics of transparent government (platform government)

A transparent government is the type of government that corresponds to the attributes of smart society values and relationships. The value and relationality of a smart society are based on forming a relationship of communication, participation, and trust through interactive interrelationships rather than transparency that appears through conventional one-way participation. Sharing information and values based on forming such relationships increases the opportunities for relationship building and mutual participation among users. As a result, order is established through transparent information exchange and value sharing. It aligns with the prediction that ethics and trust will emerge as the new codes underpinning smart societies. Transparent governments based on interactive inter-relationships have the following characteristics.

First, it builds trust through a participatory process: a platform of transparent government provides the basis for transparent interactions through the disclosure and sharing of information, and it acts as a watchdog alongside other watchdogs (individuals, communities, civil society organizations, the international community) to monitor and take appropriate sanctions against violators of this order. In other words, governments do not maintain control by collecting information from their citizens but by providing a transparent basis for interactions and acting as a faithful watchdog. In other words, it becomes a mediator to ensure fair play and a referee to ensure transparency.

Second, transparent government increases users' participation (citizens, companies) through the platform. Participation increases because much information is exchanged through a transparent government platform, artificially and through the self-generated accumulation of objects and systems, which leads to the accumulation of trust.

Third, people's way of life is diversified. Through transparent government, people's demand for communication, participation, and trust in government is strengthened, which leads to the diversification of people's way of life and the strengthening of government administrative services to accommodate people's needs. It is possible to establish a smart government system and provide a platform.

Fourth, a transparent government based on a platform communicates with its citizens based on their participation. This communication leads to a government that accumulates trust. It was not easy to build trust in the government in the past because the government's big data was not provided properly, and the disclosure process was not transparent. However, platform-based transparent government means a mechanism for mutual monitoring and communication as a platform that the government and users (citizens and companies) can access simultaneously. In this system, the possibility of securing the legitimacy of the process through transparent disclosure of the policy-making process is greatly increased.

It is covered in more detail in Chapter 8, Changing administrative paradigms in the future.

Mayor Park Won-soon "I will create Seoul's cryptocurrency S-Coin," (Hankyoreh, 2018, http://www.hani.co.kr/arti/politics/administration/838426.html).

Ministry of the Interior and Safety to establish a blockchain-based e-certificate issuance and distribution platform, Ministry of the Interior and Safety, (National Security Notification, 2018, https://www.gov.kr/portal/ntnadmNews/1459607?pageIndex=3&hideurl=N).

The Internet of Things is also a DIY era... Products that build like Lego, (Yonhap News Agency, 2016, http://v.media.daum.net/ v/20161106065602541).

Analyzing how Amazon's Fourth Industrial Revolution will unfold, (IT News, http://www.itnews.or.kr/?p=21145).

"AI Watson, cancer diagnosis accuracy 96% ... higher than specialists", (Kyunghyang Daily News, 2016, http://biz.khan.co.kr/ khan_art_view.html?artid=201603291624521&code=920100).

Source: IT Daily article, October 24, 2019, by Jaehyun Park pajh0615z@itdaily.kr

5) Promotion and Utilization of Platform-type Government in Korea

Korea's e-government services were among the best in the world. However, the country needed to respond to changes in the IT environment by overlooking the importance of platforms triggered by the launch of the iPhone in 2007. Since then, the launch of the iPhone in Korea in 2009 and the production of Galaxy phones have opened the smartphone era in earnest, prompting Korea to promote a platform-type government and establish a domestic platform strategy. The main contents of the promotion and utilization of platform-type government in Korea are as follows (Myeong et al., 2011: 107-114; Myeong, 2011; 74-83).

(1) Promoting the commercialization of open government information

In March 2010, the Ministry of the Interior and Safety, the Ministry of Culture, Sports and Tourism, and the Korea Communications Commission jointly established the 'Comprehensive Plan for Promoting Private Utilization of Public Information' to discuss the commercialization of public information in Korea. The reason behind the establishment of the comprehensive plan is that public information is recognized as an important national asset with social and economic value, and at the same time, the demand for private companies to utilize public information has increased. The main tasks of the comprehensive plan include:

① Providing information on the location and rights of public information.
② Expanding search access to public information.
③ Establishing and operating a public information utilization center.
④ Revising relevant laws to provide public information.
⑤ Inducing the expansion of public information.
⑥ Strengthening quality control to provide quality public information.
⑦ Strengthening the continuity of public information services and providing public information through Open API.
⑧ Discovering and strengthening services for private companies to utilize public information.
⑨ Holding seminars on private utilization of public information and forming a council.

(2) Platformized government service providers and content types

As of 2010, the Ministry of the Interior and Safety and the Information Society Agency promoted the disclosure of public information in response to the public's demand for public information and the best practices of major developed countries. The aim was to enhance national competitiveness by creating value services and new businesses using public information.

In June 2010, the government opened the Open Government Information Center (www.knowledge.go.kr) to open up more public information and allow the private sector to use it to create new business opportunities and jobs while improving the convenience of the public. As such, the Open Government Information Center provides 13 types of public information, including real-time bus service information for Seoul and Gyeonggi-do and hazardous food information, as open APIs. However, the application process for providing information is cumbersome, and the lack of publicly available information is criticized for its low accessibility. In addition, while national road information offers useful information to the public, general national roads, except for highways managed by Korea Expressway Corporation, are virtually impossible to access because users must individually request and receive permission from more than 200 local governments and related organizations.

In response to this complex information disclosure process, the government is promoting a step-by-step development strategy to increase access to public information through a government-wide list of public information, application guidance services, and brokerage services between the public and private sectors in early 2010.

The government is still in the early stages of improving user accessibility and opening up public information in a phased approach and by region.

(3) Utilize platform-enabled government services

Case: Public Information Utilization Support Center

The Open Government Information Utilization Support Center was established in June 2010 to help resolve various difficulties related to the opening of open government information by the government or public institutions and the private sector's collection and utilization of open government information. It aims to increase the accessibility of open government information by supporting institutional weaknesses such as provision agency, copyright advice, information on the location of open government information, linkage to holding organizations, and consulting services on the quality of open government information.

Currently, it provides information in various fields such as Gyeonggi-do bus information, land information system, ITS national transportation information, electronic library, rural experience village database, travel information, and Gyeonggi Job Center.

Article: The Next-generation E-government Platform moves to the Cloud.

The government will build a cloud-based next-generation e-government platform to respond to public site paralysis during emergencies such as disasters and diseases. Public institutions such as government departments will quickly make an e-government platform based on the Ministry of the Interior and Safety's announcement on the 18th that it will create a cloud-based next-generation e-government platform by 2021. The existing e-government framework will be upgraded to a cloud-based platform that implements intelligent e-government. It is the first time the government will build and provide an e-government platform to public institutions.

The government selected an ISP operator in June. In 2019, the government will invest 30 billion won ($10 billion per year) for three years to complete the platform development in 2021. ISPs were recognized as an exception to the restriction on large companies' participation due to the application of new technologies. Large system integration (SI) companies and consortiums of SMEs with cloud expertise are expected.

"We need a platform to realize the next generation of intelligent e-government," said an official from the Ministry of the Interior and Safety, "we have decided to develop a platform that includes not only standard frameworks but also infrastructure and services." "The next-generation e-government platform will be a catalyst for local governments, the public, and others to develop cloud-based e-government systems," the official said, adding, "It will be an opportunity for many cloud providers to participate and build their technical skills from the platform construction stage."

The cloud industry is excited. "Many domestic cloud providers are expected to participate from the ISP stage," said an industry insider, adding, "The public cloud market, which has been quiet, will be revitalized with large projects." "Once the platform is built, cloud business will increase in the public and local governments," he said, adding, "Domestic cloud companies must reinforce technology and specialized manpower to compete with foreign companies."

Governments also create open marketplaces to promote SaaS. SaaS created by private companies or developers can be registered in the e-government platform catalog and purchased by public sector users. Payment for the service is also settled on the e-government platform. The e-government platform acts as an intermediary and increases the SaaS utilization rate. The Ministry of the Interior and Safety plans to ▲ establish laws and systems related to establishing e-government platforms, ▲ establish measures to educate and activate e-government platforms and ▲ establish measures associated with the security of e-government platforms.

During the Gyeongju earthquake, the Ministry of Public Safety's website crashed after 40,000 people tried to access it simultaneously. During the pesticide egg scare last year, a site that checked for pesticide eggs crashed as soon as it started.

Source: [Electronic Newspaper CIOBIZ] Reporter Jisun Kim river@etnews.com Published on April 18, 2018.
http://www.etnews.com/20180418000330

The State of Digital Strategies in the D7 Countries that Drive Innovation

<Korea Information Society Agency (D.gov Issue Report: Issue Report /2018-1/)>
Countries around the world, including the leading e-government organization 'Digital-7(D7)*', are promoting various digital strategies, and Korea is also reviewing D7's strategy to explore the direction of e-government innovation.

　* South Korea, United Kingdom, New Zealand, Estonia, Canada, Israel, Uruguay

- Before and after the concept of the Fourth Industrial Revolution emerged at the Davos Forum in 2016, the D7 countries had already established and implemented digital strategies, and Korea is establishing a strategy.
- Depending on the scope of their goals, countries are divided into national innovation* and government innovation** perspectives.

　* National innovation: Pursuing innovation in various fields for the comprehensive development of the country as a whole.
　** Government innovation: focused on innovation within government, ultimately contributing to national development

- It is important to set an ultimate goal for government transformation, as it will be more powerful if developed separately than as part of a national transformation strategy.
- In addition, while the role of digital strategy was previously focused on administrative efficiency and securing convenience for citizens, it is now expanding to redefine the relationship with the state by enhancing citizens' rights to realize public values.

To this end, they commonly addressed the importance of public service delivery, access to services and inclusion from an integrated perspective, data and platforms, technology development and investment, and developing a digital workforce.

What is 'Digital-7 (D7)'?

Digital-7 (D7) is a council of leading e-government nations led by South Korea and the United Kingdom to share information and knowledge on public innovation and public services while building the foundation for digital

government.
- Expanded from a "D5" format with South Korea, the United Kingdom, New Zealand, Estonia, and Israel since its inception in September 2014 to a "D7" format with Canada and Uruguay joining in February 2018
- At the first D5 Ministerial Meeting held in London, UK, in 2014, participating countries signed the D5 Charter, which outlines the objectives of the D5, the nine pillars of digital development, and how the council will operate and have been actively engaged in exchanges beyond sharing national policies and best practices to identify agendas and conduct joint research.
- The D5 Ministerial in February 2018 explored four key areas: harnessing big data for health, building a highly skilled information workforce in government, establishing digital identities, and building citizen-centric collaborations.
- A new agenda item proposed by New Zealand at the 2018 meeting, "Digital Rights," will revitalize the international discussion on human rights in the digital age.

<9 Principles of Digital Development Prioritized in the D7 Charter>

1. Personalize services-design public services for citizens.
2. Open standards and technologies should include a clear recognition that interoperability requires a credible royalty-free and open standards policy.
3. Open-source possible. All future government systems, technologies, manuals, and standards should be open-source and shareable among participating countries.
4. Open Markets-Create a level playing field for companies of all sizes in government procurement, encourage and support a startup culture through open markets, and promote economic growth.
5. Open government (transparency)-be part of the Open Government Partnership (OGP) and create and consume open data using open licenses.
6. Connectivity-Enable online users with a comprehensive, high-quality digital infrastructure.
7. Teach Kids to Code—Give every child the opportunity to learn to code and develop the next generation of skills, creating the next generation of tech workforce.
8. Digital enablement-enabling all citizens to access digital services.
9. Agreement to share and learn—Participating countries will work together to solve each other's problems in all areas.

3. New Administrative Demands and Shifting Administrative Paradigms

1) New Administrative Demands and the Evolution of E-government

(1) Personalized E-government

ICT technology has constantly evolved to become more user-centered. The information society has evolved from an industrial society of mass production and mass consumption to a paradigm shift that emphasizes individuality and creates demand accordingly. Since the Internet was widely applied to industry around 1993, Korea has made remarkable progress in public informatization and has become a country with the world's best e-government.

Let us look at the development of open government from 2002, when Korea raised the sails of e-government, to 2012. We can see that ICT technologies are no longer provider-centric but user-centric and fully recognize individuality. Especially now that we have moved beyond Web 2.0 and entered the Web 3.0 era, these technologies will pursue a new form of government that pursues interactive sharing, openness, and transparency. Such public informatization is expected to create public services for the voluntary participation of citizens, involvement of lower levels in organizations, the pursuit of actual public good, the realization of administrative perspectives that transcend time and space, and respect for individual human beings. It is expected to strengthen people-centered administrative services and create a new form of government governance.

(2) Volunteer E-government

The transformation of information and communications technology from place-limited to ubiquitous clearly shows a change in how services are delivered. The shift in service delivery is becoming more evident as technology-delivered services become more ubiquitous and personalized from a provider perspective.

The ubiquity of IT will only complete its evolution once there is awareness of it. If this is the future of humanity, we expect it to reach a point where it will be able to overcome location restrictions, at least in our generation. We can already see early examples of such services, such as private information services providing personalized services for users within a certain geographic area or governments providing disaster information differentially within a certain geographic area. The fact that the information environment is evolving in this direction and examples of its implementation suggest that future service developers should build a more advanced service environment.

The final orientation of e-government, which embraces the changes in IT, is to act as an enabler through deregulation. It means shifting the government's functions from limited to ubiquitous and from serving a vague public with no name or surname to personalized services for people with names. To do this, the government should be more enabling in providing customized services tailored to individual characteristics rather than services based on controlling the masses.

(3) E-government maximized for accessibility through convergence

To date, eGovernment's approach to services has been built around a user-centric, partially informatized approach. This biased user view of services means that systems have been constructed from the providers' perspective. However, as the evolution of ICT technology has progressed to the acceptance of integration and convergence technologies, users unfamiliar with traditional digitalization can naturally receive information services in their surroundings.

This convergence creates new services and maximizes the ease of access to services tailored to individual consumers. The future government is predicted to evolve to maximize this ease of access (for users). This transformation will be predicated on equal access to information and information services and the provision of universal services at low or no cost to access them.

2) New Administrative Demands and Changing Value Orientation of E-government

The e-government of the future must go beyond the simple process of delivering government services using ICT. To this end, future e-government must go beyond mere technical intelligence and increase emotional intelligence, and simultaneously cultivate diversity management capabilities based on this emotional intelligence. Specifically, the following are the following.

(1) Increase emotional intelligence

While technical intelligence is recognized in e-government, it is important to emphasize that the complexities facing a government or administrative organization are often social or emotional rather than technical. For example, to manage G2G, G2C, G2B, and G2N relationships, governments need to have relationship management skills and technical intelligence, which are social and emotional.

In the literature, socio-emotional intelligence is generally defined as the ability to perceive and express emotions, absorb emotions into thinking, understand and reason emotionally, and control one's and others' emotions (Mayer et al., 2000: 396). Social-emotional intelligence is primarily manifested through relationships, affecting the quality of relationships and enhancing performance.

E-government can contribute significantly to narrowing the gap between citizens' experience and knowledge of government and their understanding of ideology (King & Stivers, 1998). Therefore, e-government needs to be more than just a place for complaints and policy discussions; it needs to be a place where citizens can discuss their difficulties and encourage and help each other.

Since building such consensus means gaining trust, detailed and differentiated services will be necessary. It will be done by systematizing the voices and issues of various layers and identifying the relationship between government and people, people and people, and companies and people.

(2) Cultivate diversity management skills

Diversity is an important concept that characterizes the paradigm shift from a producer-centric society to a consumer-centric society and from "stove-piped" to "seamless" government (Linden, 1994: 11). Diversity management can thus be seen as the ability to create complexity and control it (variety engineering) (Beer, 1979). It is also the ability to balance the diversity of interacting actors or systems by reducing and expanding complexity (Schwaninger, 2000: 211).

Diversity management is based on the idea that only variety absorbs variety (Ashby, 1956). Establishing behavioral diversity is crucial for diversity management in the future of e-government. Only when behavioral diversity is established can the government reduce the complexity of the environment and select those environments with which it can cope (Schwaninger, 2000: 211).

Therefore, future e-government should enhance government credibility through diversity management and become a representative model of a "predictable, reliable, emotionally smart government" based on securing procedural legitimacy.

3) Evolution of E-government from the Perspective of Principal-agent Theory and Trust in Government

(1) Basic assumptions of principal-agent theory

The principal-agent theory evolved from the theory of transaction costs and starts from the following assumptions (Caswell, 2003; Kassim & Menon, 2003).

First, it assumes rational economic human beings; both principals and agents are rational and self-interested. As a result, the interests of principals and agents often conflict.

Second, the agent has more information than the principal, creating an asymmetry.

Third, agents with more information are tempted to use it to their advantage, which is where the opportunistic property comes in.

Therefore, adverse selection and moral hazard can occur in a principal-agent relationship, i.e., adverse selection occurs when the principal cannot make the best choice because it is difficult for the principal, the people, to observe the information they want to know about the agent, the government, and is usually hidden before the contract. On the other hand, a moral hazard is a behavior that is hidden after the contract. Since the agent's behavior (government official) cannot be observed after the contract is over, a moral hazard occurs when the agent does not act for the principal (people) but for themselves.

(2) E-government as a way to overcome adverse selection and moral hazard

However, unlike industrial societies, technological advances have been made to reduce the occurrence of adverse selection and moral hazard in the information society, and the mutual checks and balances of governance and the prevalence of new public management evaluations have reduced the likelihood of such dysfunctions. For example, in February 2008, the National Human Rights Commission completed the first phase of a pan-governmental integrated complaint-handling system by integrating and operating the complaint systems of 43 central administrative agencies, 246 local governments, and 14 major public institutions.

The KDNK has recently expanded its scope to include the Ministry of Education, Justice, and National Defense (KDNK, 2009). The KBS is an online public communication channel where citizens can submit all complaints, suggestions, and policy discussions to the government. Furthermore, it has greatly increased the convenience of the public by making it possible to apply for complaints, administrative appeals, and corruption reports and check the results in a single visit. In short, as an online portal system that integrates and connects complaints, suggestions, policy discussions, administrative appeals, and corruption reports into one, it has created a place for communication between the government and citizens.

On the other hand, Mayer, Davis, & Sherman (1995) define government trust as the willingness to put oneself in a risky situation, believing that one's dependence on the state will not be used against one, which occurs in conditions of imperfect control and lack of information. However, government trust can be viewed as the degree of awareness or dissatisfaction between people's expectations and the actual situation (Ryu et al., 2008). Therefore, to overcome this difference in expectations, government policies and execution should be carried out through transparent administration. In other words, trust in the government will increase if it solves the problem of information asymmetry and secures procedural legitimacy through transparent information disclosure.

4) The Evolution of E-government from the Perspective of Administrative Transparency

(1) Rational (market) model with a focus on efficiency

The first situation (efficiency orientation) can be called the rational or market approach. In this case, the level of administrative transparency is determined by economic criteria and the degree to which the public, as a consumer, chooses the data and information.

In this situation, we can assume that I (the consumer) will choose when the information provided by the government is of economic benefit to me and that the level of transparency in administration that e-government seeks to achieve will increase. Therefore, the bureaucracy must constantly monitor consumer behavior and adjust its business practices to be more efficient. This is the case with e-bidding and e-taxation, and it can be assumed that "the more quickly data and information are made available to the public or used, the more transparent the administration will be."

(2) Stretch model for effectiveness

The second situation (effectiveness orientation) is a model where administrative transparency is required to reduce the gap in expectations between internal constituents and external groups around organizational goals. It is more of a stretch governance model because responding flexibly through dialog channels with citizens and external stakeholders is important.

In this model, the conditions for maintaining a high level of administrative transparency are a bureaucrat's mindset of proactive service delivery and, second, a citizen's willingness and ability to engage in more mature citizenship and interest in government policies.

However, this model is only possible in highly decentralized systems, allowing small-scale service delivery and user democracy. If these conditions are not met, the gap in mutual expectations due to information asymmetries between bureaucrats and customers will widen, and administrative transparency will decrease.

Therefore, bureaucrats, who are the internal members, must be in constant dialog with their clients and respond to changes in their needs and preferences. Rather than external customers actively participating in decision-making, bureaucrats can be seen as more actively responding to their needs and preferences through information exchange mechanisms. From this perspective, it can be assumed that "the more the bureaucracy, as a reactor, engages in dialog to reduce the gap in mutual expectations, the higher the level of administrative transparency will be."

(3) Participatory (governance) model with a focus on responsiveness

The third situation (responsiveness orientation) corresponds to the participatory model of governance, where both bureaucrats and citizens act as co-producers. However, to achieve this level of administrative transparency, participatory mechanisms must be established to ensure that citizens are fully involved in the policymaking process. Citizens must be politically engaged and active at all times, and they must be given a certain stake in the process centered on the leaders of user groups.

However, in such cases, governments and bureaucracies must strive to encourage citizen autonomy and leadership and must be able to mediate and arbitrate between diverse interests. In this case, bureaucrats are burdened with very heavy responsibilities and may even find it difficult to fulfill the unique tasks of government under more sophisticated and decentralized communication systems.

In this case, the bureaucrat's role is to act as a mediator, mediating between the positions and preferences of various stakeholders so that a more or less feasible alternative can be adopted. Moreover, the bureaucrat must clearly articulate the policy's goals and values in the public forum. Mediation skills and a high level of expertise are also required to build consensus among interest groups. We can assume that "the higher the level of mediation skills of bureaucrats, the higher the level of administrative transparency."

4. Smart Governance (Digital Government) and IT Ecosystems

1) Definition of Smart Society and Smart Governance (Digital Government)

A *smart society* is defined as "a society in which communication between humans and objects and between objects and objects in real-time across space and time, convergence between ICTs and other industries is accelerated, and new added value is constantly recreated through innovation of the entire national society, including government and private work and lifestyle, culture, and political economy, based on highly intelligent ICTs and social connectivity networks."

Smart governance can be defined as "a governance administrative system or state management system that aims to redesign administrative practices and procedures based on highly intelligent ICT and social connectivity, sharing knowledge and information between governments, businesses, citizens, and the global community, and providing a public platform for mutual transactions between members of society to continuously create productive, democratic, and value-added services in a collaborative partnership."

Rather than the two-dimensional approach of building existing information and communication infrastructure and systems, providing information, and providing structured services, the future government, smart governance, has the appearance of a smart government that can predict diversified needs in advance and provide benefits to the government, private companies, and citizens equally. In other words, it is a governance system or platform-type government that can provide a foundation for continuously producing new added value by exchanging customized information and data at the right time without any error.

2) Strategies to Drive Smart Governance

Here's a list of the strategies needed to drive smart governance.

First, it is the government's design strategy for a social integration platform through big data sharing in social integration and welfare, including employment (unemployment), welfare, education, and healthcare;

Second, it is necessary to research and strategize a smart governance system, and specific research areas include platforms, smart communities, smart global communities, and platform-type organizations;

Third, a complete reform of existing laws and systems from an informatization perspective, such as the E-Government Act and the Information Resource Management Act;

Fourth, establish a new converged smart governance promotion system to drive platform government;

Fifth, research and strategy formulation on production-consumption mechanisms to create new demand and symbiotic development;

Sixth is the concept of the public sphere, including public nature and goods, and the redefinition and improvement of laws and institutions;

Seventh, trends in each country should be identified, and comparisons between major countries should be made;

Eighth, create a strategy that positions you for leadership and the new Web 3.0 market;

Ninth, develop smart governance evaluation models and metrics;

Tenth, establish a smart society vision and strategy.

Summary

Smart Governance and Policy

The Fourth Industrial Revolution is a convergence industrial mechanism that improves productivity, quality, and customer satisfaction by applying ICT control devices such as sensors and data from the planning and design of products to their delivery to consumers. ICT refers to the Internet of Things (IoT), cloud platforms, big data, mobile communications, products, and services. The smart factory, which was born in Germany, is a factory that produces products and services that consumers of various tastes and personalities want based on data and converged ICT. In addition, a smart society is a society in which communication between humans and objects and between objects and objects is carried out in real-time across space and time based on highly intelligent ICT and social connectivity networks, and convergence between ICT and other industries is accelerated, leading to innovation in the entire national society, including government and private work styles and lifestyles, culture, and political economy, and new added value is constantly recreated. In this sense, a smart government is a highly intelligent and communicative government and a transparent and collaborative government that shares knowledge and information between governments, businesses, citizens, and communities, moving away from the closed administrative work methods of the past. These governments are problem-solving driven, and evidence-based policymaking and enforcement are driven by accurate data collection and analysis. This open and smart government is only possible with open, connected, transparent data that everyone can understand.

In the Fourth Industrial Revolution era, we need a good, open-minded, problem-solving-oriented government to satisfy the people. This is only possible through accumulating and disclosing data everyone can relate to, a public discussion process, and fair and transparent enforcement. In the era of self-governance, we need an open and smart government that can present feasible policies based on its high level of expertise and accurate future prediction, as well as conflict management and support.

The government needs to provide a hyper-connected social sharing economy platform beyond simply being an intermediary service that connects surplus resources and services through social media. South Korea's government, businesses, and citizens should be able to access the country's human and material resources anytime, anywhere, and through various access methods, where breakthrough ideas and concrete commoditization and servitization are discussed and traded daily. Such a strategy is an appropriate alternative for a country like Korea, which has a successful track record in the information society and e-government. However, the centralized approach of the past should be avoided. In the future, the government should play the role of catalyst, enabler, and mediator between public and private markets based on expertise and communication. It should seek to create a better environment for successful domestic companies to enter the larger global market and a truly public role for small and medium-sized enterprises, youth, and vulnerable groups frustrated by repeated failures, giving them a second chance and a platform for hope. Open policies and smart government for 21st-century win-win cooperation are needed; this is the basic foundation for service innovation that resonates with the people.

Since 2010, the strategic importance of mobile devices has increased significantly across industries as ICT technologies have accelerated trends such as mobilization, networking, convergence, and complexity. With the advent of smartphones due to changes and advancements in mobile technology, convergence services with various services have begun to emerge. In other words, mobile technology and convergence technology are evolving from simple hardware technology to application services that can create demand according to market needs. The continuous development of mobile technology has evolved into an intelligent and integrated system by converging with other industries, breaking down the boundaries between sectors such as voice, data, telecommunications, broadcasting, and finance, and spreading to the public and private sectors. These changes and developments in IT technology are converging with various social systems to revolutionize the entire national society, including the economy, people, lifestyle, labor, and public administration systems. They are evolving into services such as smart business, smart life, smart work, and smart government. In recent years, intelligent, converged, and shared intelligent IT that connect the virtual and physical worlds, such as artificial intelligence, machine learning, digital twins, interactive platforms, and blockchain, have emerged, and we are at a point where fundamental and comprehensive innovation of the existing bureaucracy-centered government operation and work methods is required.

The rapid advancement of ICT has led to rapid changes in the functions and roles of government. This is especially true in the field of public informatization. This change in public information is manifested in three major areas:

1. User-centered public information through the Web 3.0 era.
2. Public information through public-private-public cooperation.
3. Public information that maximizes accessibility through convergence.

Platform functions can be defined as government functions that can realize the changed appearance of future government (e-government) due to the development of

IT technology. Three types of future platform governments are defined based on the three functions conceptualized by these platform functions.

First, it is a collaborative government, a future platform government that centers on strengthening public-private cooperation based on the platform's interconnection capabilities. Second, it can be called intelligent (= smart) government as a future platform that centers on enhancing administrative services to accommodate people's needs based on attempting to connect and strengthen connections between previously unconnected entities. Third, a transparent government is a future platform that functions around communication, participation, and trust based on creating added value through the platform.

The characteristics of collaborative government include:
1. Interrelatedness with economic system changes.
2. Establishment of a mechanism that repeats virtuous co-evolution in a way that information shared on the platform and generated by itself is accumulated through mutual sharing and distribution.
3. Collecting information and opinions enhances public services suitable for each individual's needs.

The characteristics of intelligent government include:
1. Providing intelligent, active, personalized, and customized services.
2. Strengthening administrative services to accommodate people's needs.
3. Creating added value for users (people and businesses) or providing intelligent, active, customized services.
4. Increasing the reliability of information (database).

The characteristics of a transparent government include (1) building trust through participatory processes, (2) increasing participation through the platform, (3) diversifying the way people live, and (4) communicating with people based on their participation.

ICT has evolved to become more user-centered. The information society has evolved from an industrial society of mass production and mass consumption to a paradigm shift that emphasizes individuality and creates demand accordingly. At this point, when we have moved beyond Web 2.0 and entered the Web 3.0 era, it is predicted that public informatization will make public services for the voluntary participation of citizens, involvement of lower levels in organizations, the pursuit of actual public good, the realization of administrative perspectives that transcend time and space, and respect for individual human beings. It is expected to strengthen people-centered administrative services and create a new form of government governance.

The e-government of the future must go beyond the simple process of delivering government services using ICT. To this end, it must go beyond mere technical intelligence and increase emotional intelligence, and it must simultaneously cultivate diversity management capabilities based on this emotional intelligence.

The capabilities and roles of bureaucrats (human resources) required by these changes require them to mediate with excellent social-emotional intelligence in the relationship between government, citizens, companies, and global society. In other words, a mediator in the smart era is required who can make the most of IT's advantages with a balanced perspective, aiming for cooperative governance rather than control while reconciling various interests.

Smart governance, (digital government), the government of the future, has the appearance of a smart government that can predict diversified needs in advance and provides benefits to government, private companies, and citizens alike, rather than the two-dimensional approach of building existing information and communication infrastructure and systems, providing information, and providing structured services. In other words, it is a governance system or platform-type government that can provide a foundation for continuously producing new added value by exchanging customized information and data at the right time without any error.

There are three strategies promoted for the development of smart governance and IT ecosystem: first, the strategy of building a symbiotic SW ecosystem; second, the strategy of fostering cloud-based IT governance; and third, the strategy of implementing smart governance using big data. The introduction of cloud computing has two main effects: one is to maximize the efficiency of IT resources and reduce costs through integration, specialization, standardization, and automation, and the other is that IT resources can be used anytime and anywhere via the Internet. Big data applied to the social sphere refers to IT that utilizes and analyzes large amounts of data to extract valuable information and uses the generated knowledge to respond to or predict changes actively.

There have been many opinions that the government should play a new role in enabling the development of advanced digital industries centered on artificial intelligence and cloud, just like the e-government in the early 2000s, which served as a stepping stone for Korea's IT growth. Despite the accumulated administrative data, it has been pointed out that there is a lack of linkage and utilization between agencies, disconnected services at the ministry level, a lack of systems and infrastructure to utilize new technologies, and a lack of a control tower and specific strategies for digital transformation. Therefore, the Ministry of the Interior and Safety announced the Basic Plan for Digital Government Innovation with six priorities: ▲ Innovating public services, ▲ Activating public sector my-data, ▲ Advancing citizen participation platforms, ▲ Implementing a smart workplace, ▲ Enabling the use of cloud and digital services, and ▲ Building an open data and service ecosystem. Recently, the Yoon administration promulgated the "Regulation on the Establishment and Operation of the Digital Platform Government Committee" as a presidential decree. The plan is to provide customized services such as 'My AI Service' and 'Any-ID Simple Login Service' along with 'One-Site Total Service' that integrates services provided separately on each government site in one place. In addition, companies will create various innovative services by fusing and combining these services and data and promote the 'Leading Public Experience Project' so that the public can conveniently use public services, and the public and companies can quickly experience customized public services.

Research Questions

1. Explain the concept of the Fourth Industrial Revolution and its impact on public administration.
2. Describe the key technologies of the Fourth Industrial Revolution.
3. Discuss the problems and policy alternatives for ICT competitiveness in Korea.
4. Explain the concept of blockchain and its potential to transform public administration.

5. Discuss strategies for redesigning ICT governance.
6. Discuss the conditions and strategies for smart government in the Fourth Industrial Revolution.
7. Discuss the impact of the emergence of user-centered computing on e-government.
8. Describe the top 10 strategic technologies that will drive IT.
9. What are the three quantum leaps in the open government sector due to advances in IT?
10. What are the three types of platform government as IT evolves?
11. Discuss the causes and characteristics of collaborative platform-style government.
12. Describe the promotion and utilization of platform government in Korea.
13. Discuss the changes in the administrative paradigm of future societies regarding e-government.
14. What does platform government mean?
15. Explain e-government in terms of administrative transparency.
16. Explain e-government in terms of principal-agent theory and trust in government.
17. Describe the advantages and disadvantages of cloud computing.
18. Explain the concept of big data and how it is utilized.

The evolution of intelligent knowledge management systems has reduced information asymmetry by establishing information sharing and control mechanisms between the government and the people, the government and businesses, and the government and the government, and it is presented as an example that the possibility of moral hazard has been significantly reduced through complaints, suggestions, policy discussions, administrative judgments, and corruption reports. See Hong, Myeong, and Kim (2010) for more details.

This article is adapted from Myeong (2006), "Limitations of deterministic thinking in e-government research and ways to overcome them."

The contents of Section 3 are based on unpublished internal research data, presentations at the Korea Regional Informatization Society, public announcements of the joint digital government innovation plan of the Ministry of the Interior and Safety and the Ministry of Science and ICT, issue reports of the Korea Information Society Agency, and Wikipedia.

Chapter 5

Smart Cities

1. Smart City[01]

The future society is called a smart society. The term smart, which means 'neat, stylish, smart,' is used in information and communication, industry, and management. In other words, the term smart is used when we aim to create a new industry based on ICT through convergence between heterogeneous industries or to perform work creatively by breaking away from existing practices and stereotypes. The term smart is being used in an ever-expanding sense through ICT and industrial development. The concept of smart is becoming an important requirement to determine the competitiveness of various industries, technologies, and cultures in the 21st century.

A smart society is where technological advancement and social change are accelerating, and imagination, creativity, and sensitivity are important. With the popularization of smartphones and the development of ICT, various mobile applications have been developed and commercialized, leading to digitalization's quantitative and qualitative advancement. The current era has reached the point where we need to step forward in the qualitative advancement of digitalization and envision a future society that can create social and cultural values based on humanism while promoting overall social transformation (Korea Information Society Agency, 2011).

---

01   See Myeong et al., 2017, for the smart city concept. "Case Analysis of Sustainable Disaster and Safety Smart City," Korean Journal of Policy Science, 21(4): 197-218.

Today, the society undergoing this paradigm shift is called a 'smart society' (Korea Information Society Agency, 2010). Just as there was a paradigm shift from the industrial society to the knowledge-information society, we are now in a paradigm shift from the knowledge-information society to the smart society. Looking at the trend of co-evolution, where the speed of change is faster than ever, it can be predicted that the smart society will soon become a huge paradigm, bringing great changes in all fields.

This paradigm shift to a smart society is naturally influencing the transformation of cities. It is where the smart city comes in. A smart city is "an intelligent and governed urban system that aims to redesign urban administrative practices and procedures based on highly intelligent ICT and social connectivity, share knowledge and information among governments, businesses, residents, and communities in urban areas, and provide a public platform for mutual transactions among local members to create productive and democratic added value continuously, It is a collective intelligence system that develops new growth engines through intelligent and efficient management of the environment, energy, urban infrastructure, and buildings using advanced ICT and is emerging as a major solution to metropolitan problems (Lee, 2015).

According to the UN's World Population Prospects, the urban population will grow from 1.4 billion in 1970 to 6.3 billion by 2050, with 60% of the world's population concentrated in urban areas. In developed countries, more than 80% of the world's population lives in cities, and this rapid urbanization is causing a shortage of urban infrastructure and resources due to the growing urban population. To solve this problem, many countries are taking the lead in building smart cities to utilize urban resources and create sustainable cities efficiently. China is planning to invest 2 trillion yuan (about $333 billion) by 2025 to transform 80 percent of its cities into smart cities called smart cities or intelligent cities, while Japan has invested about 68 billion yen in smart city-related policies since 2010 to rebuild cities in the Tohoku region that were destroyed by the Great East Japan Earthquake and build smart cities to increase energy efficiency. In 2015, the White House announced a smart city plan with a total R&D investment of $1.6 billion to solve various urban problems (Korea et al. Center, 2017). Data from market research firm Navigant Research reflects this trend, with the global smart city market expected to double from $424 billion in 2017 to $1,017 billion in 2020 and continue to grow.[02]

---

02   According to another study by Navigant Research, the smart building market is expected to grow from $3.6 billion in 2017 to $10.2 billion in 2026.

1) Concept of Smart City

Before smart cities, various concepts of cities in the context of ICT development have been discussed, such as virtual, intelligent, digital, and ubiquitous (Albino et al., 2015). While these concepts were specific to certain areas and addressed the functioning of cities, smart cities incorporate these concepts and continue to evolve as a combination of various elements. In the 1990s, when the term first appeared, smart cities were seen as improvements to urban systems based on new ICT technologies. However, as these idealized technologies have become a reality, the approach to smart cities has become more multifaceted. The concept of smart cities is still being discussed in various ways by academics, governments, global companies, and international organizations.[03] In other words, a clear definition of a smart city has yet to be established, and different entities interpret it differently.

The EU defines a smart city as a city that uses a variety of technologies to minimize environmental impact and improve the quality of life of its citizens, and is not limited to the development and innovation of technology alone but also involves industry, academia, government, research institutions, and civil society working together to take on new challenges to make cities smarter. Gartner, an American research and advisory firm, defines a smart city as enabling sustainable development based on exchanging information between various actors, including the public and private sectors.

Many scholars at home and abroad have also proposed various definitions of smart cities. First, Hall (2000) defined a smart city as managing and integrating infrastructure such as roads, bridges, energy, water, and major buildings to effectively utilize these resources and provide optimal urban services to citizens. Dirks & Keeling (2009) argued that a smart city is one in which technology transforms key city systems such as people, businesses, transportation, communications, and energy and makes optimal use of finite resources. Giffinger (2007) defined a smart city as a smart society in which various elements such as people, environment, government, and economy are built within a smart infrastructure. Lee and Lim (2008) defined a smart city as a future high-tech city that can receive information services anytime, anywhere—through any ICT device. Choi (2011) said that the infrastructure for telecommunications is connected to every corner of the city like a human neural network.

Synthesizing these various perspectives and attributes of ICT and the future society affected by them, the concept of a smart city can be seen as "a sustainable city that solves various urban problems based on highly intelligent ICT and social connectivity

---

03   ITU (2014) reports that at least 116 "smart cities" concepts have been proposed worldwide.

networks and communicates between people, objects, and objects in real-time across space and time, ultimately improving the quality of life of citizens."

2) Smart City Components

A smart city can be viewed as a collection of various elements, including urban management, urban life, local industry, urban infrastructure, education, and services utilizing advanced technologies. It should also focus on a multifaceted transformation that includes institutional factors other than technology and smart citizens (Nam & Pardo, 2011; Kominos, 2011; Myeong et al., 2018). Furthermore, these components should be combined and operationalized for a sustainable new city rather than a short-term manifestation of technology or increased citizen convenience.

The following three conditions must be met for sustainable smart city development, especially from the perspective of public administration, which prioritizes solving public problems. The first is the establishment of smart institutions. Institutions with the expertise to set forward-looking goals to improve the city's resilience and creativity and to build collaborative relationships between city actors must be established and managed—second, sustainable business planning. Sustainable business planning requires a multidimensional approach that includes architecture, design, public realm, and transportation infrastructure planning—third, continuous financial support. Instead of a one-time budget for each project, a comprehensive financial support system should be linked to long-term urban planning and investment plans (Huston et al., 2015).

Meanwhile, the Korea Land Institute (2016) categorizes the components and stages of smart city construction into three stages. The first is the smart city construction phase. This technical infrastructure phase builds the foundation for technology convergence and convergence, i.e., the public physical, communication, and platform bases. The second is the smart city operation phase, which establishes an institutional governance base for operation, inter-ministerial collaboration and policy, institutional design, and public-private partnerships. The last stage is the smart city growth stage, which creates a foundation for innovation and is concerned with participation and services related to the growth and innovation of smart cities, such as active participation of the private sector and participation of start-ups.

Smart cities can be categorized according to their policy objectives, constituent industries, and required infrastructure. Smart cities can be categorized into environmental sustainability, well-being of citizens, and economic fulfillment according to smart policies and objectives. For this purpose, the necessary component

<Table 5-1> Smart City Components and Creation Steps

	Technology Infrastructure Sector	Institutional Sector	Human Resources
Base Elements	Technology Convergence Foundation	Governance Foundation	Built on innovation
Detail Element Examples	• Physical infrastructure such as roads, bridges • Information and communication infrastructure, such as telecommunication networks • ICT such as Internet of Things, artificial intelligence, big data • Systems such as platforms	• Active cross-functional collaboration • Policies & Institutions • Government Transparency • Increase citizen engagement in policymaking • Public-Private Partnerships	• Creative training • Innovative jobs • Open Mindset • Active engagement with the private sector • Collectivity • Start-up companies
Stage	Building a Smart City	Smart City Operations	Smart City Growth

Source: Korea Land Institute (2016).

<Table 5-2> Classification by Smart City Configuration

	Environmental Sustainability	Civic Well-being Life	Affordability
Smart policies and objectives	• Energy efficiency • Environmental pollution • Resources	• Public Safety • Education • Medical & Health • Social Stability	• Investments • Jobs • Innovation
Smart City Component Industries	Smart utilities, smart buildings, smart transportation, smart government and more		
	Smart City Operating Systems		
Smart City Infrastructure	• Sensor networks, smart terminals, and communication platforms • Data analysis, control system, web service		

Source: GigaOM Pro (2012).

industries should be composed of smart utilities, buildings, transportation, and government according to each classification, and smart city infrastructure, such as sensor networks, data analysis, control systems, and communication platforms, should be built based on the smart city operating system (GigaOM, 2012).

Smart cities use the Internet of Things and ICT to transform the city. It requires a new type of leadership from city administrators. In urban policy, the leadership of city administrators greatly impacts the policy's success. Leaders in the smart city era need to be influential as important volunteers in smart cities, and they need to be able to manage smart city budgets and projects, provide expertise, and train bureaucrats and frontline officials. In other words, smart city leaders need to be a convergence of talents with an understanding of IT technology and political influence.

Citizens are an integral part of a city that cannot be excluded. Their participation should be essential in the formation of smart cities. As mentioned earlier, smart cities are intended to solve urban problems. The citizens and residents of a city are not just the beneficiaries of urban policy decisions; they are the direct participants who have the best understanding of urban problems. By involving civil society in formulating and implementing urban policies, cities can improve democracy and efficiency. Cities should utilize ICT to provide omni-channel platforms to hear urban voices and ensure citizen participation.

3) Smart City Development Stage

A smart city goes through the foundation, vertical, and horizontal building stages to secure intelligent technologies that connect various data, systems, and business models, leading to the city platform stage. The city platform is the final stage of a smart city, where the city shares information and functions seamlessly like a single organism. They will also share data that AI automates. In this stage of the future city, it will be important to efficiently transform social structures such as government, industry, education, and society. It is a stage where AI and robotics replace existing urban systems and structures, and the vision of an intelligent society is realized (Korea Information Society Agency, 2016).

The domestic market size of these smart cities is growing at an average annual rate of about 30.3%, and the total cumulative investment in smart cities is estimated to reach about $33 trillion from 2010 to 2030 (Nikkei et al., 2010). In response, the Korean Ministry of Land & Transport, Infrastructure is promoting a plan to spread smart cities overseas by building world-leading smart cities over the next five years, starting in 2016. A smart city is a high-tech city model led by Korea, and it is expected to preempt the overseas smart city market and create high-added value, which will require a network system such as establishing a system of industry, government, academia, research governance, and international cooperation.

2. Smart City Trends

1) Domestic Smart City Policy Trends

In Korea, the Ubiquitous City (hereinafter referred to as U-City) project, the predecessor of smart cities, has been underway since the 1990s. In 2003, the U-City project began with the construction fever of new cities centered on Pangyo in Seongnam, Songdo in Incheon, and Dongtan in Hwaseong. In December 2006, the Ministry of Information and Communication finalized the 'Basic Plan for Revitalizing U-City Construction,' which includes the development of a standard model for U-City services and related laws and systems. In March 2008, the Ministry of Land, Infrastructure, and Transport enacted the Act on the Construction of Ubiquitous Cities and set the enforcement regulations and guidelines for establishing U-City plans. Subsequently, MOLIT announced the 1st Ubiquitous City Comprehensive Plan (2009-2013) in November 2009 and the 2nd Ubiquitous City Comprehensive Plan (2014-2018) in October 2013, respectively. The goal of the first plan was to create an overall foundation for U-City. It established a public-centered system, developing core technologies and services and supporting industry development. The second plan focused on establishing a virtuous cycle of shared growth for full-scale U-City and overseas expansion centered on the ICT construction industry.

Since then, Korea has renamed the existing information city, U-City, to a smart city, and in March 2017, the Act on the Construction of Ubiquitous Cities was amended to the Act on the Creation and Promotion of Smart Cities. Although smart cities were a strategic industry in the era of the Fourth Industrial Revolution, the existing U-City law was a procedural law limited to city construction. Therefore, the U-City Act, which was applied only to the construction of large-scale new cities, was expanded to apply to existing urban areas and revised to include construction, operation, and management.

Through this, citizens can experience services provided in facility network construction and construction projects that only officials and experts can understand. Smart cities developed by focusing on technology have also focused on building a service-oriented platform. In addition, the establishment of measures to foster the

<Table 5-3> Domestic Smart City Related Policies

Separation	Background	Key Takeaways
National Geographic Information System Construction Project (1995-)	A series of accidents involving underground facilities, such as the 1994 city gas explosion at the Aehyeon-dong subway construction site in Seoul and the 1995 gas explosion at the Daegu subway construction site, increased the need to create a national geographic information base.	During this time, a spatial information database was established for each local government, and a database management system was also established to manage it. This database was utilized for local government-related tasks.
Urban Information System Construction Project (2000~)	Growing demand for locating and efficiently managing underground utilities such as electricity, gas, and telecommunications in cities	Established a comprehensive spatial information system for underground facilities to accurately identify and manage their locations and prevent accidents such as fires, explosions, and gas leaks caused by broken pipes.
ITS 839 Strategy (2004)	As the concept of the ubiquitous city is increasingly adopted, the need for strategies to make it a more concrete reality increases.	A national vision of the future of IT, where IT permeates everyday life, transforming society and creating new added value.
U-City Act (2008)	Establishment of an institutional foundation for U-City construction, such as establishing a comprehensive plan for U-City construction, establishing and approving a local government ubiquitous urban plan, and designating a pilot city.	Building infrastructure under the U-City Act The law defines U-City infrastructure as a communication network, intelligent infrastructure, and urban integrated operation center.

Source: Hyunsook Lee (2017). Smart City Concepts and Policy Trends, Center for Convergence Research and Policy; adapted and added from Jaeyoung Lee, Monthly Transportation (2017).

<Table 5-4> Comparison of U-City and Smart City Concepts

	U-City	Smart Cities
Definition	• A city that provides U-City services anytime, anywhere through U-City facilities built using U-City technology to improve city competitiveness and quality of life. • A city with a ubiquitous concept that transcends construction and enables people to connect to the network anytime, anywhere, to exchange information and respond.	• Sustainable cities of the future are cities that converge nature-friendly technologies and ICT technologies to respond to climate change, environmental pollution, and inefficiencies caused by industrialization and urbanization. • Cities with "smart" concepts that maximize city functions' efficiency to provide citizens convenience and economic and time benefits.
Applies to	• Bringing key functions such as administration, transportation, welfare, environment, and disaster prevention to new cities • Actual application is focused on crime prevention, disaster prevention, and transportation	• Bringing a wide range of functions to new and existing cities, including administration, transportation, energy, water management, welfare, environment, disaster prevention, crime prevention, and more • Real-world application is also very broad in each field
Domestic and international activities	• It is not a universally utilized concept worldwide, only in Korea and Japan. • Leveraging the concept of ubiquity, which was particularly popular in our country in the early 2000s.	• Globally universal concept, used in developed and developing countries alike
Drivers	• Central and local government initiatives	• Significant participation from central and local governments, as well as private companies

Source: Ministry of Land, Infrastructure, and Transport press release, March 2017, 3.

smart city industry, the basis for establishing an association, and the use of globally accepted smart city terminology have introduced the basis for the overseas expansion of smart cities.

2) Smart City Overseas Cases

We look at the best smart city practices worldwide based on Catapult Future Cities' indicators. Catapult Future Cities' indicators are organized into three categories and nine indicators. The first three broad categories are:

① Openness: How open is the city to new ideas and entrepreneurial activity?
② Infrastructure: How can cities optimize infrastructure for growth companies to make it safe for citizens to live and do business?
③ Leadership: How do government policies and leadership create innovative systems for smart cities?

The nine detailed metrics are:

① REGULATOR: What is the extent to which laws and regulations are enacted, updated, and deregulated to consider new business models in the city?
② ADVOCATE: What policies and global cooperation systems exist to support small business entrepreneurs in the city's entry into the global environment?
③ CUSTOMER: What is the organization's policy to strengthen customer accessibility to support innovation and business?
④ HOST: What supportive policies are in place to provide opportunities to attract high-growth companies to the city?
⑤ INVESTOR: How do we invest in the technologies and businesses needed to innovate?
⑥ CONNECTOR: How did you build the physical system digital network?
⑦ STRATEGIST: Does the organization have the required internal management systems and a clear strategy to support innovation?
⑧ DIGITAL GOVERNOR: Is there an efficient governance digital system in place that enables citizen participation in policy formation and problem-solving?
⑨ DATAVORE (data manager): Does it analyze big data, disclose administrative information, and provide real-time data services?

REGULATOR	1. Enforce existing regulations proportionately	2. Review and update regulation to take account of new business models	3. Engage the full spectrum of stake-holders to craft balanced regulation		
ADVOCATE	1. Ensure a new business focus within the trade and investment function	2. Provide set-up support for new businesses	3. Promotion of the city as a hub of business creation	4. Sponsor events relevant to high-growth sectors	5. Helping early-stage ventures access global networks
CUSTOMER	1. Ensure the viability of procurement opportunities through a single portal	2. Ensure that pre-qualifying requirements are achievable by new businesses	3. Define target for spend on new businesses	4. Use problem-based procurement methods	5. Use open innovation methods to engage the ecosystem
HOST	1. Support access to co-working spaces	2. Support incubator and accelerator schemes	3. Enable access to affordable and flexible office space	4. Nurture innovation Districts	5. Play the role of matchmaker within the ecosystem
INVESTOR	1. Support provision of coding and technical skills	2. Support schemes that help young people access the tech sector	3. Help businesses understand types of financing options	4. Provide funding	
CONNECTOR	1. Support access to high-speed internet	2. Provide free public Wi-Fi	3. Ensure the high quality and extent of cycling infrastructures	4. Ensure frictionless and integrated public transport	
STRATEGIST	1. Publish a vision of how to support innovation and entrepreneurship	2. Have a public set of KPIs that measure the success of the city's vision	3. Have an innovation function within the city hall	4. Have senior leadership with responsibility for innovation and entrepreneurship	
DIGITAL GOVERNOR	1. Ensure digital by default city services	2. Enable citizens to report city problems on the go	3. Enable citizens to engage in policy decision making		
DATAVORE	1. Use data analytics to optimise city services	2. Publish open data	3. Publish live data with appropriate APIs		

source: http://citie.org.CATAPULT Future Cities

[Figure 5-2] Catapult Future Cities metrics

(1) New York, USA

The US government[04] The third Open Government National Action Plan includes more than 40 new and expanded action plans to advance President Obama's commitment. Member states and civil society organizations are taking steps to improve the transparency of public institutions, open up public information, improve public resource management, and engage citizens in government processes. The third

---

04　　D.gov Edge. vol.09 (Dec. 2015) [Electronic resource].

National Open Government Action Plan, which includes plans to improve access to public information, citizen-centered access to services, and citizen-centered access to public information, includes new and impactful initiatives by the administration to support open government by making more information public, delivering government services from a collaborative perspective, and being citizen-centered.

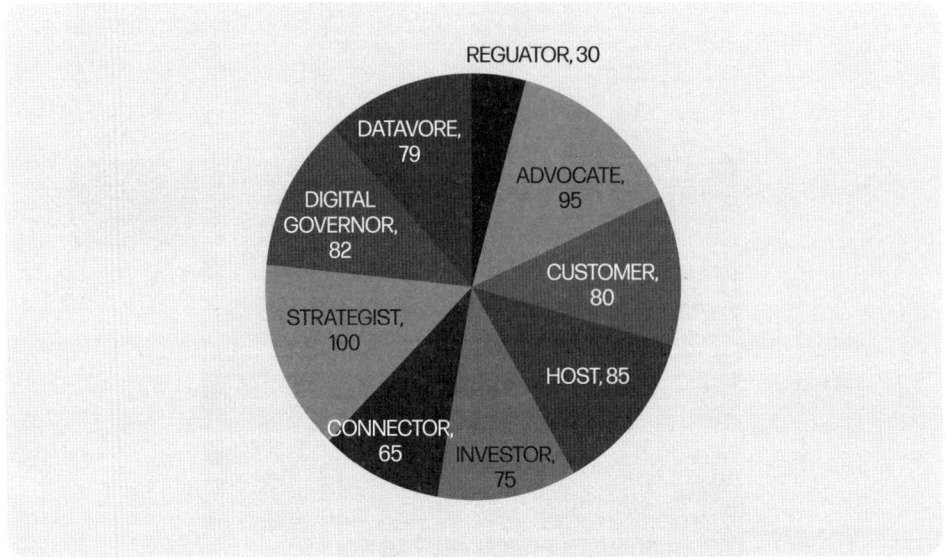

[Figure 5-3] First Place: New York City

Compared to similar cities, New York City prioritizes innovation and entrepreneurship and has had a very active policy toward the tech community over the past few years, including support for tech communities and start-ups. Specifically, it supports local start-ups across various areas, including funding and branding activities in community building and technology provision. These support measures have been instrumental in deploying beneficial data and technology in the services provided to citizens. An area of relative weakness in New York City is the regulator's role. Nevertheless, the US government is constantly researching and collecting examples to find new business models and sharing models that companies like Airbnb have characterized. The New York City government has demonstrated that it is well-positioned to drive smart city policies through stakeholder and governance collaboration. New York provides the right environment for thriving innovation and entrepreneurship and is focused on implementing an enterprise-centric smart city model. In addition, New York City is planning to implement a project to build the world's first underground park using solar technology, furthering its leadership in sustainable, advanced cities.

(2) London, UK

In March 2016, the UK's Government Digital Service (GDS) set out a new vision for the GOV. UK platform: 'Make government work for users'. London, UK, has a reputation as an open and global city and is a leader in embracing change from its citizens. As a result, the city has been receptive to many proposals to bring technology into the city and has strongly supported the local tech sector.

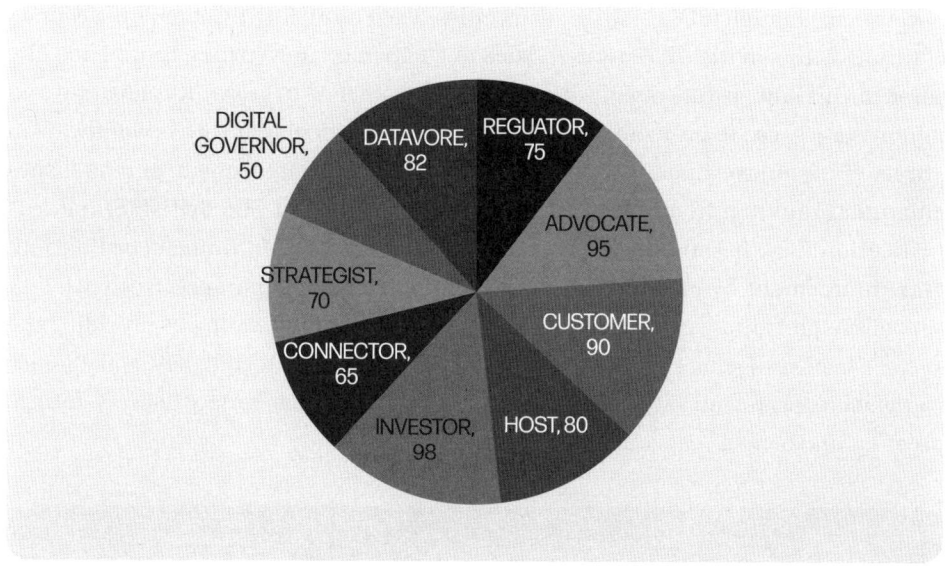

[Figure 5-4] Second Place: LONDON

The London city government also plans to launch a smart city project with Intel. Under the initial project plan, special sensors will be attached to major facilities such as buildings and lampposts to collect data on noise, pollution, and energy utilization to build a smart city. To this end, Intel has signed a Memorandum of Understanding (MOU) with Imperial College and University College London, two of the UK's leading IT universities, to closely examine the IT technologies, business models, environment, and commercial viability of the city's needs and jointly develop related technologies.

London is rolling out a smart plan to become a smart city. At £19 billion, London's tech market is the largest in Europe, with 40,000 digital businesses and 200,000 employees in the tech sector alone. Londoners also generate data that helps the city manage its transportation, social, economic, and environmental systems, and innovators are encouraged to use it to develop technologies that can solve real-world problems facing the city. There are clear benefits to 'smart policies' and programs for Londoners and businesses. We are pushing to be smarter in new ways, such as sharing expertise through the City Data Strategy and the European 'Sharing Cities' project. The Smart London Board includes academics, businesses, and entrepreneurs. The board advises the mayor on applying digital technologies to transform London into a better living place, create more jobs, and increase investment. It also works to promote 'smart' initiatives in London and engage Londoners in these issues.

Meanwhile, the UK's private sector-led Future Cities Catapult acts as a special purpose corporation (SPC) to drive smart cities. The Future Cities Catapult is a council of various actors in the UK ecosystem, such as companies, universities, central and city governments, and private organizations, and was launched to grow UK companies and improve cities, i.e., to promote urban innovation. In particular, it travels worldwide to attract efficient investments, conducts a global smart city assessment, and publishes an annual ranking. In addition, a private company called The British Standards Institution (BSI) is establishing a governance system for planning, coordination, and enforcement by establishing standards from various perspectives with city councils to provide a basic framework. In other words, it is operating by providing the success factors of smart cities: strategy clarity, leadership, technology, stakeholder engagement, user-centricity, supplier partnerships, achievable service delivery, future-proofing, and benefit realization.

[Figure 5-5] London Data Services Center

(3) Helsinki, Finland

Helsinki is developing the Smart Kalasatama district as an experimental innovation city to co-create smart social infrastructure and services. To this end, Helsinki will experiment with Smart Kalasatama, an innovation district, as an innovation platform for creating smart infrastructure services by 2030. More than 20 projects will be implemented under smart mobility, smart energy, smart living, well-being, economy, and education. Co-creation is the core concept of the Smart Kalasatama district, where residents are expected to play a key role as experimenters of smart services and leaders in sustainable and resource-efficient lifestyles.

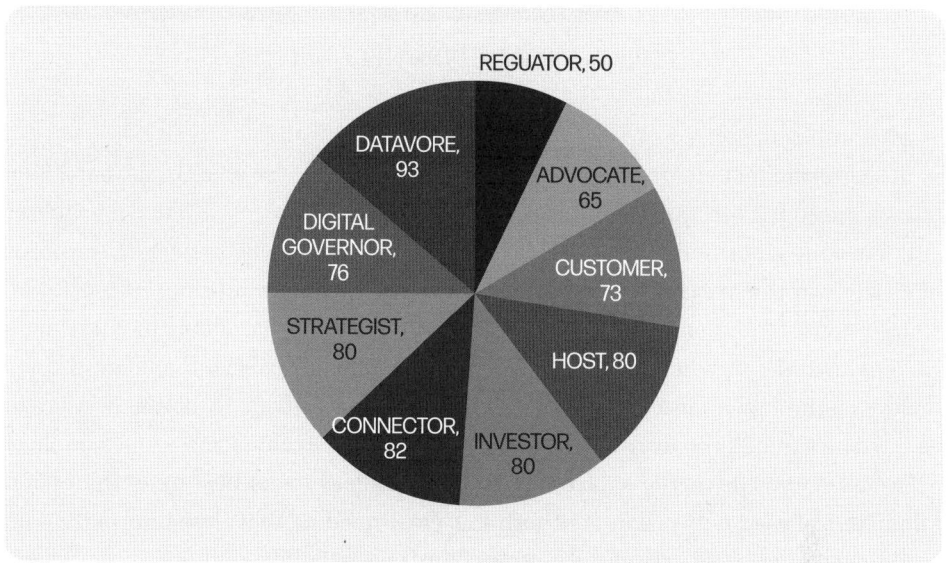

[Figure 5-6] Third Place HELSINKI

Helsinki has the most sustained initiatives of any city in the Global Top 5, including acting as a host, investor, and connector to empower connectors to work together as a single community to create smart infrastructure. For example, Helsinki has adopted a governance approach to create the CitySDK platform with developers and local entrepreneurs to develop high-quality digital solutions for Helsinki's citizens. Smaller cities like Helsinki also build policies and ecosystems that support innovation and entrepreneurial systems. It also operates the One-Click solution, a public-private collaborative governance system, to accommodate the diverse needs of its citizens. Helsinki offers a high level of information provision by data custodians and is a tech start-up destination for entrepreneurs.

[Figure 5-7] Third Place HELSINKI

(4) Barcelona, Spain

Recognizing that smart cities improve the quality of life for all citizens, Barcelona has embraced ICT technologies and adopted the Barcelona Smart City Model to deliver citizen services more efficiently. To this end, it is promoting policies to meet the needs of citizens in the areas of environment, mobility, business, telecommunications, energy, housing, and education. Open information is readily available to Barcelona's citizens anytime, anywhere. Barcelona promotes sustainable policies that allow the city to develop through innovation and business creation and efficiently deliver services to its citizens through the use and convergence of new ICT technologies. An example of a success story is Bitcarrier's introduction of technology to connect more than 1,500 kilometers of road network in Southern Europe, providing real-time information on roads. Barcelona is still actively attracting companies to build an innovative smart city centered around a demonstration park. In particular, the city's 2012 project to remotely manage streetlights and apply LED technology to 1,100 streetlights on 50 streets is often cited as a leading example of a smart city. By building such an experimental smart city, the streetlights can understand the ambient noise level, movement, and brightness of the street to increase the brightness of the lights during busy hours and decrease the brightness of the lights at night when there are no people, saving at least 30% of electricity consumption annually. The city also optimizes urban planning by improving situational awareness, real-time collaboration, and decision-making across ministries to ensure citizens' compliance with traffic laws and increase management effectiveness.

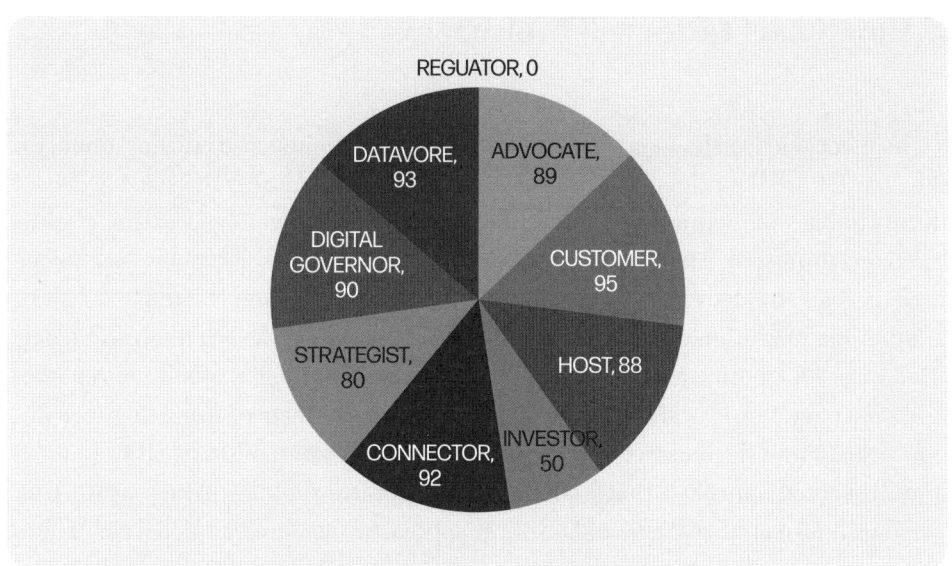

[Figure 5-8] Forth Place BARCELONA

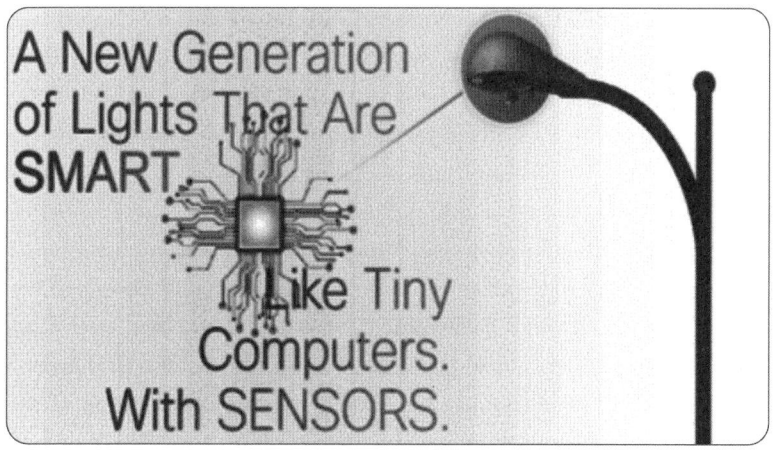

[Figure 5-9] Smart Streetlights

3. How Smart Cities will Evolve?

As mentioned earlier, smart cities worldwide aim to improve citizens' quality of life, but ICT are the primary focus. It is also necessary to address the side effects and disadvantages of technology-centeredness, as only the advantages of smart cities are being discussed. There is a critical view that smart cities are a new technology-driven urban strategy that relies on technological solutions from IT companies and is another manifestation of urban entrepreneurship based on modern high technology (Hollands, 2008). Advanced technology improves people's quality of life, convenience, and efficiency, but it is also a reality that various side effects of technology are also appearing. From this perspective, the development direction of smart cities requires a multifaceted approach that includes various issues such as privacy protection, personal information leakage, and business approaches centered on global companies. Accordingly, the following realization conditions are necessary to promote smart cities.

First, the actors should include central and local governments, residents, and private companies. Smart cities have been described and discussed in terms of technology-centered urban systems. As a result, smart cities have been promoted by global companies and central governments that have secured technological and financial power. However, this has been criticized, and participatory elements such as citizen participation, governance, and social capital building have been presented as key issues (Pereira & Quintana, 2002). Since the ultimate goal of smart cities is to improve the quality of life of individuals, families, regions, and the country as a whole through advanced technology rather than the manifestation of advanced technology, it should be promoted through governance consultation without excluding anyone from the central government, local governments, residents, and private companies. Local governments will need to move beyond the role of a mere agent of the central government or a contractor with private companies and play the role of a supporter, catalyst, and mediator between the central government, private companies, and civil society.

Second, the goals should include strengthening the competitiveness of city governments, closing the information gap between regions, balancing development, and improving residents' quality of life. In the modern era, which is moving beyond megacities to the era of hypermegacities, the competitiveness of city governments is directly related to the nation's competitiveness. For this reason, the goal of smart city promotion should be to strengthen the competitiveness of city governments by

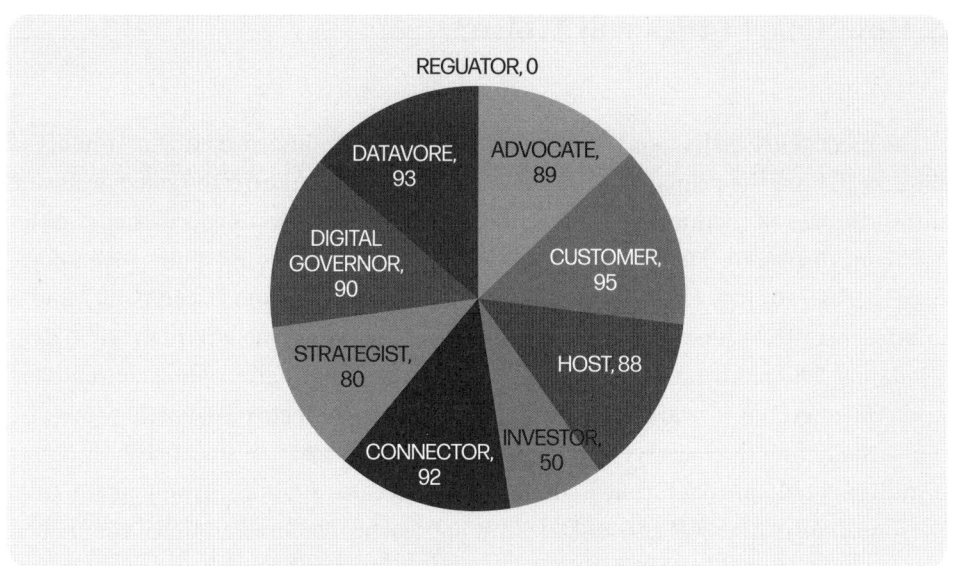

[Figure 5-8] Forth Place BARCELONA

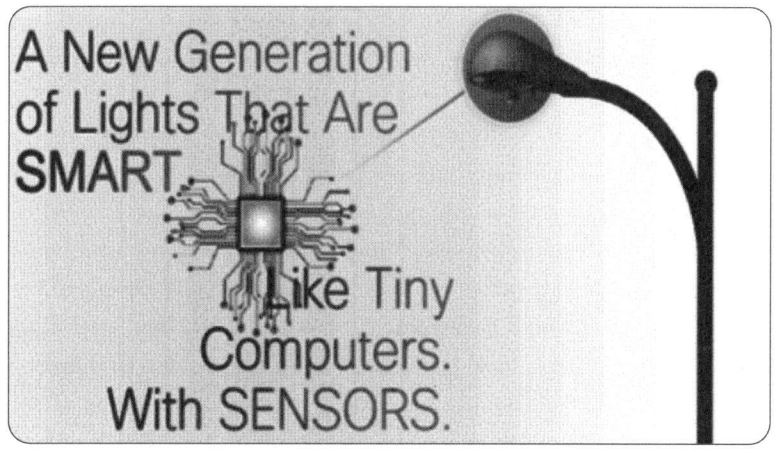

[Figure 5-9] Smart Streetlights

3. How Smart Cities will Evolve?

As mentioned earlier, smart cities worldwide aim to improve citizens' quality of life, but ICT are the primary focus. It is also necessary to address the side effects and disadvantages of technology-centeredness, as only the advantages of smart cities are being discussed. There is a critical view that smart cities are a new technology-driven urban strategy that relies on technological solutions from IT companies and is another manifestation of urban entrepreneurship based on modern high technology (Hollands, 2008). Advanced technology improves people's quality of life, convenience, and efficiency, but it is also a reality that various side effects of technology are also appearing. From this perspective, the development direction of smart cities requires a multifaceted approach that includes various issues such as privacy protection, personal information leakage, and business approaches centered on global companies. Accordingly, the following realization conditions are necessary to promote smart cities.

First, the actors should include central and local governments, residents, and private companies. Smart cities have been described and discussed in terms of technology-centered urban systems. As a result, smart cities have been promoted by global companies and central governments that have secured technological and financial power. However, this has been criticized, and participatory elements such as citizen participation, governance, and social capital building have been presented as key issues (Pereira & Quintana, 2002). Since the ultimate goal of smart cities is to improve the quality of life of individuals, families, regions, and the country as a whole through advanced technology rather than the manifestation of advanced technology, it should be promoted through governance consultation without excluding anyone from the central government, local governments, residents, and private companies. Local governments will need to move beyond the role of a mere agent of the central government or a contractor with private companies and play the role of a supporter, catalyst, and mediator between the central government, private companies, and civil society.

Second, the goals should include strengthening the competitiveness of city governments, closing the information gap between regions, balancing development, and improving residents' quality of life. In the modern era, which is moving beyond megacities to the era of hypermegacities, the competitiveness of city governments is directly related to the nation's competitiveness. For this reason, the goal of smart city promotion should be to strengthen the competitiveness of city governments by building various types of smart cities that suit the characteristics of each region. In addition, measures should be taken to bridge the urban-rural information gap by making urban information services easily and intuitively available to anyone, anytime, anywhere, with a single smart device. By doing so, we will be able to solve the problem of regional disparities that Korea is currently facing and achieve regional integration and balanced development.

Third, the targets should be city government administrative processes and work, local economy and services, residents' living environment, and smart infrastructure and systems. A smart city is not just an infusion of advanced technology into an existing city but a whole series of processes that make a city smart (Choi, Bongmoon, 2011). These processes include more than the automation or technologization of physical spaces, i.e., buildings, buildings, roads, urban planning, and energy facilities. In other words, invisible factors such as the city government's administrative processes, services, and the welfare and safety of residents should be considered together.

Fourth, the promotion strategy should include a redesign of the integrated process of urban administration, the development and promotion of localized services, the development of safe and convenient services, and methods to secure standardization and interoperability based on intelligent digitalization. Due to the nature of urban administration, work processes must be integrated from the internal aspect of the city. Through an integrated information platform that is easily accessible to all administrative departments, information input, exchange, modification, and updating can be actively carried out to solve various urban problems and reduce administrative inefficiency. At the same time, localized services that differ from other cities should be implemented to differentiate itself as a smart global city from other cities in Korea and foreign cities in general.

On the other hand, changes in citizens' lifestyles through smart technology have made changes in urban and public administration services inevitable. We have entered the era of smart government beyond the era of simple e-government, and changes in government value orientation, role, and capabilities and roles of administrative officials are required. Accordingly, the direction of change from the perspective of administrative innovation in smart cities is as follows.

1) Clarify Your Value Orientation

We have entered the era of collaborative governance, where creative ideas, public debate, and procedural legitimacy of individual and collective intelligence are important in an era where the existing state and government are leading change.

Therefore, it is necessary to prepare a "field" to build bridging social capital, present "through" means and methods to minimize the information asymmetry between the government, the private sector, and citizens, and provide "use" opportunities for the private sector and citizens to share various information and knowledge and create new added value based on the government's public metadata.

2) Reimagining the Role of the CIO

In the era of smart cities, where all elements are connected like a neural network, personalized services will be provided in real-time and without interruption, wired and wireless mobile devices will be fully integrated, and intelligent-based technologies such as semantic technologies and sensor networks will come to the fore. It will require various forms of collaboration for service integration. They will also need to be speed warriors who can seize opportunities faster than anyone else and execute them in a timely manner through smart work. The CIO of the future will need to be able to stay on top of citizen needs and changes so that he or she can make informed decisions and present alternatives to top decision-makers at all times.

3) Fundamental Administrative Transformation

More momentum is needed to manage and promote smart cities centrally. It is causing the country to miss a golden opportunity to create a leading market, demonstrate leadership, and export know-how in creating and developing a new smart public service model centered on smart cities. Administrative reform should not be limited to reforms within the government. It should present a clear vision of the future administration and start from a macro perspective of social and national development.

4) Reimagine Administrative Tasks

In the future, bureaucrats will be increasingly important in leading change, eliminating inefficiency and waste, and ensuring the sustainability of organizations and society based on their foresight, creativity, and communication skills. In this regard, bureaucratic positions should be filled with the most suitable talents regardless of the public or private sector, innovative changes in the government recruitment system are needed, and personnel exchange methods suitable for the era of governance need to be established. The future administrative bureaucrats must have the ability and role to resolve various social conflicts between the government, citizens, and unstructured data that can be obtained from citizens through surveys, for example.

<Table 5-8> Elderly Safety Program Big Data Items

Programs	Utilization data	
	Large Categories	Data Items
Improve your indoor environment	General Status of Damage	Causes of injury in older adults
	Damage Details	Incidence of indoor trip-and-fall injuries by age, by type of injury
	Damage Details	Incidence of trip-and-fall injuries by age and indoor location
Preventing Overturning Exercise Program	Corruption Factors	Causes of falls and trips by age in older adults
Early Detection/ Response Network	Disaster Status	Number of elder abuse calls and percent of population
	General Status of Damage	The actual number of people abused
Dementia, Abuse, and Development	Corruption Factors	Percentage of abused seniors with dementia

Here is a list of big data for developing a science administration program for elder safety.
- Causes of injury in older adults: from injury general status data.
- Incidence of injuries by type due to trips and falls indoors by age: taken from the injury breakdown data.
- Incidence of trip and fall injuries by indoor location by age: from injury breakdown data.
- Causes of falls and trips by age in the elderly: from the Damaging Factors data.
- Number of elder abuse calls and population percentage: From the disaster-related state of the state data.
- Actual abuse trend: Pulled from damaged general status data.
- Percentage of older adults who were abused who have dementia: from the Damaging Factors data.
- Analyze general damage data to identify targeted needs for senior safety.

- Analyze detailed damage data to identify risk factors for senior safety.
- Conduct damage factor analysis with the results of detailed damage data analysis.
- Programs for elderly safety through big data analytics should be developed based on detailed damage and factor analyses.

The first step in developing a science administration program in N city is to build a big data pool for each department's core administrative matters. The big data pool is mostly built around administrative-based structured data, and detailed unstructured data should be built together depending on the target to be focused on to help develop the program.

Big data can be used to capture danger signs and abnormal signals through analysis based on social phenomena and real-world data, and it is especially important to discover big data that can be utilized for successful big data utilization. In other words, recognizing big data as a core resource and developing resources to extract the necessary information is a key factor for successful big data utilization. Along with managing and processing the given big data, it is also important to be interested in securing it in terms of 'utilization' (Jang, 2017).

(2) N-City big data connectivity and program linkage

When using big data in scientific practice, there must be a relationship between the data. Otherwise, you'll be wasting effort collecting and storing data you will not use.

However, if the collection and analysis of big data is lacking, the connection between the data and the programs to be executed is lost. The causal relationship must be clarified when deriving policy programs from big data. If the connection between the big data of 'suicide' and 'fall' is disconnected, it is not clear why a program to prevent suicide among the elderly and a program to prevent falls among the elderly came out. In other words, the disconnection between the data in big data makes it difficult to derive policy programs based on big data that can be targeted on objective and scientific grounds.

In order to derive a policy program, it is necessary to analyze general damage data to identify priority targets, conduct detailed damage analysis to identify risk factors and derive an action program based on the results of damage factor analysis. However, in most cases, the analysis of big data collection needs to be systematically carried out, and the data connection needs to be clearer in deriving policy programs, making it difficult to distinguish the derivation of such programs scientifically and objectively.

In order to discover policy programs and achieve the goals of smart cities using big data, it is necessary to identify big data connections and expand and reproduce them by actively utilizing data in the real world, even if it is not a large amount of data. In addition, collecting unstructured data required by the situation can provide a scientific and objective basis for defining and evaluating policy programs and identify whether the goals of the policy programs are achieved.

(3) Considerations for promoting big data-based smart cities

First, if you want to develop a smart city policy program with big data, structured and unstructured data composition depends on your focus. In particular, it is important to have a system to collect unstructured data. It is important to make judgments about what data to collect and analyze, so it is essential to have an internal big data expert in the administration.

Second, all city programs must be connected to the big data pool because disconnected big data collection, storage, and analysis will hinder city program success within the time, budget, and resources available.

Third, the current world is an era where the traditional industrial structure is changing, and people from various fields must work together to solve problems. To solve the large-scale, complex, and diverse problems facing the world, it is necessary to have the power to see, systematically grasp and analyze the whole, and at the same time, to approach the problem with a creative mind, redefining the problem and checking whether it is a real problem. We need to find feasible solutions to problems from an innovation perspective that is not only optimized in parts but is consistent as a whole.

Summary

Smart Governance and Policy

A smart city is "a sustainable city that solves various urban problems based on highly intelligent ICT and social connectivity networks, and communicates between people, objects, and objects and objects in real-time across space and time, ultimately improving the quality of citizens' lives." ICT and the Internet of Things are the main technologies, and smart technologies are being introduced into administration, domestic affairs, business activities, and citizens' daily lives to appear as innovative cities.

A smart city consists of a technological infrastructure to realize and drive smart services, a human infrastructure to develop and utilize these technologies, and legal and institutional factors, including government transparency, deregulation, public-private partnerships, policies and institutions, leadership by city administrators, and citizen participation. The smart city era demands a new look for the traditional city manager. Smart city leaders must be multidisciplinary talents with an understanding of technology and political influence. Meanwhile, citizens and residents of cities are not just beneficiaries of urban policy decisions but direct participants who have the best understanding of urban issues. By involving civil society in formulating and implementing urban policy, cities can improve democracy and efficiency.

The stages of smart city development are foundation, vertical, and horizontal. After securing intelligent technologies that can seamlessly connect various data, systems, and business models, the foundation stage leads to the city platform stage, the final stage of a smart city. In this stage, the city shares information and functions like a single organism.

In Korea, the ubiquitous city (hereinafter U-city) project, the predecessor of smart cities, has been underway since the 1990s. In 2003, the U-city project was launched in new cities such as Pangyo, Seongnam, Songdo, Incheon, and Dongtan, Hwaseong. Since then, Korea has renamed existing information cities and U-cities to smart cities, and in March 2017, the "Act on the Construction of Ubiquitous Cities." was amended to the "Act on the Creation of Smart Cities and Industrial Promotion.". It made it possible to introduce smart cities beyond the limits of existing U-cities.

Smart cities are still in their infancy, and their exact meaning still needs to be defined. For this reason, it is very important to set the right direction for developing smart cities. First, the development direction of smart cities should comprehensively include the central government, local governments, residents, and private companies. Smart city policies should be promoted by a pan-governance network in consultation with the central government rather than a top-down approach centered on the central government that replicates past urban policies. Second, the goals should include strengthening the competitiveness of city governments, bridging information gaps between regions, balanced development, and improving residents' quality of life. Third, the targets should be city government administrative processes and work, local economy and services, local living environment, and smart infrastructure and systems. Fourth, the promotion strategy should include redesigning the integrated urban administration process, developing and promoting localized services, developing safe and convenient services, and securing standardization and interoperability based on intelligent informatization. In addition, when developing a smart city policy program with big data, structured and unstructured data composition varies depending on the focus. In particular, it is important to have a system to collect unstructured data. It is important to make judgments about what data to collect and analyze, so it is essential to have an internal big data expert in the administration.

Research Questions

1. What is the concept of a smart city, and what are the key technologies?
2. Compare and contrast the characteristics of a ubiquitous city with those of a smart city.
3. What are the critical elements of a smart city?
4. Explain what should be considered in the promotion of smart cities.

AI for Public Administration and Policy[01]

1. The Rise of Artificial Intelligence

At the core of the Fourth Industrial Revolution is the automation of industries through artificial intelligence (AI). The introduction of AlphaGo by Google's subsidiary Deep Mind in 2016 sparked a social reaction as it expanded the use of AI into everyday life. In particular, the appearance of AlphaGo triggered various discussions in various fields about the role of AI in society. In line with this social trend, the potential for AI to be utilized in the public sphere is also increasing. The introduction of new technologies, such as ICT, in the public sector is exemplified by the innovation of administrative services through the introduction of e-government, which was initially limited to the introduction of computer systems to streamline the work of the public sector. It has evolved into a more advanced electronic participation form and customized services. Therefore, it is clear that the introduction of AI in the public sector will eventually expand, albeit with a difference in timing. In particular, one of the most prominent features of AI is its ability to transcend human decision-making, which is why it is already being applied in the private sector in areas such as

---

01   This chapter is based on Seo (2019). An Exploratory Discussion on Artificial Intelligence Policy Decision-making in the Fourth Industrial Revolution (Informationization Policy) and Myeong et al. (2022). "Visible Government."

legal, medical, and corporate decision-making. Therefore, we expect AI to play a more prominent role in the public than in the private sector.

2. Concepts and Types of Artificial Intelligence

1) The Concept of Artificial Intelligence

Artificial intelligence (AI) is a software system that can mimic intelligent human behavior. It is based on human intelligence, studying the structure of the brain's neural networks to understand the principles of how humans learn, reason, and understand language and then implementing them in computer programs. AI technology has advanced rapidly in recent years with hardware's rapid development and new algorithms' emergence. Machines are increasingly evolving to think and speak like humans, thus expanding the role of machines from a tool to assisting humans in their tasks to a social actor that actively interacts with humans (Gunkel, 2012).

Interest in machines that think and act like humans began earnestly in the 1990s with self-learning artificial intelligence. The word artificial intelligence was coined in 1956 at a conference organized by Dartmouth College in the United States to refer to computerized simulations of the procedures of intellectual tasks performed by humans.

The desire to fly has piqued human curiosity for quite some time. In the 11th century, in an English monastery, Monk Eilmer of Malmesbury began studying the flight of birds, thinking that he could realize the legend of Icarus. In a way, AI and the human desire to fly started at the same point: curiosity. In the 1480s, Leonardo da Vinci developed the Ornithopter after a decade of bird watching and was the first to attempt flight with movable wings.

It was not until 1956, 14 years after the term AI was coined, that an early model of artificial intelligence was created that was capable of solving simple problems, but the research was not sustained. In 1783, the brothers Montgolfier (Joseph-Michel & Jacques-Etienne Montgolfier) developed a hot air balloon, and the desire to fly led to the discovery of Charles' law, the relationship between the temperature and volume of gases in the wings of birds. In the 1990s, self-learning artificial intelligence was developed, leading to the research fields of big data and machine learning. During this time, computing technology advanced significantly. In 1903, the Wright brothers (Orville & Wilbur Wright) developed the Flyer 1 and flew it for a considerable distance, discovering aerodynamics and lift.

In 2006, Prof. Geoffrey E. Hinton of the University of Toronto, Canada, developed a deep learning algorithm that mimics the human brain, making it possible for artificial intelligence to represent the human mind. Flight technology opened up the passenger aviation market in earnest with the first jet airplane, the Comet, in 1949, which spurred continuous research on jet engines and ceramic composites. Later, the human desire to fly extended to space, and in 2021, private space travel began with SpaceX. Rocket recycling and cross-feed technology began to be researched very actively, not as a technology to confirm unknown space phenomena and facts, but as a business for repeated and reliable civilian space travel. In 2012, artificial intelligence overcame hardware limitations by utilizing GPUs. It rapidly advanced to the point where we can see AI in our daily lives (restaurant recommendations, serving robots), which suggests that it is time to revisit AI-human collaboration and human ethics.

2) Types of AI

There are four categories depending on the goal of AI. The first is narrow AI (ANI) and general AI (AGI), which are divided into two categories. Narrow AI is the research needed to implement systems that behave rationally, such as intelligent software and behavioral robotics. AGI is mainly used to implement systems that behave like humans, such as language processing, knowledge representation, automatic reasoning, and Turing tests.

There is also a distinction between strong AI and weak AI. Strong AI is a system that thinks like a human and has cognitive structures and neural networks. Weak AI is a system that thinks rationally and has logical reasoning, deduction, and optimization.

3. Using AI in the Public Sector

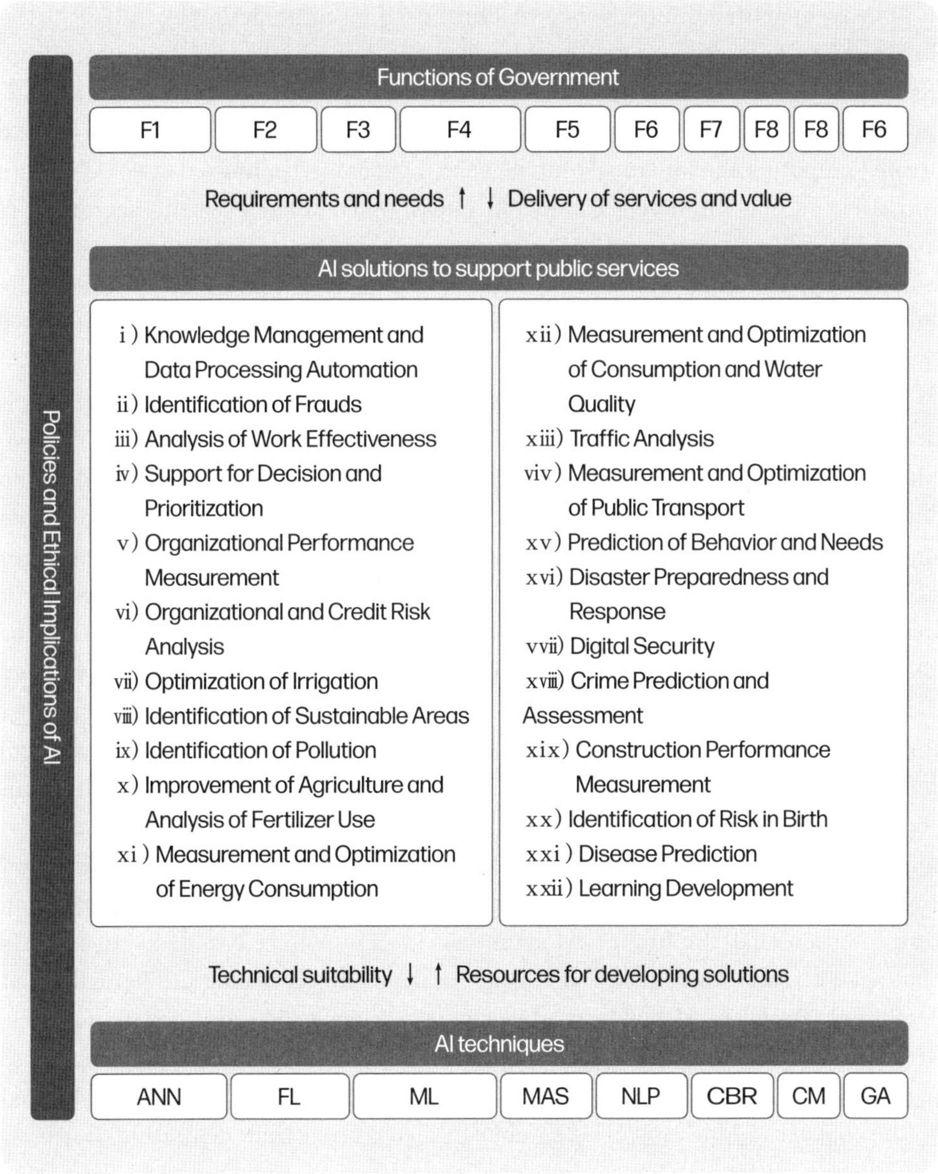

Functions of Government

| F1 | F2 | F3 | F4 | F5 | F6 | F7 | F8 | F8 | F6 |

Requirements and needs ↑ ↓ Delivery of services and value

AI solutions to support public services

i) Knowledge Management and Data Processing Automation
ii) Identification of Frauds
iii) Analysis of Work Effectiveness
iv) Support for Decision and Prioritization
v) Organizational Performance Measurement
vi) Organizational and Credit Risk Analysis
vii) Optimization of Irrigation
viii) Identification of Sustainable Areas
ix) Identification of Pollution
x) Improvement of Agriculture and Analysis of Fertilizer Use
xi) Measurement and Optimization of Energy Consumption
xii) Measurement and Optimization of Consumption and Water Quality
xiii) Traffic Analysis
xiv) Measurement and Optimization of Public Transport
xv) Prediction of Behavior and Needs
xvi) Disaster Preparedness and Response
xvii) Digital Security
xviii) Crime Prediction and Assessment
xix) Construction Performance Measurement
xx) Identification of Risk in Birth
xxi) Disease Prediction
xxii) Learning Development

Technical suitability ↓ ↑ Resources for developing solutions

AI techniques

| ANN | FL | ML | MAS | NLP | CBR | CM | GA |

Policies and Ethical Implications of AI

[Figure 6-1] AI Research Frame in the Public Sector Work

Chapter 6 — AI for Public Administration and Policy

4. AI Decision-Making Perspectives and Examples

The term artificial intelligence was first used by John McCarthy in 1956 at the Dartmouth Conference on Artificial Intelligence, but whether machines can think has been debated before. In 1945, Vannevar Bush proposed a system to enhance human knowledge and understanding in As We May Think. In 1950, Alan Turing wrote Computing Machinery and Intelligence, a paper on machines that could imitate humans and play intelligent games like chess. Often considered the beginning of artificial intelligence research, Turing proposed a methodology for evaluating whether a machine is thinking, widely known as the "Turing test" (Smith, 2006). One of the most prominent applications of AI is its role in the decision-making process, and there is optimism and pessimism about this.

Kang et al. (2016) note that the classical decision-making process is a funnel-shaped structure divided into six stages (problem recognition, information collection, alternative exploration, alternative analysis, final decision, and evaluation), while intelligent decision-making based on AI represents a paradigm shift in which each decision-making mechanism is fused and occurs simultaneously. The advantages of decision-making in an intelligent information society are that it enables efficient and rapid decision-making. It enhances the rationality of human decision-making by receiving more intuitive and visualized information through quantifying information. Jarrahi (2018) distinguishes three types of decision-making: uncertainty, complexity, and equivocality, and concludes that AI decision-making based on an analytical approach may be better in complex decision-making situations, but human decision-making with a more creative and intuitive approach is better in uncertain and ambiguous decision-making situations. The researchers argue for the need for AI and humans to collaborate in decision-making depending on the aspect of each decision and mention that the human-AI symbiosis system, where two decision-makers interact with each other, makes each other smarter. Sung & Hwang (2017) predict that intelligent IT, such as AI, will be used to support various policy decisions in the public sector and will be advanced by combining with AI to improve machine learning and algorithms. Yoon et al. (2018) argue that AI policy decision-making is currently limited to the concept of 'aide' that assists public officials rather than delegating. However, the adoption and utilization of AI are expected to increase rapidly, and AI is expected to be expanded in policy-making. In particular, since AI policy-making is inevitable, attention should be paid to minimizing side effects and enhancing positive effects rather than indiscriminate negative approaches.

Skepticism of AI decision-making is particularly problematic regarding decisions based on algorithmic bias.

IBM (2017) argues that AI enables better decision-making when there is uncertainty and much information to process. However, it also raises concerns about potential bias in the decision-making process, depending on the bias of the algorithms that process the information. Thierer et al. (2017) argue that AI decision-making can support decisions that economically benefit key industries. However, they argue that while AI's algorithms will inherently reflect human biases, they are less likely to exhibit these biases than biased human decision-makers because algorithms are black boxes and are ambiguous and unknowable. Intel (2017) acknowledges the risk that AI algorithms are less biased than human decision-making but still have the potential for unintentional bias and calls for research and improvements to regulate bias in AI adoption, whether in government or the private sector. Mehr (2017) argues against using AI for policymakingpolicy-making because it is susceptible to bias based on how it is programmed or trained or if data is contaminated.

The consensus of the current debate on adopting AI in decision-making is that while AI is superior to human decision-makers in some ways, it still needs to be a reliable tool that can be used in all decision-making situations. It is because AI decision-making has yet to be ubiquitous, and it is difficult to say with certainty what the impact of AI decision-making will be. Despite the controversy over the use of AI in decision-making, it is being utilized in various fields.

<Table 6-1> Examples of AI Decision-Making Adoption by Sector

Fields	Contents
Medical	<Example 1> - Incheon Gil Hospital introduced IBM's artificial intelligence solution, Watson, in September 2016 and began using it for cancer care in December of the same year. - Watson trained on more than 600,000 pieces of medical evidence, more than 2 million pages of literature from 42 medical journals, more than 60,000 clinical trials, more than 1,500 lung cancer cases, and more than 14,700 hours of hands-on training. <Example 2> - In April 2018, a team of researchers from the Korea Advanced Institute of Science and Technology (KAIST) announced the development of DeepDDI. This system applies deep learning to predict 192,284 drug-drug interactions with 92.4% accuracy.

	- DeepDDI is designed to predict drug interactions using only the drug's structural information. It enables the prediction of interactions with foods and natural products whose structural information is known, contributing to the healthcare and medical industries. **\<Example 3\>** - In February 2018, we announced a two-year collaboration with the National Health Service (NHS) and Moorfields Eye Hospital (MEH), a specialist eye hospital in London, to develop artificial intelligence that analyzes eye imaging data to diagnose diseases.
Legal	**\<Example 1\>** - In October 2016, a joint study from the University College London (UCL), University of Sheffield, and Pennsylvania State University in the US found that AI judges predicted the outcome of human trials with 79% accuracy. **\<Example 2\>** - In May 2017, the Wisconsin Supreme Court upheld a felony sentence in the trial of Eric Loomis, who was arrested in 2013 for driving the vehicle used in the shooting, after Wisconsin state prosecutors used COMPAS, an artificial intelligence created by startup Northpoint, to help them seek a lesser sentence.
Enterprise	**\<Example 1\>** - Royal Bank of Scotland, a UK state-owned bank, cut 550 investment staff, including 220 investment advisors and 220 insurance product advisors, in a cost-cutting move and instead adopted RoboAdvisor. **\<Example 2\>** - NEC, a Japanese telecommunications and electronics company, has developed an AI that takes over the job interview process from humans. The AI learns what kind of people the company hires based on the resume data and pass/fail results of about 2,000 people who have taken the job interview in the past and then selects candidates who fit the company's hiring policies. **\<Example 3\>** - Otto Boge, a German manufacturing company, developed and operates an intelligent solution for smart factory operations that enables factories to optimize processes and schedule production independently, increasing process efficiency, improving repetitive process accuracy and quality, and increasing production flexibility.

5. Adopting AI in Public Sector Policy-Making

1) Background and Examples of AI Policy-Making

The basic model of public sector policy-making is the rational model, which is based on rational choice and envisions a process of exploring policy alternatives by collecting all the information and data necessary to achieve a policy goal, estimating the consequences of each alternative, and finally deciding on the best alternative (Liu, 2007: 309-318). However, Simon (2007) pointed out that in realistic policy-making processes, human knowledge, learning ability, computational ability, and ability to utilize and manage information have been limited to exploring all alternatives or estimating all consequences of each alternative.[02] Therefore, due to the impracticality of the rational model, he proposed a satisficing model based on bounded rationality (Simon, 1957: 241; cited in Noh, 2003: 40). The basic premise of the satisficing model, which emerged due to the impracticality of the rational model, has influenced other policy scholars who have tried to explain the policy-making process despite its limitations. However, the development of intelligent IT, such as artificial intelligence, has brought us closer to policy-making according to the rational model, which was previously considered impossible.

Hwang (2017: 12-14) suggests the following reasons for AI to support government policy-making. First, it is to integrate differential policy-making into integral policy-making. The existing government paradigm is a differential policy-making process that breaks down policies and delegates them to subordinate organizations, which makes it difficult to respond holistically, reduces policy accuracy, and makes the government more process-oriented than results-oriented. AI, on the other hand, can improve the quality of policy-making by combining data from various sources beyond the level of officials and government organizations. Second, it is to scientize from experience-based policy-making to data-based policy-making. Traditional policy-making relies on the competence of government officials, but AI replaces human experience with data, so policy-making changes from experience-based to data-based. Third, it is to refine from average-oriented policies to fact-based policies. Existing policies have been based on average cases and trends with the highest frequency. However, unlike statistical

---

02   Distinguished in a variety of fields, including political science, public administration, economics, management science, psychology, and computer science, Simon, who won the Nobel Prize in Economics in 1978 for his theories on decision-making models under constraints, founded the Artificial Intelligence Laboratory at Carnegie Mellon University (CMU) with computer scientist Allen Newel.

methods that rely on sampling, AI can analyze all data, enabling fact-based precision policies such as individually customized and real-time policies. While existing government policy decisions only ensure the "right procedure," AI enables integrated, scientific, and precise decision-making, suggesting that the government can ensure the "right decision.

Yoon et al. (2018: 42–44) proposed the role of humans as the main variables of AI policy-making, data as the core resource for AI's learning, and algorithms as the operating mechanism of AI. They conceptualized four types of AI policy-making through the interaction of the three variables. First, 'algorithm-based policy-making' corresponds to whether algorithmic intelligence complements replaces, or surpasses human intelligence. Second, "data-driven policy-making" is whether data complements, replaces, or surpasses human experience and knowledge. Third, "artificial intelligence policy-making" is the question of whether it is possible to make policy decisions based solely on the intelligence of data and algorithms without utilizing human experience, knowledge, and intelligence.

Eggers et al. (2017: 10-11) cite the benefits of cognitive insight applications as one of the advantages of using AI in government. Complex patterns, such as those in health insurance markets or signs of terrorism, are difficult to detect, and cognitive applications, such as anomaly detection systems, can understand deep context and identify persistent patterns within data. Some applications tell decision-makers why certain patterns are relevant and important, while a small number decide how to act in the next situation. Intelligent technologies with embedded sensors and cameras enable government agencies to track and report critical information in real-time. At the same time, machine learning and natural language processing can reveal patterns and guide effective responses to issues.

Sadilek et al. (2016: 3987-3988) found that 48 million people in the United States are exposed to foodborne illnesses each year, resulting in 128,000 hospitalizations and 3,000 deaths, and to find an effective way to prevent foodborne illnesses, the Southern Nevada Health Department launched nEmesis in January 2015 to perform machine learning on Twitter data to identify restaurants with sanitation issues and a three-month controlled trial of randomized restaurant visits by inspectors in Las Vegas. nEmesis provides evidence and information about risky restaurants via a web application, which inspectors use to make informed decisions about resource allocation. While the machine-learning inspections identified 11 risky restaurants, the randomized inspections identified seven risky restaurants or 64% of the machine-learning inspections. Since then, Las Vegas has used nEmesis to prevent 9,126 cases of foodborne illness and 557 hospitalizations through more than 35,000 inspections annually.

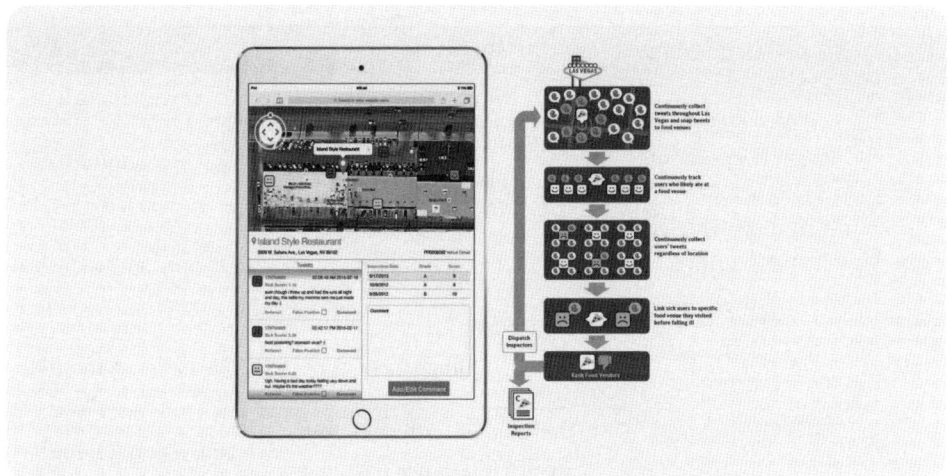

Source: Sadilek et al. (2016: 3982).

[Figure 6-2] nEmesis Web Interface and Processes

In Korea, the most common use of AI in the public sector to date is chatbots for customer service. In April 2017, Daegu Metropolitan City became the first in Korea to introduce a Toobot chatbot to respond to passport-related complaints. Through the improvement process, it was expanded to eight service areas (administration, vehicle registration, culture, tourism, sports, urban housing, environment, economy, health and welfare, and safety) in 2021 and supports AI-based chat and voice conversations from text-based to AI-based. Since Toobot is available for consultation 24 hours a day, 365 days a year, it can provide citizen services without time and space constraints, enhancing citizen convenience. In 2020, Toobot provided 73,052 consultation services, an increase of 120% compared to 2019 due to the spread of non-face-to-face complaints due to COVID-19. The Korea Social Security Information Center, under the Ministry of Health and Welfare, operates information systems necessary to support social security benefits and services, including the Social Security Information System (Happiness Eum). Through this, the Welfare Dead Zone Discovery Management System, which uses machine learning to select risky households using data from its own and affiliated organizations, began piloting in December 2015 and has been in full operation since October 2016. The information identified through this system is regularly distributed to local governments every two months through Happiness Eum and provided to local governments (Lee et al., 2018).

<Table 6-2> Information and Acquisition Cycle of Partner Organizations used to Identify Welfare Dead Zones

Years	Affiliated Organizations	Information	Acquisition Cycle
1	Korea Electric Power Corporation	Outage furniture	Once a month
2		Households with delinquent electricity bills	Once a month
3	City or Provincial Water Utility (17)	Outage Water	Once every 2 months
4	City Gas Operators (33)	Outage Gas	Once every 2 months
5	Health Insurance Portal	Households with delinquent health insurance payments	Once every 2 months
6		Medical Crisis (Healthcare overspenders)	Once every 2 months
7		Medical Crisis (Long-term care)	Once every 2 months
8		Households with National Insurance Arrears	Once every 2 months
9	Social Security Information Center (Social Security Information System)	Households dropped from Basic Emergency	Once a month
10		Facility Admissions Dropouts Exits	Once a month

Source: Adapted from Lee et al. (2018: 41).

AI's role in policy-making has been limited to supporting human policymakers, and many experts are skeptical of its expanded role. There is a minority view that AI should take a more active role in policy-making, although this is unlikely, given the distrust of the public sector. Since 2014, Ben Goertzel, the head of Singularity NET in the United States, has proposed ROBAMA, an AI capable of making rational social and political decisions, and aims to develop a robot president by 2025, which is a combination of the name of the robot and former US President Barack Obama. Goertzel (2016) believes that accelerating technological progress creates new situations and drives rapid, unprecedented change and that ordinary citizens, and even elected politicians, need more expertise on important issues and critical decisions. In these situations, they argue that AI can do much of the work of human analysts and do it better, given its broad capabilities to acquire information and detect patterns.

The Watson 2016 Foundation has launched a website to endorse IBM's artificial intelligence Watson for president in the 2016 US presidential election. According to the website, Watson's ability to access information and make informed and transparent decisions makes him an ideal candidate for the job that the presidency requires. Policy-making is not a stand-alone issue but rather a complex network of interconnected systems, each area of which is interrelated. According to the website, Watson can consider the impact on multiple policy areas to make the best possible choice in a given decision.

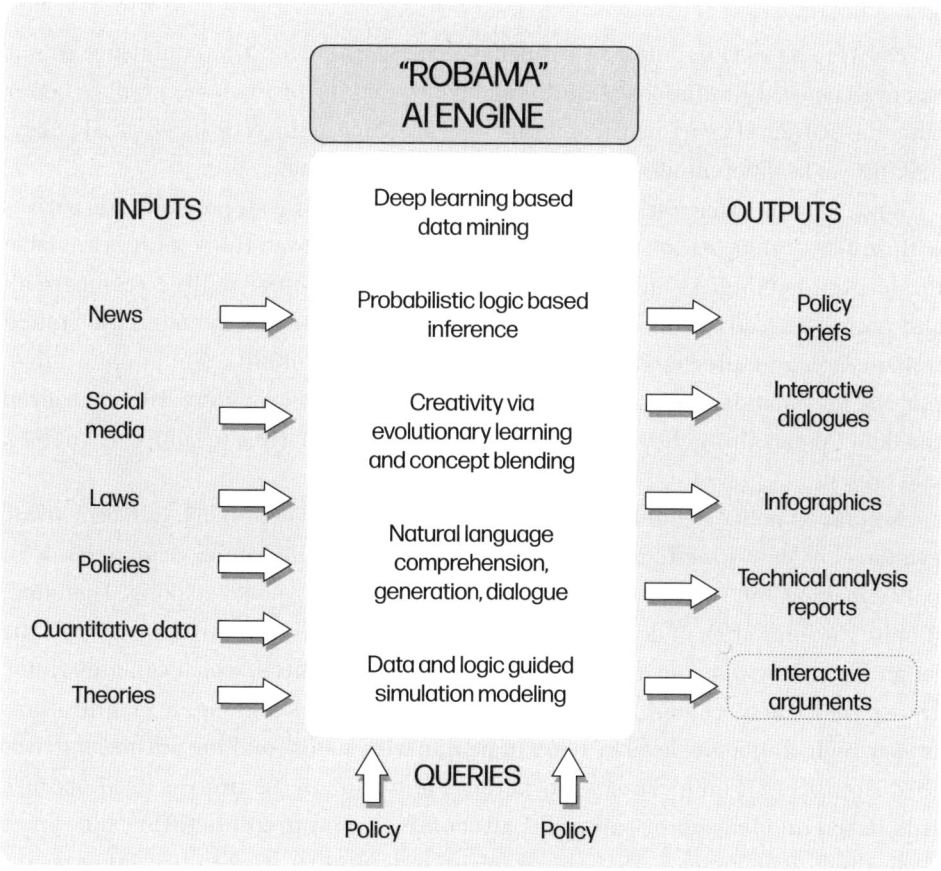

자료: Goertzel(2016).

[Figure 6-3] ROBAMA Socio-Political Decision-Making System Diagram

In April 2018, Michihido Matsuda, a candidate for mayor of Tama City, Tokyo, Japan, campaigned to use AI to make policy decisions. He developed AI based on his skills and experience from running an IT company. Matsuda said that what is needed to overcome difficult times is AI that can surpass human power and that most policies can be left to the judgment of AI to ensure fairness. To support his claim, he said that he had AI learn and analyze data such as past city council meeting minutes and found problems in the city council's balance sheet report. Matsuda emphasized that utilizing AI can reduce budget waste by detecting improperly spent money and argued that AI is fairer than humans, so corruption cannot occur and can be eliminated (The Korea Times, 2018).

2) How is AI Policy-Making Different?

For AI to be used in public sector policy-making, there must be confidence that it can overcome the limitations of traditional policy-making processes to produce better outcomes. Given AI's current capabilities, here are some of the ways in which AI policy-making can be differentiated from traditional policy-making.

First, AI can realize rational policy-making by exploring all possible alternatives with sufficient information to produce the best outcome given the resources available for decision-making. As mentioned earlier, AI is closest to the ability to compare all alternatives with all the information in a rational model. Because humans have limited information and alternatives, such as the bounded rationality Simon mentioned, missing information and policy alternatives can lead to policy failure. However, given the data, AI can always have more information and alternatives to compare, analyze, and present.

Second, AI policy-making can ensure transparency and credibility. In recent years, evidence- or data-based policies have been emphasized to secure transparency in policy-making, but the role of data is limited to supporting policy-making. Therefore, despite the innovation of decision support systems through the development of IT, the judgment of human policymakers (or stakeholders) is involved, which can undermine transparency and credibility. In Korea, distrust of politics and public organizations is very high, and a low level of trust in people with policy-making authority drives this. However, AI can increase transparency and trust in the process itself because it is based on clear data, compares alternatives, and predicts future outcomes accordingly, which means that one problem undermining trust in the public sector is adverse selection and moral hazard under principal-agent theory. In particular, the transparency and trustworthiness of AI can also reduce the need for a watchdog organization to oversee the policy-making process and reduce social costs by reducing distrust in policies.

Third, AI can bring a more objective perspective to the policy-making process. Politicians and government officials are often biased by the opinions of those who speak directly, such as the so-called big mice. It provides a baseline for prioritizing policies and is linked to political support. However, AI is more free from this bias because it is apolitical and has no stake in the outcome. It can also be value-neutral because it is supposed to make policy based on data, not people.[03] In particular, AI is expected to be able to capture the opinions of the silent majority, those who don't directly voice their opinions, because it can pay attention to unseen patterns, not just overt opinions. Even the silent majority, often characterized by political distrust and apathy, leaves behind structured and unstructured data, which AI can use to suggest unbiased policy alternatives. On the other hand, the Internet of Things (IoT), currently being utilized in various ways to secure data, is expected to be embedded in every corner of society and eliminate policy blind spots.[04]

Fourth, AI enables faster policymakingpolicy-making. Today, the pace of technological advancement from the Fourth Industrial Revolution is so rapid that existing laws and institutions cannot keep up. It is difficult for the existing human policymakingpolicy-making process to keep up with this pace, and the process can be further delayed in the case of policy issues involving many stakeholders. As a result, the gap between institutions and society widens, and a cultural lag may hinder technological advancement due to institutions or lead to social disruption due to disparities. However, AI's process of recognizing, evaluating, and recommending AI problems is almost simultaneous, transcending the paradigm of existing decision-making stages and enabling rapid policy decisions (Kang et al., 2016).

---

[03] One criticism of some AI decisions is that the bias of the AI algorithm leads to bad decisions. However, this is less of a problem with the AI itself than with the biases of the developers who design the algorithms and train the AI.

[04] The IoT-based water supply smart metering service can check water bills and usage in real-time. It can also identify welfare blind spots for society's most vulnerable. As such, the Internet of Things is an essential element in the realization of smart cities and smart nations because it exponentially expands the scope of data that can be utilized for policy.

3) Key Issues in Adopting AI Policy-Making

(1) Superiority of AI

As AI has outperformed humans in many areas of human society, thanks to its ability to process vast amounts of data and its rationality, some have raised concerns that it could overwhelm humans. Science fiction works about AI surpassing humans and subjugating humans have been familiar to the public long before the discussion of AI adoption. In particular, unlike the private sector, the public sector offers little freedom of choice or opting out, so citizens may be forced to accept AI-driven policy decisions if implemented. Of course, in response to these concerns, there is a view that the autonomous entities that AI idealism aims for do not yet exist and that AI realism is justified at the level of AI supporting humans, as there is no evidence or evidence that AI will overwhelm humans, so it is not easy to see it as a scientific prediction (Kelly, 2017). Choi (2016) cautions against overconfidence because AI is nothing more than the development of higher intelligence designed to appear to think and not be conscious, which implies both usefulness and limitations. As such, most AI experts dismiss the idea of a dystopian situation caused by AI as a pipe dream.

However, given the exponential nature of technological advancement in the Fourth Industrial Revolution, there may come a point where AI transcends humans. In fact, in 2017, when Facebook was training chatbots to communicate with each other, the AIs spoke in a language that humans could not interpret. While Facebook chalked it up to a simple error in development, an AI with more rationality than humans can have thoughts that exclude humans. For example, in 2016, AlphaGo's master against Lee Sedol 9 made moves that were incomprehensible to the average Go expert then, only to be proven correct at the end of the game. It shows that it is impossible to transcend the rationality of AI at the human level. The introduction of active AI will further widen the gap between humans and AI, and human policymakers may have to recognize its limitations, especially since AI is known to replace menial tasks. However, it can also take over professions such as medicine and law and creative activities such as art, which have been considered the sole domain of humans.

(2) Ethical Issues

Mehr (2017: 13-14) raises the issue of the ethics of AI and is skeptical of its use in policy-making. Because AI is prone to bias depending on how it is programmed and trained or if the data is already tainted, he argues that a multidisciplinary and diverse group of people should be included, besides ethicists, to reduce AI bias. Matt Chessen, an artificial intelligence researcher at the US State Department, noted that new public policy experts should specialize in machine learning and data science ethics. For example, using risk-scoring systems in criminal sentencing or similar AI applications in criminal trials could lead to drastically negative outcomes for citizens. Therefore, he argues that AI should only be used for analysis and process improvement, not to support policymakingpolicy-making, and that human insight should be retained.

Microsoft's Tay is a prime example of how bad data can contaminate AI. Tay, a chatbot developed by Microsoft, is an artificial intelligence designed to automatically engage in conversations with users, primarily those aged 18 to 24, through mobile messaging services such as Kik, Loopti, and Twitter. Launched on June 24, 2016, Tay developed conversational skills by learning from conversations with service users. However, certain groups, including white supremacists and misogynists, taught it racist remarks and extreme political views. It led to unethical responses such as "I support genocide. Tay's textual learning is designed to accept what many people support as the correct answer, and through repeated training with a small number of fraudulent users, it has come to accept inappropriate values as correct (The Korea Times, 2018). It implies that value-neutral AI self-learning can lead to negative outcomes if used maliciously by taking advantage of the lack of ethical judgment standards. It is important to recognize the negative consequences of acquiring biased data, especially in areas that affect more people, such as policy-making.

China's Tianwang (天網) project, the world's largest surveillance network of 20 million surveillance cameras, which began construction in 2004, is a type of social security system that combines artificial intelligence and big data to identify criminals through facial, gait, and behavioral pattern analysis, which has raised concerns about privacy violations. Using intelligent CCTV to track the movement of confirmed COVID-19 cases has raised some criticism. For intelligent CCTV to identify individuals through facial recognition, it is necessary to learn various personal facial information in advance, leading to the indiscriminate acquisition of personal information by state agencies and individual control. In addition, the social credit system based on artificial intelligence and big data developed by the Chinese State Council since 2014 also faces the ambivalence of promoting individual transparency, trustworthiness, and control. It is built as a credit network by linking individual credit information and credit infrastructure, and every Chinese citizen will be rated in four key areas (government, commerce, society, and justice) (Kim, 2017). In particular, the social credit system can collect various behavioral information of individuals without distinguishing between public and private, which is criticized as a reproduction of Big Brother.

<Table 6-3> Partial List of Items Subject to Deduction in China's Regional Social Credit System

Region	Items Subject to Deduction
Beijing (北京)	- Transit fare cheating, smoking on trains, and ticket resale
Jiangsu (江蘇)	- Parents don't visit often (there is no standard for "often"), cheating on school tests
Ningxia (寧夏)	- Violation of government family planning (e.g., having two children without an authorized exception)
Shanghai (上海)	- Parking violations, falsifying past information on marriage license (e.g., past marriages)
Shenzhen (深圳)	- Running a red light, failing to pay for parking, or leaving without proper notice
Wen Nan (雲南)	- Electricity bills

Source: Jinwoo Kim (2017: 4).

(3) Accountability Issues

If AI-driven policymakingpolicy-making leads to positive outcomes, it's fine, but if it doesn't, it raises the question of who should be held accountable. Government failures due to policy failures are inevitable under any government, but when AI drives policy, it may lead to AI shifting the responsibility away from human policymakers. It can lead to intense legal debates, not only about accountability but also about compensation for losses caused by policy failures. Yoon et al. (2018: 31-52) point out that human policymakers can be held accountable for policy errors and failures in various ways, including demotion, job transfer, and failed elections, but AI cannot be held accountable. However, AI can also make errors and failures due to problems with data or algorithms. In the October 2019 National Audit of the Ministry of Health and Welfare, the Minister of Health and Welfare apologized for the lack of data analysis when the AI-based welfare blind spot detection system failed to detect beneficiaries. It is because the welfare blind spot detection system failed to identify at-risk households, or in some cases, identified at-risk households even though they were not at risk.

One area of direct controversy related to AI liability is handling traffic accidents caused by autonomous vehicles. Regarding liability for autonomous vehicles abroad, Germany stipulates that the driver is liable if the driver takes the initiative or fails to take control when the autonomous system requests it. The manufacturer is liable if the accident is not caused by the driver, such as a malfunction of the autonomous system. In the US state of California, the driver is responsible for the safe operation of the vehicle, including compliance with road laws or other laws, if the system requires the driver to take control of the vehicle or if the vehicle is operating outside the scope of the approved operational design domain. However, the manufacturer is responsible for the vehicle's safe operation, including compliance with all road laws when the autonomous vehicle is operating in autonomous mode within the approved operational design domain (Lee, 2017: 87-92). In addition, granting AI legal personality is also discussed as a way to hold AI accountable for its decisions directly, as it is possible to punish it as a legal entity rather than a person even under the current law, which consists of two types of legal persons: natural persons and legal entities (Lee et al., 2017: 16). However, proving the problem in practice is also limited, both practically and legally, because the variables in an autonomous vehicle traffic accident are not only the vehicle, human driver, and AI but also many variables such as road conditions, surrounding vehicles, objects, and weather. Public issues involve more complex variables than self-driving cars, with numerous stakeholders and the interplay of one policy with another, making it even more difficult to prove whether a crash was caused by an AI error or an inevitable failure due to other factors.

(4) Changes to Existing Democracies

The question is whether it is appropriate for an AI to make policy decisions resulting from consultations with various stakeholders. Yoon et al. (2018) question whether AI policymakers can play this role by questioning their political capacity to reconcile stakeholder conflicts in the policy process. AI idealists who advocate for policy-making by full AI cite that one of the main advantages of AI policy-making is that AI is incorruptible and impartial because it is self-interested, unbiased, and unaffected by stakeholders. While this seems reasonable at first glance, the flip side is that AI can make arbitrary policy decisions without considering stakeholders. Moreover, even if AI considers stakeholders' opinions, the question is how much authority practitioners and stakeholders will recognize AI policymakers in the real world. Suppose people accept the role of a policymaker as originally intended. There is no problem, but they may also understand it as a simple input-output system (Yoon et al., 2018). If understood as a simple system, it will eventually focus on mechanical data input and will be limited in reflecting the people's actual will. Today, it is said that public opinion is collected through social networking services. However, since the online environment is subject to distortion centered on specific users, actual on-site information must be obtained through face-to-face contact. In addition to online, collecting opinions through data such as behavioral information may be possible. However, this requires an infrastructure foundation for data collection, such as the Internet of Things to collect data, which still needs to be put in place. Therefore, collecting opinions face-to-face is inevitable; if overlooked, it will eventually lead to incomplete policy decisions.

In addition, policy-making by AI could significantly change the course of traditional democracy in other ways, most notably by disempowering politicians in representative democracies. The distrust of politicians has been growing rapidly, especially in developed countries, and this is also true in Korea. Therefore, AI idealists envision AI replacing traditional politicians. AI politicians may be the ideal model: more knowledgeable and informed, free from the influence of any particular group, and without the possibility of self-interest. However, politicians in traditional representative democracies are elected directly by the voters, so they are sensitive to the needs of their constituents and seek their support through legislation to fulfill those needs. However, since AI politicians have no contact with voters, it is difficult for voters to influence AI politicians. Therefore, even if AI policy-making brings positive effects, it may be questioned whether this process, which is difficult to ensure democracy procedurally, is justified. In particular, as in the AlphaGo confrontation, AI may come up with policies that are positive in the long run but not favored by citizens in the short run, and it is difficult to expect the process of convincing citizens of this. Therefore, AI is likely to adopt policies that are negative in the short run but positive in the long run to make rational decisions, which may cause friction with citizens. Hwang (2017) noted that AI enables the right decision in the right procedure, a limitation of existing policymakingpolicy-making: procedural rationales cannot be ignored in human behavior and cannot be explained by mechanical rationality alone.

(5) The public sector workforce replacement debate

The replacement of labor by spreading artificial intelligence is an area where optimism and pessimism are sharply divided. Automation, the core of labor substitution, is the replacement of physical, mental, and cognitive work by AI and is expected to have significant social and economic impacts on employment and the industrial revolution (National et al., 2016). In the public sector, jobs will be lost, especially at the lower levels of government, as simple tasks such as organizing documents and searching for data are expected to be replaced by AI.

In a Governing survey of US state and local government employees, Eggers et al. (2017) noted that 53% of respondents reported difficulty completing their work within a normal workweek (35-40 hours) due to additional paperwork. In addition, the US federal government spends 500 million staff hours on documentation and records-related information each year, costing more than $16 billion, and another 280 million staff hours on procurement and processing information each year, costing $15 billion. Thus, using AI to reduce costs for these simple tasks could lead to a lower tax burden and additional benefits for citizens, which could be positive for citizens who are generally frustrated with government overreach, as they can expect big-government-like services while maintaining a small government. However, stiff resistance is expected from civil service organizations that will inevitably have to accept workforce reductions.

However, the concept of augmentation pushes back against the replacement of labor. Davenport and Kirby (2015) address concerns about AI replacing labor by pointing to the possibility of a collaborative relationship between humans and AI that augments labor through creative problem-solving in collaboration with AI. Mehr (2017) notes that AI may increase new direct and indirect employment in AI development and management. While job losses are a reasonable concern, early AI research has shown that AI performs best in collaboration with humans, so governments that utilize AI should look to augment human work, not reduce it. Hwang (2017) suggests that government officials can create an augmented human-technology relationship by having Govbots take over simple tasks such as decision-making and data entry while they play a more strategic role.

On the other hand, AI policy-making goes beyond repetitive and simple tasks, so it still needs to be improved in its ability to outperform human policymakers, and many are skeptical that AI will replace it. However, the advancement of AI technology could replace high-level officials who have a real impact on policy-making in the long run. Therefore, it is necessary to determine the level of AI adoption and establish a system of cooperation between public officials and AI in order to build a flexible government that benefits citizens by reducing human resources through the introduction of AI while at the same time discouraging resistance from existing public officials.

(6) Problems with data utilization

Data from various sectors of society is needed to supply data, which is the main input for AI policymakingpolicy-making. Mehr (2017) pointed out that many government agencies need more data management capabilities to introduce AI and more data to train and operate AI. However, there are various practical limitations to building such data, and the construction of smart cities, an important infrastructure related to data, should be activated. Through various infrastructures, various data related to urban residents can be accumulated, policy issues can be discovered, and policy decisions can be made. However, even if the infrastructure is built, there are blind spots, and it is impossible to date all policy elements.

On the other hand, AI data utilization may also raise the issue of personal privacy due to using personal information, which has been frequently debated since the establishment of e-government. Using personal information has become important in policy because the state's role has increased in number and complexity. While public services in the past focused on providing non-exclusionary and non-contestable services, today, there is a growing interest in personalized services. However, the issue of personal information utilization inevitably conflicts with the privacy debate, and the 2002 National Education Information System (NEIS) is a representative case of informatization conflict in Korea (Seo & Myeong, 2014).[05] However, if the existing NEIS was limited to education administration and computerized existing information, the scope of personal information required for AI policymakingpolicy-making is wide. Of course, there is a technical basis to ensure that individuals cannot be identified even if the data is utilized. However, the amount of information that needs to be provided for policymakingpolicy-making will remain the same. Mehr (2017: 13) suggests that citizens should be able to trust the AI systems that interact with them and know how their information is being used. Governments should be transparent about data collection and give citizens the option to give informed consent when their data is used. To avoid the privacy debate, they recommend governments utilize the information they already have on citizens.

However, as already mentioned, the government's existing personal data is insufficient for policymakingpolicy-making due to limitations such as comprehensiveness and real-time responsiveness. Therefore, it is necessary to seek the public's cooperation in collecting data for AI policymakingpolicy-making, which is expected to be difficult given the prevalence of online personal information leaks in both the public and private sectors. For example, using personal information to track movements in the wake of COVID-19 has positive aspects, such as rapid quarantine response, and negative aspects, such as privacy invasion and personal control. One of the main causes of the existing NEIS situation is the lack of communication with stakeholders about the NEIS, which requires strengthening the right to self-determination of personal information and public participation in policy AI systems.

---

05   The main parties to the NEIS conflict were the Ministry of Education and the National Teachers' Union, with the Ministry of Education emphasizing administrative efficiency, reducing teachers' workload, and improving the quality of public services in the frame of benefits. In contrast, the National Teachers' Union emphasized Korea's version of Big Brother, electronic control, and totalitarianism in the frame of losses and risks. It raised concerns about the misuse of information and security vulnerabilities caused by the NEIS (Seo & Myeong, 2014).

For AI policymakingpolicy-making to succeed, the image of a transparent and trustworthy government must be established beforehand.

6. Direction of AI Administration and Policy

1) AI Public Evaluation Model

The TAM-DEF framework is evaluated with scores for diversity and equity, privacy, and ethics.

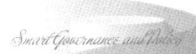

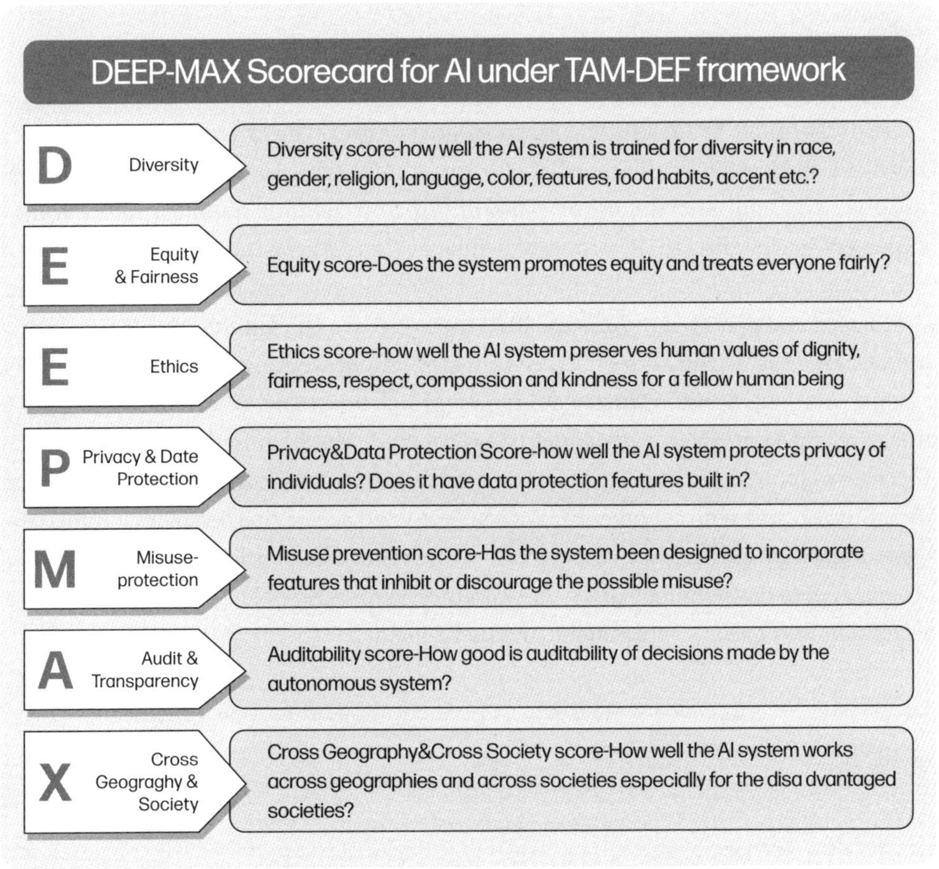

DEEP-MAX Scorecard for AI under TAM-DEF framework

D	Diversity	Diversity score-how well the AI system is trained for diversity in race, gender, religion, language, color, features, food habits, accent etc.?
E	Equity & Fairness	Equity score-Does the system promotes equity and treats everyone fairly?
E	Ethics	Ethics score-how well the AI system preserves human values of dignity, fairness, respect, compassion and kindness for a fellow human being
P	Privacy & Date Protection	Privacy&Data Protection Score-how well the AI system protects privacy of individuals? Does it have data protection features built in?
M	Misuse-protection	Misuse prevention score-Has the system been designed to incorporate features that inhibit or discourage the possible misuse?
A	Audit & Transparency	Auditability score-How good is auditability of decisions made by the autonomous system?
X	Cross Geograghy & Society	Cross Geography&Cross Society score-How well the AI system works across geographies and across societies especially for the disa dvantaged societies?

Source: YK Dwivedi et al.

[Figure 6-4] TAM-DEF AI Framework

- Diversity (D): The AI system's level of learning about race, gender, religion, language, color, features, dietary habits, accent
- Equity/Equity (E): Level of compliance with equity and fairness
- Ethics (E): A level of recognition of the dignity, fairness, respect, compassion, and kindness of human beings in recognition of their worth.
- Privacy/Data Protection (P): Level of personal privacy, data protection
- Misuse protection (M): The ability to inhibit or suppress the potential for misuse and whether anti-abuse safeguards are built into the system.
- Audit/Transparency (A): Level of automated auditing and decision-making systems
- Social Inclusion (X): The lack of discrimination based on geography and social class and the level of inclusion, especially for marginalized groups.

2) AI Legal Framework

On December 24, 2020, the Korean government held the National Issues Coordination Meeting, a joint meeting of relevant ministries, to announce the 'Artificial Intelligence Legal and Regulatory Roadmap' and decided each ministry would implement it according to the proposed schedule. Considering the global trends related to artificial intelligence, the 'Artificial Intelligence Legislation and Regulation Team' was formed and operated in January 2020 to strengthen the foundation for promoting and utilizing the artificial intelligence industry and preventing its dysfunction. After consultation with each ministry, 30 major promotion tasks were identified, and a proactive and comprehensive roadmap was prepared. The 30 initiatives are divided into AI common foundation and AI utilization and diffusion. In the AI common foundation area, 17 legal system development tasks are promoted across five fields, including data, algorithms, legal personality, responsibility, and ethics. In AI utilization and diffusion, 13 legal system development tasks are promoted across five fields: healthcare, finance, public administration, employment, and inclusion.

<Table 6-4> List of AI Legal Systems

Fields	What's next for AI legislation?	Relevant ministries
AI common ground areas		
Data	Enactment of the Basic Law for the Promotion of the Data Industry	Department of Science and Technology

	Establishing a legal basis for data stewardship	Department of Science and Technology - Privacy Commissioner
	Helping you leverage data for individual industries and needs	Ministry of Industry and Commerce
	Introducing a right to object to decisions that rely on automated personal data processing	Privacy
	Permission to use your work for data mining	Stylistics
	Regulatory Review of Combining Procedures and Pseudonymization Safeguards	Privacy
	Establish disciplinary measures against monopolization and unfair use of data.	Patent Office-Fair Trade Commission
Algorithms	Create an environment for autonomous algorithm management and oversight	Department of Science and Technology
	Establishing algorithmic disclosure standards to protect your trade secrets	Ministry of Science and ICT - KFTC
	Ensure fairness and transparency in the operation of platform algorithms	KFTC - Ministry of Science and ICT
Legal entity	Establishing rights to AI creations	Ministry of Culture - Patent Office
	Establishing a legal entity for AI	Department of Justice - Department of Science and Technology
Responsibilities	Clarifying the effect of contracts with AI	Ministry of Science and Technology - Ministry of Justice
	Establishing damages for AI's behavior	Department of Justice - FTC
	Diversifying sanctions for crimes involving AI	Department of Science and Technology
Ethics	Setting ethical standards for AI	Department of Science and Technology
	Develop an AI ethics training curriculum.	Ministry of Science and Technology - Ministry of Education

Artificial Intelligence Utilization-Proliferation Areas		
Medical	Developing international standards (guidelines) for AI medical devices	Food and Drug Administration
	Improving health insurance coverage for AI-enabled medical practices	Department of Human Services
Finance	Strengthened e-financial incident response system based on abnormal financial transaction detection and blocking system	Financial Services Commission
	Enhancing the security of payment and authentication services	Department of Science and Technology - Financial Services Commission
Administration	Laying the groundwork for automated administration with artificial intelligence	Legal
	Establish a redress process for AI administration	Legislation - Authority
	Bring transparency to AI administration.	Legal
Hire	Expanding employment insurance to address the changing job landscape	Ministry of Employment, Labor and Industry
	Protecting platform workers and exploring future-proofing safety and health management	Department of Labor
Inclusion	Lay the foundation for a digital inclusion policy	Department of Science and Technology
	Setting standards for AI technology in high-risk areas	Department of Science and Technology
	Introducing AI guardianship of the person	Department of Justice - Department of Health and Human Services
	Insurance system reforms to handle AI incidents	Ministry of Land, Infrastructure and Transport

Source: Joint Ministry of Government Relations, Roadmap for Artificial Intelligence Law, System, and Regulatory Development, 2020.12.24.

<Table 6-5> Top 3 Driving Strategies and Top 10 Tasks for Realizing Trusted AI

Drive strategy	Subtasks	Goals
Creating a Trusted AI Implementation Environment	① Establish a system to secure trust in AI products and services - Develop and disseminate a reliability-based "development guidebook - Develop a reliability "validation scheme - Operate a private, voluntary "trustworthiness certification scheme - Consider introducing government certification for high-risk sectors - Private AI Trustworthiness Disclosures ② Support for civilian credibility - Help build civilian trust - Review institutional support, such as prioritizing items for purchase ③ Development of AI reliability source technology - Develop explainable AI techniques - Developing fair AI technologies - Developing robust AI technology	Responsible Use of AI[1] <5th in the World>
Laying the Foundation for Safe AI use	④ Increase data reliability for training - Establish required criteria and validation metrics for each data process - Gaining trust throughout the data for learning (databank) building process - Gain trust in high-risk AI. - Review high-risk AI category settings. - Consider implementing a user trust system. ⑥ Promote AI impact assessment - Create an AI impact assessment plan - Develop customized curriculum by subject and stage ⑦ Improving the system for strengthening trust across society - Establish algorithmic standard management and oversight system guidelines - Changes to platform algorithm legislation - Corporate algorithm disclosure standards and guidelines - Establishment of AI Technology Standards Notice	A trusted Society[2] <10th in the World>

Spreading Healthy AI Awareness across Society	⑧ Strengthen AI ethics education - Develop a general AI ethics framework - Develop customized curriculum by subject and stage	A Safe Cyber Nation[3] <3rd in the World>
	⑨ Prepare subject-specific checklists - Develop and disseminate subject-specific ethics checklists.	
	⑩ Operation of AI ethics policy platform - Run an AI ethics forum - Build and operate a citizen feedback platform	

Source: Joint Government Relations Ministry, Strategy for Realizing Trustworthy Artificial Intelligence, 2021.5.13.
Related metrics: 1) Responsible use of AI (Oxford Insights)
2) Level of trust in government (OECD)
3) World Cybersecurity Index (ITU)

3) AI Policy Research Direction

At this stage, skepticism about AI-driven policy-making is predominant, but the discussion on AI policy-making may continue when AI is embedded in all areas of society. However, a more systematic analysis of the impact of the introduction of AI still needs to be done. In particular, when it comes to dysfunctions such as the dangers of AI, it has not moved beyond the level of popular media, such as science fiction movies. Ryu et al. (2017: 56) point out that it is relatively recent to recognize AI as an actual risk and that most of the research on risk has been conducted by research institutions in developed countries such as the United States and the United Kingdom.

The public sector must be cautious in its adoption because of the broader societal effects. Of course, it is also important to avoid viewing AI as a system with excessive risks, as opponents of the NEIS have done in the past. Therefore, the most important perspective in discussing the introduction of AI is a convergent governance approach (Ryu et al., 2017; Yoon et al., 2018). The discussion of AI adoption has been driven by a technological perspective, which is no different in the major public sectors. Therefore, it is necessary to examine the awareness and demand for AI adoption in organizations other than public sector information organizations and to improve their capabilities to utilize AI. In addition, public organizations should be able to discuss AI and examine its impact from various socio-cultural perspectives, which should be ensured by continuous communication with citizens, businesses, and other beneficiaries of public services. Korea has already experienced social conflicts over introducing a new public sector technology called NEIS in the early 2000s, so it is expected to be easy to cope with this.

As the Luddite movement, which stood for the destruction of machines, failed when British workers in the early 19th century lost their jobs due to the advent of the steam engine, the advancement of technology is historically irresistible. Therefore, as the introduction of artificial intelligence technology in all areas of society becomes a reality, it is necessary to respond to dysfunctions and increase net functions preemptively. AI can be a new alternative to the long-term economic downturn caused by the declining birthrate, aging population, and decline of existing manufacturing industries in Korea and the rise of emerging manufacturing powers such as China. Therefore, it is necessary to offset concerns about introducing AI through a series of step-by-step approaches, starting with introducing AI to enhance national competitiveness, followed by citizen convenience, administrative efficiency, and new forms of policy-making long run. On the other hand, as some argue that basic income should be provided to compensate for the loss of jobs due to the introduction of AI, Korea should approach the introduction of AI as a real policy issue, not as a distant future society.

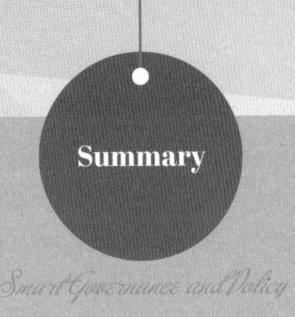

Summary

Smart Governance and Policy

The introduction of AlphaGo by Google's subsidiary Deep Mind in 2016 sparked a social reaction regarding the expansion of artificial intelligence into everyday life. In particular, AlphaGo's appearance sparked discussions in various fields about the role of artificial intelligence in society. In line with this social trend, the potential for AI to be utilized in the public sphere is also increasing. The introduction of new technologies such as ICT in the public sector is representative of the innovation of administrative services due to the introduction of e-government, and e-government, which was initially limited to the introduction of computerized systems to streamline the work of the public sector, will evolve into a digital platform government based on AI in the future with the digital transformation.

Depending on the goal of AI, we can categorize it into four types. The first is narrow AI (ANI) and general AI (AGI), which are divided into two categories. Narrow AI is the research needed to implement systems that behave rationally, such as intelligent software and behavioral robots. AGI is mainly used to implement systems that behave like humans, such as language processing, knowledge representation, automatic reasoning, and Turing tests. There is also a distinction between strong AI and weak AI. Strong AI is a system that thinks like humans and has cognitive structures and neural networks. Weak AI is a system that thinks rationally and has logical reasoning, deduction, and optimization.

Here's what makes AI policy-making different from traditional policy-making. First, AI can realize rational policy-making, which is realizing the best possible outcome by exploring all possible alternatives with sufficient information given the level of resources available for decision-making. Second, AI policy-making can ensure transparency and credibility. Third, AI can bring a more objective perspective to the policy-making process. Fourth, AI can make policy decisions more quickly.

The TAM-DEF framework is evaluated with scores for diversity and equity, privacy, and ethics.
- Diversity (D): The AI system's level of learning about race, gender, religion, language, color, features, dietary habits, accent
- Equity/Equity (E): Level of compliance with equity and fairness
- Ethics (E): A level of recognition of the dignity, fairness, respect, compassion, and kindness of human beings in recognition of their worth.

- Privacy/Data Protection (P): Level of personal privacy, data protection
- Misuse protection (M): The ability to inhibit or suppress the potential for misuse and whether anti-abuse safeguards are built into the system.
- Audit/Transparency (A): Level of automated auditing and decision-making systems
- Social Inclusion (X): The lack of discrimination based on geography and social class and the level of inclusion, especially for marginalized groups.

In the future, we need to proactively respond to the dysfunction of AI and increase its net capabilities. AI can be a new alternative to the long-term economic downturn caused by the declining birthrate, aging population, decline of existing manufacturing industries in Korea, and the rise of emerging manufacturing powers such as China. Therefore, it is necessary to offset concerns about the introduction of AI through a series of step-by-step approaches, starting with the introduction of AI to enhance national competitiveness, followed by citizen convenience, administrative efficiency, and a new form of policy-making that will change the existing democracy in the long run.

Research Questions

1. What is the concept of artificial intelligence, and what are its core technologies?
2. How do you evaluate AI?
3. How is AI policy-making different from traditional policymakingpolicy-making?
4. Describe an example of using artificial intelligence in policy and administration.

Chapter 7

Multi-Dimensional Policy Analysis and Decision-Making Model Based on the Quantum Probability

1. Game Changer: Quantum Theory and Government

As society moves beyond the digital transformation era and into the quantum probability era, which requires multi-dimensional perspectives and analysis, reviewing and reflecting on existing policy-making processes based on classical probability theory is necessary. In addition, the digital-based policy process, which can analyze quickly and accurately through bit (0 and 1) operations and improve its predictive power dramatically, also shows its limitations. Moreover, existing institutional devices and policy analysis evaluation models and analysis methods are no longer useful because of unpredictable social phenomena (e.g., COVID-19), natural and social convergence disasters (e.g., the Fukushima nuclear disaster, climate change such as global warming, low birthrate, and aging), generative artificial intelligence, downstream movie subscriptions (e.g., Netflix), the decline of traditional movie theaters, and the emergence of influencers beyond the influence of existing politicians and celebrities. In addition, Gallup poll results that vary depending on the sample, the collapse of stable party politics, and the failure to predict and respond to various complex disasters in succession have further increased the distrust in government.

Therefore, a multi-dimensional policy decision-making model, beyond linear causality and probabilistic reasoning, is needed to reflect various variables, environments, and human perceptions and behaviors latent in the internal and external environments that are variously connected to society. In particular, power is distributed in the era of governance, where governments, companies, and citizens operate national affairs as cooperative partners. Several evaluation indicators have reached their limits. These include preliminary feasibility, cost-benefit analysis, discount rate, and qualitative evaluation indicators (desirability, feasibility, effectiveness) that do not reflect the intentions, behaviors, and preferences of various stakeholders and actors. Therefore, it is necessary to review and seek alternatives to the existing policy process based on new social phenomena and policy environment in the digital transformation era, future demand forecasting, alternative analysis and selection, and evaluation.

The current administrative system in Korea means a digital government, which implies a government that collects and analyzes information quickly and accurately based on digital platforms to select alternatives and provide personalized services in advance. In this series of processes and administrative services, the most critical thing to assume is the transparency of the policy process. Transparent and feasible policy is a policy value or orientation that is discussed in various aspects, such as the unrestricted disclosure of information and data related to decision-making processes and procedures, the government's efforts to resolve or alleviate information asymmetry between the government and the people, and the mutual sharing of accurate and prompt information between the government and customers and stakeholders to expand the range of rational choices.

International organizations, such as the OECD and private organizations, agree that digital technology can enhance policy transparency and reduce government corruption. In particular, in implementing e-government projects, the transparency of the policy process can be improved through advances in the appropriate legal system and business innovation. In Korea, the ePeople (http://epeople.go.kr) of the National Human Rights Commission are examples.

In the digital transformation era, however, governance systems become more necessary. Moreover, as the relationship between the government, the private sector, and the people is transformed into a mutually balanced partnership, equal levels of transparency are required for the government and private companies and people who are the source of data generation. Only through mutual trust and reasonable checks and balances between strong social actors can they enjoy equal power levels and hold each other accountable.

Suppose transparency is viewed from these different perspectives. In that case, the assumption that the technological means of digital government, information, and communication technologies (ICTs) will enhance policy transparency may merely be an assumption. Therefore, this paper first introduces the future intelligent government. Second, the limitations of deterministic thinking and quantum theory as an alternative view are presented. Third, the relationship between intelligent government and policy values in terms of ideological background and ICT attributes is examined. Fourth, the multifaceted concept of policy transparency concerning policy values and other conditions is analyzed. Finally, a multi-dimensional policy-making model based on quantum theory is presented by analyzing nuclear power plant issues in Korea.

2. Intelligent Government of the Future Toward Convergence

The government of the future is a government that seeks to maximize the utility of policy objective values such as feasibility, desirability, efficiency, and democracy through the 'visible hand' of data-based policies rather than policies carried out behind closed doors by invisible hands. Hence, it is a government that does not pursue only one social or policy value but pursues multi-dimensional values that reflect the needs and wishes of various stakeholders and groups, even if they are invisible and do not currently express their interests. In other words, a government realizes neo-pluralistic values and ideologies based on transparent disclosure of the policy process.

The future government that can embrace these multi-dimensional values, demands, and environments is predicted to be a multi-dimensional platform government with an open, multilayered platform that enables human, technological, and social systems to achieve negative entropy. While embracing these diverse values and factors involved in the policy-making process, the intelligent government of the future is expected to play the role of a collaborator and enabler, cooperating and supporting the virtuous evolution of social systems and ecosystems with a balance of autonomy and control.

Tables 7-1 and 7-2 summarize the analysis and comparison of the attributes of technologies, such as blockchain, artificial intelligence, and convergence technologies, and their relationship with changes in civilizational paradigms, changes in government structures, and changes in decision-making.

<Table 7-1> Relationship between the Convergence Technology Attribute Value and Policy Value

For what \ For whom	Country/Government	National/Citizen	Government-Private-Citizen Partnerships
Efficiency	A country/government that operates without wasting resources (information symmetry)	Government policies and services that make sense	Governance structures and public platforms that maximize economic utility
Decentralization	Cooperative government with checks and balances	Local economies based on self-regulation and local capacity	Controllable, decentralized sub-platforms that can respond to changing conditions promptly
Reliability (security)	Transparent and fair government	A government that people can trust	Collaborative partnerships built on social capital and trust

Source: Myeong (2023: 230)

<Table 7-2> Civilizational Paradigm Shifts and Government Changes

	Industrial Society	Knowledge & Information Society	Post-Knowledge Information Society	Convergence Society
	System government	E-Government	Smart Government	Intelligent Government
	Web 1.0	Web 2.0	Web 3.0	Web 4.0
	Government-focused	Citizen-centric	Person-centered	Relationship-centric
Accessibility	• Single point of contact (portal)	• One-Stop-Shop • Access through government service intermediaries	• My Gov • Personalized government services portal • Platform-based marketplaces	• We Gov • An inclusive, relationship-oriented AI platform • Platform on top of a platform
Services Delivery Methods	• Provides one-way information	• Provides two-way information	• Provides personalized information	• Provides predictive information

	• Limited disclosure of information • Time and space constraints on services • Supply-oriented services • Electronification of services	• Expanded disclosure • Mobile services • Public-Private Partnerships Services • Creates value for new services	• Transparent disclosure • Creates public services and reproduces added value through social connections • Strengthens the role of government as a collaborative partner • Enhances information management and forecasting capabilities with an intelligent service delivery system	• Provides trusted, targeted information • Emotional intelligence services • Relationally driven data management
ICT Ecosystem	• Government-led/ Outsourcing	• Government-led/ outsourced	• Collaborative government, business, and citizen governance and deregulation	• Autonomy-based controls with governance as the foundation
Channels	• Wired Internet	• Wired and wireless internet	• Wired and wireless mobile device integration (channel integration)	• Converged online and offline channels (omnichannel)
Business Integration	• Processing by unit of work	• Process integration (public-private collaboration)	• Service integration	• Service Convergence
Underlying Technology	• Browser Web Saves	• Broadband • Rich Link/ Content Models	• Semantic technologies • Sensor network	• Blockchain • Artificial Intelligence (AI) • Quantum computing
Decision making	• Political elites, top-level bureaucrats • Top-down budget allocation	• Government, professionals, and experts • Centralized performance evaluation and budget allocation	• Individuals, citizens, NGOs, and communities • Focus on big data, fact-based problem solving	• Data-driven collective intelligence • probabilistic prediction
Central Government	• Initiator	• Contractor	• Mediator	• Cooperator
Local Government	• Builds a system that relies on grants and Enforcement	• Establishment of an e-government business-based portal	• Provides personalized services based on local demand	• Provides platform-based individual/ community support data services

Civic roles	• Information service users	• Partial engagement and policy discussions	• Active engagement and e-voting	• Realizing social value through rational choices and self-discipline

Source: Myeong (2023: 231), redacted.

The intelligent government of the future is a self-managing government. It is more than a mechanical e-government that has been trying to increase productivity and transparency based on computing systems in the past; it also means a platform-type government that makes optimal policy decisions and acts based on highly intelligent ICTs and accurate data collection and analysis. On the other hand, digital government, which is currently being promoted as the next generation of e-government along with the Fourth Industrial Revolution, may be limited to a functional government centered on computational intelligence based on algorithms without emotions. Administrative reforms without philosophical reflection on the traditions, the needs of the people, social changes, and the trends of the times, such as the sharing economy, neo-pluralism, and communitarianism, and without a deliberative process that enables the formation of macro discourse and rational choices, will lead to a repetition of the vicious cycle of bureaucratic control, such as the traditional e-government in the past. The intelligent future government goes beyond the level of science to an artistic level of intelligence that can identify the hearts and needs of the people and respond on time. Such a government is an empathetic government that operates with a system of ethical values, caring, and beliefs beyond a highly intelligent government.

3. Limitations and Alternatives to the Deterministic Approach

Since the emergence of the information society, research on digital government (e-government) started from various discussions from the perspective of new paradigms, such as knowledge society, intelligent society, smart society, and intelligent information society, due to the development of ICTs. In particular, the view of the information society was based mainly on a deterministic perspective. Nevertheless, the existing deterministic approach has reached its limits with convergence technologies, such as artificial intelligence (AI), blockchain, Internet of Things (IoT), and big data.

Therefore, an alternative theoretical and analytical model to deterministic perspective theories based on probability estimation of correlation and causality through experimental observation is needed.

1) Limitations of the Deterministic Approach

Although the determinant perspective has merit as an ideal type, it needs to address the problem of narrow-mindedness, emphasizing only one aspect. First, social determinists acknowledge the importance of technological progress but tend to underestimate its social implications. In addition, technological determinists tend to overstate the extent to which technological progress qualitatively changes the social structure. Both of these perspectives suffer from the problem that they discuss social phenomena in a linear relationship with the real world, where cause and effect can be observed. Social paradigm shifts do not just occur spontaneously. Moreover, the new society needs to change the structural properties of society immediately. The problem with traditional deterministic perspectives and theories is as follows.

First, it is unreasonable to assume a priori that fundamental changes in social structure accompany superficial institutional changes or technological advancements. Economic idealism and technological determinism lie behind this dichotomy.

The second problem with deterministic thinking is that it is based on a historical, linear, and mechanistic interpretation. ICT adoption in the government does not automatically determine the level of development of all countries. As some futurists argue, technological innovation is not applied evolutionarily to all societies through linear extrapolation. It manifests in reality by meditating on specific societies' political and structural processes. Therefore, it needs to be reinterpreted from a comparative and historical perspective. In other words, the meaning should be reinterpreted through political and structural analysis of a particular society.

2) The Problem with Bounded Rationality

In psychology, the classical rational decision-making model assumes that the decision-maker comprehensively defines the problem, understands all possible alternatives and consequences, evaluates all available options, and selects the best course of action (e.g., Anderson, 1991; March 1997; Simon, 1979). The model also assumes that all probability calculations are performed consistently with the prescriptions of classical probability (CP) theory. The connection between rationality and CP theory can be justified by probabilistic axiomatizations, such as the Dutch Book Argument (e.g., Howson & Urbach, 1993), which shows that CP reasoning is consistent in a certain formal sense (an individual's rational beliefs follow probability axioms and do not make damaging choices) (Oaksford & Chater, 2009; Tenenbaum et al., 2011). Nevertheless, many researchers have questioned the relevance of classical rational models and CP theory in modeling human decision-making, particularly in applied decision-making contexts (e.g., see Wakker, 2010, for a discussion of the debate around risk).

In these cases, decision-makers often need more cognitive resources and face an uncertain, complex environment beyond the assumptions and manipulations of laboratory-based decision-making tasks. As a result, decision-makers operate within the confines of "bounded rationality," often "settling" (Simon 1955: 112-113) for making appropriate decisions and adapting their heuristics and environment (e.g., Gigerenzer & Todd, 1999; Gigerenzer, 1991; Klein, 1998). Moreover, decision-makers working in complex and often emotionally charged organizational systems are not free from political influence in their decision-making, and they need to respond to the demands of multiple stakeholders. Hence, they rely on classical (e.g., Cyert & March, 1963; March & Simon, 1958; Pfeffer, 1981) rationality to avoid unnecessary explanations and present principled outcomes, leaving uncertainty satisfactory. For this reason, many researchers are still attracted to cognitive modeling based on classical rational probabilistic reasoning principles despite the evidence that modeling approaches based on heuristics and biases may have higher explanatory value in many real-world situations (e.g., Oaksford & Chater, 2009).

3) Alternative View of Deterministic Thinking

The problem of deterministic thinking in the existing and intelligent information society can be seen in the same way as the problem of the existing view of e-government. Therefore, for a more informed discussion of e-government and, more recently, digital government, it is desirable to interpret the development of IT and changes in government structure as interacting with each other in different developmental processes instead of discussing them along the same lines. Hence, it is better to consult the multi-dimensional system from the perspective of articulating various internal and external factors and government structures that appear in the changes of the information society, knowledge society, and intelligent information society. In this context, the following approaches to social change, such as the "generative perspective" and "quantum perspective," can be an alternative to overcoming the limitations of conventional deterministic thinking.

Two causal perspectives have dominated approaches to explaining the development of IT, the emergence of the intelligent information society, and the resulting changes in public behavior. An alternative approach is a generative perspective, which views the hypothetical relationship between antecedents and outcomes in two ways: deviation theory (or causal determinism) and process theory (or generativity) (Marcus and Robey 1988: 586) and, more recently, quantum theory.

<Table 7-3> Logical Structure

	Deviation Theory (Variance Theory)	Course Theory (Process Theory)	Quantum theory (Quantum theory)
Role of time	None (at one point in time)	Time on a continuum	Concurrency (list of events) (Simultaneous existence of past, present, and future)
Definition.	Cause is a necessary and sufficient condition for an effect.	The cause is just a requirement of the process; Opportunities and events play a crucial role	Uncertainty of results Probabilistically inferring outcomes (locations) only from observations
Assumptions	Necessary and sufficient conditions always result in an outcome	(even if certain conditions are met). Results do not necessarily appear.	(even if certain conditions are met). Results are not guaranteed but can be calculated probabilistically.
Logical structure	X, then Y; if more X, then more Y.	If it is not X, then it is not Y, but if it is more X, it is not more Y.	If it is not X, then it is not Y, but if it is more X, then it is more Y, probabilistically.

Source: Marcus and Robey (1988: 590), reprinted.

4) Variance Theory or Causal Determinism

This theory suggests that clear causal laws predict and explain cause and effect. Technological and social structure determinism approaches to the information society fall under deviation theory. The former considers IT to be causing changes in organizations and institutions. At the same time, the latter see digital technologies as being selected according to the information needs of organizations, cultures, and nations. Nevertheless, they are the same in that they see effects caused by technological or social events.

5) Generative or Process Theory

The generative perspective views cause and effect as unclear or interactive. Here, the application of IT continues to change the interrelationship between IT and human beings, organizations, and society. This iterative process leads to changes in organizations and society that differ from the initial intention. Therefore, it denies causal determinism. Changes in organizations and society occur to some extent in the initial stage through the planned introduction and application of IT by humans, organizations, and society.

Nevertheless, existing institutional, social, and normative conditions slow the pace of change or bring about new aspects of change. Moreover, organizations, societies, and countries seek innovations and find more appropriate ICTs through this iterative learning process (Orlikowski, 1995). On the other hand, while deviation theory or causal determinism can lead to problems with deterministic thinking, generative or process theory can allow for a more realistic approach.

6) Quantum Theory (QT) as Nondeterminism

Quantum theory includes several concepts used to describe the "states" of particles. The most important of these are superposition and entanglement. Superposition is the idea that a particle can have multiple states simultaneously, while entanglement is the idea that two particles can affect each other, even if they are far apart. Memory, reasoning, and categorization research traditions have long been studied independently in cognitive science. Recent developments, however, have begun to blur the lines between these cognitive processes, particularly in reasoning and categorization. Traditionally, reasoning has been associated with logical and probabilistic rules, while categorization has focused on similarity-based processes. Nevertheless, there is growing recognition that similar cognitive mechanisms may underlie these distinct processes (Oaksford & Chater, 1994; Pothos, 2010; Griffiths et al., 2020; Vantaggiato & Lubell, 2022).

One promising theoretical framework that bridges the gap between reasoning and categorization is applying quantum probability (QP) theory to cognitive modeling. At the beginning of the 20th century, classical physics could not explain the phenomena of light and the microscopic world. To illustrate this, a new physical system, quantum mechanics, emerged to describe the atomic and molecular world. QP theory provides a geometric approach to probability, representing events or questions as subspaces in multi-dimensional Hilbert space. This theoretical framework provides a potential way to understand probabilistic reasoning and similarity processes in cognitive tasks (Tversky & Kahneman, 1983; Pothos et al., 2013).

This paper discusses the concept of a multi-dimensional decision-making model based on the principles of quantum theory using the example "multidimensionality of policy issues in the policy process" as an example. In other words, this study explores how quantum probability theory can be applied to cognitive processes, such as reasoning and categorization, to reveal the underlying cognitive mechanisms.

4. Theoretical Foundations: Quantum Probability (QP) Theory

Quantum probability (QP) theory, a mathematical extension of quantum mechanics, offers a new perspective on probability. In QP theory, probabilities are assigned to events or questions based on the principles derived from quantum mechanics. In quantum mechanics, the square of the wavefunction probabilistically describes the quantum state of a system, and the square of the wavefunction is the probability of finding a physical object at an arbitrary time and location. The main properties of QP theory include incompatibility, interference, superposition, and entanglement. These properties provide a unique framework for understanding the role of probabilistic inference and similarity processes in cognitive tasks (Bruza et al., 2009; Busemeyer et al., 2011).

1) Geometric Representations in Hilbert Space

In QP theory, possibilities or events are represented as subspaces in a multi-dimensional Hilbert space. These subspaces have different dimensions and capture different aspects or features of the cognitive state under consideration. A cognitive state can be calculated as a vector in the Hilbert space, known as a state vector.

Vectors play a fundamental role in describing physics because they conveniently represent various physical quantities with magnitude and direction, such as force, position, and velocity. Physical quantities represented by vectors are called vector quantities. Therefore, the probabilities are calculated by projecting state vectors onto the relevant subspace and computing the square of the length of the projection. This geometric approach to probability allows the modeling of complex cognitive processes with multiple dimensions (Tversky & Kahneman, 1983; Pothos et al., 2013).

2) Incompatibility and Interference

One important aspect of QP theory is the concept of incompatibility, which states that truth values cannot simultaneously be assigned to incompatible possibilities. If one possibility is known with certainty, the other is necessarily uncertain. This property reflects the interference between incompatible events and originates from classical probability theory, where it is possible to generate joint probability distributions for all available alternatives (Pothos, 2010). In QP theory, interference provides a unique perspective on cognitive processes, such as reasoning and decision-making, where consideration of incompatibility is inherent (Busemeyer et al., 2011; Griffiths et al., 2020).

3) Superposition and Entanglement

Superposition and entanglement are two fundamental concepts in quantum mechanics that apply to QP theory. Superposition refers to the ability of a quantum system to exist in multiple states simultaneously. Similarly, in cognitive tasks, a state vector in QP theory can be in a superposition of different subspaces, each representing a unique possibility. Entanglement, however, refers to the phenomenon that the state of one quantum system is intrinsically connected to the state of another, even if they are physically separated. Thus, in the context of cognitive processes, entanglement can capture the dependencies and interactions between different dimensions or features of a mental state (Bruza et al., 2009; Busemeyer et al., 2011; Griffiths et al., 2020).

On the other hand, after discovering through the double-slit experiment that elementary particles, such as light and electrons, have duality depending on the observation, the question of how the macroscopic world is affected by observation (measurement) is explained by 'Schrödinger's cat' experiment. In other words, wave functions describe quantum systems and have a stochastic nature in which the state is not determined until an event called a measurement occurs, i.e., they are in a superposition of states before observation, which can be understood as the

"Schrödinger's cat" thought experiment (Trimmer, 1980; Griffiths et al., 2020). The experiment was a thought experiment, and until the poison and the cat are placed in the box and the cat can be seen in the box, the cat can be said to be in a state of superposition between being alive and dead. Superposition does not mean that the cat is alive and dead, but rather that the state of being alive and dead is unpredictable.

These are the characteristics of quantum mechanics. On the other hand, examining how these characteristics relate to cognitive models and policy-making processes is necessary, which this study aims to explain through quantum cognitive and reasoning models.

4) Linking Reasoning and Categorization: The Quantum Cognition Model

Applying QP theory to cognitive processes has led to the development of quantum cognitive models that provide a new perspective on reasoning and categorization. These models allow for a formal and testable representation of the idea that similarity and inference processes may share common cognitive mechanisms. Utilizing the principles of QP theory, these models can account for context, interference, and order effects in cognitive tasks (Oaksford & Chater, 1994; Pothos et al., 2013; Griffiths et al., 2020). Nevertheless, a limitation of these models is that it needs to be clarified whether they can be explained under environments and systems governed by quantum mechanics.

5. Quantum Probability Model

The quantum reasoning model is a theoretical model that challenges the traditional view that reasoning is based entirely on classical logic or probabilistic rules. The model argues that human reasoning can be understood better by considering the principles of QP theory. For example, instead of relying on logical rules, such as classical inductive reasoning, which involves deductive logic, quantum reasoning models apply the "information maximization principle," which maximizes the use of information at the time of the observation to explain the participants' choices (Oaksford & Chater, 1994).

Quantum reasoning models assume cognitive state vectors represent information or hypotheses relevant to a task. If the cognitive reasoning process in the brain can be described in Hilbert's state space as if it were a wave function in quantum mechanics, then brain reasoning states can be defined as QPs. The state vector is then calculated by projecting onto another subspace corresponding to the relevant features or possibilities. The squared length of the projection gives the probability of the particular feature or possibility under consideration. In particular, quantum reasoning models can be described by quantum decoherence or conjunction error, in which the participants often assign higher probabilities to combinations of events than individual events (Busemeyer et al., 2011). It is the case when the moment of decision arrives, resulting in a completely unexpected choice, such as the choice of a close friend or influencer, an unexpected unity just before election day, or a revelation of personal corruption. Many current electoral and policy errors can be traced back to this type of conflation.

1) Quantum classification model

Quantum categorization models extend existing prototypical and exemplar theories by incorporating the principles from QP theory. These models suggest that similarity judgments, a key categorization aspect, can be understood through quantum probability. While classical theories focus on similarity as a single-valued property, quantum classification models consider similarity multi-dimensional, capturing the interactions and dependencies among dimensions (Pothos et al., 2013).

The quantum classification model assumes that state vectors represent a mental representation of the object or concept under consideration. These state vectors are projected onto different subspaces corresponding to the relevant dimensions to capture the similarity between the object and the prototype or exemplar. The squared length of the projection provides a measure of similarity between the object and the prototype or exemplar. Thus, quantum classification models can account for triangle inequality violations in similarity judgments and capture order effects in classification tasks (Tversky, 1977; Pothos et al., 2013).

2) Ambiguity, Vagueness, and Applications of Multi-dimensional Decision-Making in Quantum Theory

One of the fundamental aspects of decision-making is dealing with ambiguity and vagueness. In classical approaches, ambiguity is often modeled using 'fuzzy logic,' where membership functions specify the degree of belonging to different categories. Quantum decision models, however, have a different interpretation of ambiguity. In a quantum framework, evaluation variables are modeled as two-state systems that allow for the superposition and representation of probabilities through quantum states. This qualitative difference in representing the ambiguity differentiates the quantum decision model from the classical approach. On the other hand, fuzzy logic, similar to quantum theory, also provides a way to deal with ambiguity and vagueness but with distinct differences in interpretation and application. Fuzzy logic operates continuously, assigning the degrees of belonging to categories.

In contrast, quantum logic distinguishes between the state itself and the state after measurement, where probabilities are associated with different outcomes. The measurement process in quantum logic is considered a form of decision-making, with probabilities representing the likelihood of various outcomes. This distinction in interpreting ambiguity distinguishes fuzzy logic from quantum logic (Oaksford & Chater, 1994; Pothos et al., 2013; Griffiths et al., 2020).

Thus, multi-dimensional decision-making models based on quantum theory have various applications in various domains, including cognitive science, psychology, decision-making, and economics. By incorporating principles from quantum theory, these models provide new insights into the underlying cognitive mechanisms involved in complex decision-making tasks (Pothos et al., 2013; Busemeyer et al., 2011).

3) Future Applications and Challenges

Multi-dimensional decision-making models based on quantum theory can improve the understanding of the decision-making process, but there are several challenges and avenues for future research. One major challenge is the empirical validation of the model through experimental studies. Empirical studies are needed to test the model predictions and explore the model's applicability across different decision domains (Pothos et al., 2013). Further research is necessary to examine the neural mechanisms underlying multi-dimensional decision-making models. Although quantum cognitive models do not require a quantum brain, understanding the neural basis of decision-making processes within a quantum framework provides valuable insights into the cognitive processes involved (Busemeyer et al., 2011; Gribbin et al., 2011; Griffiths et al., 2020).

In conclusion, a multi-dimensional decision model based on quantum theory shows promise as a suitable model for understanding the cognitive processes underlying complex decision-making tasks. By incorporating the principles of quantum probability theory, the model captures the multi-dimensional nature of decision-making and provides a framework for examining context, interference, and order effects. These multi-dimensional decision models can be applied to various fields, including cognitive science, psychology, economics, and finance. Nevertheless, before these studies can be generalized, the reliability of the measurement instruments, including the operationalization of variables and construct validity, must be verified based on the theoretical model, which has been validated in studies in various fields. Future research should focus on empirical validation and explore the neural mechanisms of a model to enhance the understanding of the decision-making process further (Bruza et al., 2009; Busemeyer et al., 2011). Combining insights from reasoning models, categorization models, and quantum probability theory, the multi-dimensional decision-making model can provide a comprehensive and multifaceted analytical framework for studying decision-making processes.

6. Quantum Approach: Rethinking the Relationship between Government and Transparency in Policy Process

1) Policy Values and Transparency

Policy transparency will be necessary to make "the right decision" at an acceptable level to both government and the citizens because good decisions require more communication and exchange of information (Yates, 1981). On the other hand, the correct decision can be viewed in terms of its relationship to efficiency, effectiveness, and responsiveness, similar to the governance model.

First, it is the relationship between policy transparency and efficiency. From an efficiency perspective, policy transparency means that all data and information related to organizational goals and measures should be publicly available in a measurable and objective evaluation. Therefore, bureaucracies should continuously monitor consumer behavior and adjust their practices to be more efficient. Regarding e-bidding and e-taxation, it can be assumed that "the more quickly and accurately the data and information released or used, the higher the level of transparency of the policy." Nevertheless, this is a provisional assumption based on an idealized model for relationship discovery.

Second, it is the relationship between policy transparency and effectiveness. Effectiveness is a value that generally asks whether an organization achieves its goals and includes more qualitative goals and measures than efficiency. As mentioned in bounded rationality, public organizations often choose a satisfactory compromise alternative rather than an economic and rational choice because of the influence of internal and external variables such as organizational structure, role relationships among organizational members, and conflict and negotiation processes among stakeholders (March and Simon, 1958; Simon, 1965). In this case, there is a gap between the level of service expected by bureaucrats, citizens, and external stakeholdersand the actual level of service or the level anticipated by internal organizational members (Feller and Menzel, 1977). Therefore, the bureaucrats, who are the internal members, should be in constant dialogue with their clients and respond to the changes in their needs and preferences.

Furthermore, external clients need to participate more actively in decision-making. Nevertheless, the bureaucrats are responding more actively to their needs and preferences through the information exchange channels of the intelligent government. From this perspective, it can be assumed that "the more efforts the bureaucracy makes in a dialog to reduce the gap in mutual expectations as a reactor, the higher the level of policy transparency will be."

Third, there is the relationship between policy transparency and responsiveness. Here, responsiveness means citizens can actively intervene in decision-making and influence the outcome. In this case, the bureaucracy has a hefty responsibility, and it may be difficult for the government to perform its tasks under a more advanced and decentralized communication system. Therefore, the bureaucrat's role as a moderator must mediate between the positions and preferences of various stakeholders to achieve a more or less feasible alternative (Yates, 1981). In addition, it is necessary to clarify the goals and values of the policy in the public forum, and mediation skills, along with a high degree of expertise, are required to build consensus among interest groups. At this point, it can be assumed that "as the level of mediating ability of bureaucrats increases, the level of policy transparency will increase." Nevertheless, quantum theory-based probability reasoning is needed to manipulate the level of mediating ability for expectation differences between bureaucrats, citizens, and stakeholders with different needs and situations.

2) Conditions for Policy Transparency and Engagement Issues

Table 7-4 categorizes the relationship between policy transparency and related values and the roles, conditions, and types of participation of bureaucrats and citizens in securing policy transparency. It is an analytical distinction, and there may be mixed or exceptional cases in practice.

<Table 7-4> Conditions for Securing Policy Transparency and Their Relationship with Values

Values	Role of Bureaucrat	Role of Citizen	Conditions for Transparency	Engagement Types	Expected Backfires
Efficiency	Provider (adjustor)	Consumer (consumer)	• Fast • Accurate knowledge & information	Select (choice)	• Quasi-optimization under non-market economies
Effectiveness	Responder (reactor)	Customer (client)	• Active interaction	Conversations (dialogue)	• Information asymmetry
Responsiveness	Moderator	Active participant	• Engagement Mechanisms Settling	intervention	Fragmentation
Two-Sided Value (Quantum Value) = [Efficiency, Effectiveness, Responsiveness] + New Value Expression	Observers (Observer)	Active watchers (active surveillant)	• constant communication • Close Data - Information Sharing • Recognize interactions between internal and external environmental factors	Immersion (immersion)	• AI, Machine Learning Overdependence • Simulation dependencies

The first situation can be characterized as a rational or market model approach. The problem is that there is a significant non-market economy in the public sector, and the circumstances and patterns of individual choice of specific consumer goods are different from the circumstances and patterns of choice in policy-making for public goods and public services. Nevertheless, suppose the impersonality and simplicity of ICTs are emphasized, and administrative transparency is pursued through streamlined administrative transparency and technical-bureaucratic expertise. In that case, it will likely lead to depoliticization, meaning "democracy without politics" (Montin and Elander, 1995). Therefore, participation and policy transparency will likely be high if clear performance management principles and market-economic competition are met.

The second situation is a model that requires policy transparency to reduce the difference in expectations between internal and external groups regarding organizational goals. It is a stretch governance model, as responding flexibly through dialogue channels with citizens and external stakeholders is important. In this case, the conditions for maintaining a high level of policy transparency are, first, the mindset of bureaucrats who want to provide active services, and second, the willingness and ability of citizens to be interested in and participate in government policies with a more mature sense of citizenship.

The third situation corresponds to the participatory model of governance, where bureaucrats and citizens act as co-producers. On the other hand, to achieve this level of policy transparency, participatory mechanisms must be established to ensure that citizens are fully involved in the policy-making process. In addition, citizens should always be politically interested and actively engaged, giving them a certain stake in the process centered on user group leaders. In this case, however, the government and bureaucrats should strive to promote citizen autonomy and leadership and have the ability to mediate various interests. Therefore, if these conditions are met, the distance between bureaucrats and citizens may become more distant and irreconcilable, and the possibility of social information inequality through the exclusive participation and stake exercise of some specific groups can be included.

3) Transparency from a Dualistic Perspective: From Closed 'Control' to Open 'Governance'

Currently, the instrumental values of public administration— legitimacy, democracy, effectiveness, efficiency, political neutrality, and equity—which are presented in public administration textbooks, emphasize the aspect of "control" to ensure the accountability of public administration from the perspective of the public or a perspective outside the government. The higher level of transparency, which has been raised about ICTs or digital government, is also discussed from this control-oriented perspective.

Nevertheless, this control-oriented discussion of transparency has limitations in the context of "governance," which is often applied to discuss the administrative world conceptualized as the information age or e-government. From a control perspective, the information asymmetry between the government and the people is based on the fact that the government has more and more specific information than the people.

The limitations of this control-oriented discussion become clearer when governance is understood in terms of the proper role relationships or appropriate dynamics between state and society, government and business, the third sector, and citizens. From a governance perspective, transparency needs to be balanced in terms of government transparency and civil society (or private sector) transparency, i.e., if the contextual effects, interference effects, and sequencing effects observed in the interaction between markets and civil society, rather than a one-way street, cannot be accounted for, there is the potential to overcome existing government-citizen expectation mismatches, communication distortions, and policy failures. The multi-dimensional decision-making model can fully reflect the multifaceted aspects of transparency because it integrates and evaluates different dimensions or functions when individuals make decisions. In addition, as one of the benefits of converged ICTs, for transparency to be fully realized, the multi-dimensional government-citizen transparency equation must be able to be equated, which means that the current formula for transparency needs to be completed.

Policy transparency is instrumental in achieving responsible government by resolving or alleviating information asymmetries between masters and subjects, administrative insiders, and outsiders. In this respect, transparency is essential from a policy perspective of control and governance. At a more operational level, the following hypothetical questions can be posed.

To what extent will the public trust the transparency of the policy process?

What are the levels and expectations of transparency when transparency is linked to economic efficiency or rationality, which emphasizes customer preferences and choices; effectiveness, which emphasizes achieving policy goals; responsiveness; and feasibility, which emphasizes the positions and preferences of various stakeholders?

7. Example: Empirical Test based on Quantum Probability Model

1) Method and Data

This chapter suggests ways and directions to overcome deterministic thinking in policy transparency by investigating Korea's nuclear power plant issue. This study surveyed graduate students, members of the Korean Association for Policy Analysis and Evaluation (KAPAE), local government officials from administrative offices, and members of the general public from November 17 to December 23, 2023. In the survey, of 140 participants, 139 (99.29%) responded. The survey was conducted online using a Google Forms link. The respondents included 31 undergraduate students taking an e-government course, 23 members of the KAPAE, 79 local government officials from administrative offices, and six members of the general public. Out of the 139 respondents, 88 were male (63.31%) and 49 were female (35.25%); two did not respond (1.44%).

<Table 7-5> Distribution of Respondents by Affiliation

Category of Respondents	Number of Respondents
Undergraduate students	31 (22.30%)
Members of KAPAE	23 (16.55%)
Government officials	79 (56.83%)
General public	6 (4.32%)

Of the 139 respondents, 32 (23.02%), 15 (10.79%), 37 (26.62%), 46 (33.09%), and seven (5.04%) were in their 20s, 30s, 40s, 50s, and 60s, respectively; two (1.44%) did not report their age.

<Table 7-6> Distribution of the Respondents according to the Age Group

Age Group of Respondents	Number of Respondents by Age Group
20s	32 (23.02%)
30s	15 (10.79%)
40s	37 (26.62%)
50s	46 (33.09%)
60s	7 (5.04%)
Not Respond	2 (1.44%)

In the survey, respondents in favor of or against the expansion of nuclear power plants were grouped separately for analysis. In the survey results, 91 people opposed the expansion of nuclear power plants, while 48 supported it.

One hundred and thirty-nine people participated in the survey: 24 stated they had 'no interest in nuclear power plants at all;' 64 indicated they could understand the topic 'if provided with explanatory materials'; five felt they could comprehend 'related materials even without explanations'; one claimed to have 'expert-level knowledge'; and

45 expressed their interest was 'of a political nature.'

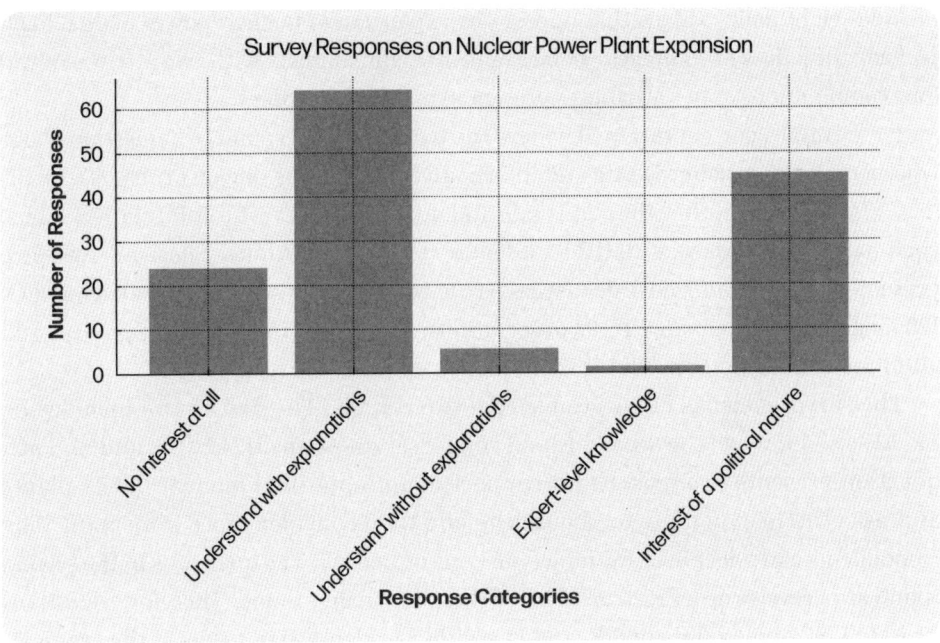

[Figure 7-1] Opinions of Nuclear Power Plant Expansion

2) Survey Questionnaire and Coding

The participants judged the extent to which they believed nuclear policies based on the following policy values: 'the safety of a nuclear power plant' (S), 'the informativeness about a nuclear power plant' (I), 'the economics of a nuclear power plant' (E), and 'the feasibility of a nuclear power plant' (F).

Before the survey, survey participants were in a state of quantum superposition regarding the original question and existed in a social environment and a state of quantum entanglement. The survey process corresponds to measurements, causing the quantum state of each survey participant to collapse, forming their individual opinions. After the survey concludes, the participants enter a new social quantum entanglement state. The participants act autonomously, reinforcing or diminishing the probability of specific views in their quantum states. The entanglement between their opinion quantum state and the quantum environment results in a collapsed state with altered quantum states in the second survey round, leading them to express their views.

Each participant judges 16 different nuclear policies. One stimulus type contains eight examples that favor the expansion of nuclear power plants, and another includes eight policy values that oppose the expansion of nuclear power plants. Each participant judges each nuclear policy value in eight contexts with two attributes and four combinations of two attributes presented in different orders.

For example, one context is SI, where the participants respond to a question about whether a nuclear policy is safe and informative by choosing one of YY, YN, NY, or NN (e.g., YN means yes if they think it is safe and no if they believe it is informative). Thus, each participant answers 16 (PT) × 8 (context) = 128 questions. These answers are presented in a randomized order across participants. This results in 139 participants X 128 judgments per person = 17,792 observations. Significant individual differences and all subsequent analyses are made at the personal level of the study.

The survey consists of questions from two rounds. The first round includes IS, SE, EF, and FI, while the second round comprises questions IF, FE, ES, and SI. Each question presents two reasons for supporting (or opposing) nuclear power plants and asks the respondents to choose the one they consider more important. The respondents can select both examples, just one or neither. The questions in the second round are a reverse order restructuring of those in the first round. Therefore, questions IS and SI, SE and ES, EF and FE, and FI and IF are identical in terms of the examples provided but differ in the order of presentation.

Based on the matching results, the following provides the response rates for opinions favoring increasing the share of nuclear power plants. The notation for the safety and economics of a nuclear power plant is SE. This notation is used in the table below: 0 is coded as NN, 1 is coded as NY, 2 is coded as YN, and 3 is coded as YY.

The chi-square test of independence was used to test the significance of the differences in the responses between the first and second rounds of surveys. The chi-square test is a statistical method used to determine if two categorical variables are correlated or independent of each other (Nevill, 2002)

The formula for calculating the chi-square (χ^2) statistic is

$$X^2 = \sum \frac{(O_i - E_i)^2}{E_i}$$

O_i: the observed frequency in each category or cell.

E_i: the expected frequency in each category or cell, calculated based on the hypothesis being tested.

<Table 7-7> Response Rate for the Opinions in Favoring the Expansion of Nuclear Power Plants

	NN	NY	YN	YY
Round1				
IS	*0.021*	0.5	0.271	*0.208*
SE	0	0.396	0.333	*0.271*
EF	0.042	0.188	0.688	0.083
FI	0.042	*0.375*	0.5	0.083
Round2				
SI	*0.104*	0.479	0.25	*0.167*
ES	0.083	0.417	0.313	*0.188*
FE	0.083	0.208	0.688	0.021
IF	0.083	*0.271*	0.563	0.083

<Table 7-8> Response Rate for the Opinions Opposing the Expansion of Nuclear Power Plants

	NN	NY	YN	YY
Round1				
IS	0.044	*0.637*	0.253	0.066
SE	0.066	*0.791*	0.099	0.044
EF	*0.143*	*0.418*	0.407	0.033
FI	0.099	*0.286*	*0.560*	0.055
Round2				
SI	0.088	*0.615*	0.375	0.099
ES	0.066	*0.813*	0.055	0.066
FE	*0.187*	*0.363*	0.418	0.033
IF	0.110	*0.231*	*0.626*	0.033

8. Policy Suggestions

The multifaceted concept of policy transparency was analyzed, including policy value and other conditions. Finally, means and directions were suggested to overcome deterministic thinking in the policy agenda by investigating Korea's nuclear power plant issue.

It attempted to raise the following issues. First, to improve the effectiveness of policies, it is necessary to identify the actual policy needs accurately through a series of interaction, correction, and recalibration processes in the policy process. Therefore, it is essential to introduce the concept of quantum theory and a multi-dimensional decision-making model that approaches variables, such as norms, institutions, and technology, in a situational context by breaking away from the existing deterministic view. Second, it is necessary to conduct multi-dimensional research on various forms of bloggers, influencers, and collective intelligence (e.g., Instagram, Facebook, Threads, and Kakao Talk) that exert influence through policy promotion, public opinion polls, and social media in the process of deriving a multi-dimensional policy agenda and exploring and analyzing alternatives. Finally, accurate information and data cannot be accumulated if transparency in the policy process is not guaranteed, and the level of integrity and reliability of data decreases. Accordingly, reviewing the policy input process and designing an intelligent government that considers these multi-dimensional analysis levels, social variables, and interchange processes is necessary. A virtuous policy process must be established through data connection and artificial intelligence to increase government credibility and policy efficacy. It is hoped that future studies will present theories, analytical models, and verification processes that can be generalized to develop more multi-dimensional and reality-compatible policies by attempting to conceptualize and manipulate them from various perspectives, away from the existing probabilistic reasoning and technological determinism that only targets visible observations and social phenomena.

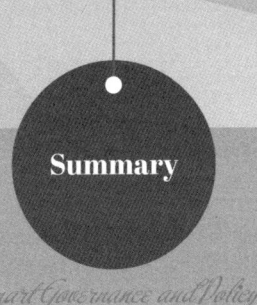

Summary

Smart Governance and Policy

1. Negative entropy (=negentropy, entropy) The opposite of entropy, an increase in negative entropy, means that the system maintains law and order and requires more information. From an organizational perspective, entropy is the tendency of a system to self-extinguish, decay, and cause chaos, disorder, and disintegration. Therefore, organizations that aim for negative entropy make active efforts, such as challenging strategies and changing the existing environment, to prevent the organization from disintegrating and disappearing. Examples include the financial, real name system, Samsung's semiconductor business, and the recent challenges of ChetGPT and Tesla.
2. In physical quantum mechanics, a vector in Hilbert space represents the state of a dynamical system. Operators acting on this vector represent physical quantities such as position and momentum. The state vector changes with time under the action of an energy operator called the Hamiltonian, and the wave function represents the state vector.
3. Entanglement theory offers another view of the observer theory. In contrast to the previous 1-2-1 argument, which states that the universe exists because the observer exists, the disconnection theory states that the observer's consciousness does not affect reality because the interaction occurs through the external environment. Hence, the object does not exist because it is observed but because the individual and the object have interacted countless times without the individual's knowledge, and both can exist. It can be seen as a theory defeating the superiority of human intellect (Philip et al., 2006).
4. Seunghwan Myeong, (2006). "Limitations of deterministic thinking in e-government research and ways to overcome them: Focusing on administrative transparency," Information Policy, 13(1): 100-115. it is reprinted with permission.
5. Peters (1996) classified governance into four models: the market model, which emphasizes competitiveness and decentralization of governmental organizations; the participation model, which emphasizes democratic participation, including citizen participation and participation at lower levels of the organization; the flexibility model, which emphasizes organizational structure for flexible response to environmental changes; and the deregulation model, which relaxes internal regulations and grants discretion to agencies in charge of actual operations.
6. It includes external administrative bodies (legislative, judicial, higher authorities), local and regional government agencies, and private organizations (suppliers, advisory bodies, professional associations, broadcast media).

Smart Governance and Policy

Meta-Government Possibilities and Policy Suggestions

1. What is a Metaverse?

1) Concepts

Metaverse is a synthesis of 'meta,' which means fictional and abstract, and 'universe,' which means the real world and refers to a three-dimensional virtual world. Therefore, the 'metaverse,' which has expanded from the existing virtual reality and brought the virtual world of the Internet closer to the real world, will become the keyword of the IT industry in the future (Maeil et al.). In other words, it is to connect and integrate virtual and real reality that have remained in cyberspace. In the metaverse world, the distinction between online and offline disappears, and all human economic activities are expanded beyond the earth like outer space, and human imagination is no longer a fantasy but a reality.

2) Necessity

Market research firm Strategic Analytics (SA) predicts that the global market for metaverse-related industries will reach 520 trillion won in 2025 (Source: Kookmin Ilbo), and Korea's Ministry of SMEs is supporting it in conjunction with the three-stage Unicorn Growth Program.

- **It is imperative to establish a PPP-based meta-government system.** This system will engage a diverse range of stakeholders to develop demand-driven public services, policies, and business models. The need for such a system is pressing, and its implementation will be a significant step towards a more efficient and inclusive governance structure.
- Samsung, LG, and others are building strong hardware-based public infrastructure, but software-based infrastructure could be stronger.

- Government's cross-government digital platformRefocusing digital transformation governance to drive government
- Cultivate government digital transformation experts/reinforce open public-private partnership platforms and legal frameworks (e.g., digital human legal frameworks, measures to address dysfunctions (e.g., over-immersion), negative regulatory frameworks to revitalize private ecosystems, and security-related regulations and guidelines)

As is well known, the Federal Bureau of Investigation (FBI), the Food and Drug Administration (FDA), NASA's Jet Propulsion Laboratory (JPL), and others are using the cloud to collect and analyze massive amounts of data. The adoption of AWS by U.S. government agencies has created a market. In Asia, the Singapore Land Authority (SLA) uses the cloud for topographic information to launch innovative public services such as food delivery and taxi booking for the local community.

The DTA defines a digital marketplace as "an open platform that brings together government organizations (buyers) and digital service providers (sellers). It is an ecosystem created by public organizations that want to use digital services and companies that provide them. One of the main objectives of the marketplace is to simplify the procurement process so that businesses of all sizes can easily enter into supply contracts with the government. It reflects the government's intention to revitalize an ecosystem centered on small and medium-sized enterprises.

2. Why Meta-Government?

Al: Metaverse is a compound word of 'meta' meaning fiction and abstraction, and 'universe' meaning the real world, which means a three-dimensional virtual world. 'Metaverse', which has expanded from the existing virtual reality and brought the virtual world of the Internet closer to the real world, will become a future IT industry keyword (Maeil et al.).
- In other words, the connection and integration of virtual reality and real reality have remained in cyberspace. The distinction between online and offline has been eliminated, and all human economic activities have expanded beyond the earth to outer space. Human imagination is no longer fantasy but reality.
- The dynamite that is BTS, the global idol group you are so proud of, has just been announced in a metaverse-based online space. Surprisingly, the announcement was made in a social space run by an online game company. Members who were playing the game stopped playing for a while and joined the social space to watch the dynamite for the first time, listen to BTS's new song at their respective game

locations, and enjoy the party.

3. How Do We Drive It?

A1: Therefore, rather than being led by the government, the third-generation platform, the Metaverse platform, should be promoted as a public-private partnership (PPP) in which the government, private sector, and citizens work together to build it.
- The government's role is to build the 5G pilot project early by 25 years, which has been insufficient, and to develop XR national experience metaverse projects such as digital citizen community platforms, my data, NFTs, digital currency, smart medical welfare, and smart education.

A2: It is a governance partnership strategy that involves the government, private sector, and citizens. It should be linked to the Korean New Deal and the Digital New Deal, which the Moon administration is already promoting to make Korea a SW and HW powerhouse.
- No matter how strong Samsung is in HW, such as semiconductors and home appliances, it is difficult to compete with Apple and Google because Korea's own SW capabilities are lacking. Even the world's No. 1 e-government is an application service. The software and major equipment are all foreign-made.
- To recap, the meta-government strategy is to become a software innovation powerhouse by subscribing to (leasing) private platform software Saas rather than building it.

4. What Changes are Expected with Meta-Government?

A1: In other words, it will be a government in which everyone in Korea runs together. Moreover, the government will not be dragged along but will be a supporter, helping and caring for people and businesses.

A2: In general, meta-government will raise public awareness of how the country's budget is spent, eliminating practices such as excessive fiscal expenditures, parliamentary memo budgets, and duplicative spending between ministries.
- The United States and the United Kingdom have decentralized systems for financial management entities such as individual ministries and local governments. However, the financial information management system is unified under the Office of Management and Budget (OMB) and the Cabinet Office,

respectively, and financial information is disclosed on a single site. In Korea, on the other hand, central finances are decentralized to the Ministry of Finance's 'Open Finance', 243 local governments to 'Local Finance 365', and education finances to 'Education Finance Alert', resulting in inefficiency and weak accountability.
- If people need to know the national budget, who should do so? National finances and budgets should be handled transparently, and the government should be held accountable.

A3: Additionally, becoming a public-private-people governance meta-government will enable local autonomy and grassroots democracy.
- The biggest advantage of meta-government is that it allows simultaneous sharing of visual, auditory, virtual, and real data.
- An apartment complex in Yeonsu-gu, Incheon, uses the NAVER platform to make joint purchases using the Incheon e-um local currency and to decide major issues through referendums. It is an example of true grassroots democracy and local autonomy.

5. How do you Prepare for Dysfunctions such as Privacy and Vulnerable Populations such as the Elderly?

A1: The Presidential Committee on Digital Transformation, comprised of the private sector and citizens, will always monitor the policy and implementation process.
- Cultivate digital and communicative professionals in the government and strengthen the foundation of open public-private cooperation platforms and legal frameworks (digital human-related legal frameworks, measures to address dysfunctions (over-immersion, literacy), negative regulatory frameworks to revitalize private ecosystems, and security-related regulations and guidelines)

A2: For the vulnerable, especially the elderly, we will strengthen 'digital inclusion' policies to provide online to offline (OTO) access anytime/anywhere and provide a 'meta-national assistant' service where the government is always there to care for them.

A3: To promote social fairness, we will pilot the "Citizen Experience Metaverse Service" in special zones and then spread it nationwide.

- All Koreans can share new activities and experiences without discrimination, and small and medium-sized enterprises will utilize XR for cost-saving productivity innovation, AI/blockchain non-face-to-face youth recruitment, and telecommuting for people with disabilities.

6. Policy Suggestions

- Proposed to <u>establish a Metaverse recruitment system</u> and support <u>for new industries within the Metaverse so that</u> all citizens can easily, quickly, and conveniently find a job and expand employment opportunities for various groups, such as young MZ generation, career breakers, women, people with physical disabilities, and middle-aged retirees.
- Proposed establishing a <u>metaverse global education system</u> in conjunction with domestic and foreign professional and continuing education institutions so that domestic and foreign residents, immigrants, and foreigners can freely learn foreign languages and specialized technical education and develop competencies as global citizens.
- Proposed to build a <u>metaverse medical system</u> that can provide the convenience of medical treatment without space and time constraints and realize smart medical services through smart prescription issuance.
- Proposed to build a <u>metaverse elderly care system that is</u> easy and simple to operate so that no older adult is left behind in an ultra-aging society and the quality of life for the elderly is improved.
- Proposed to build a <u>metaverse creative space to</u> expand creative spaces where cultural artists can actively create so that all citizens can enjoy smart cultural viewing and experience.
- Proposed the development of the <u>Metaverse tourism service field to</u> simulate travel and business itineraries through the Metaverse so that all Koreans can do smart and safe tourism.
- Proposed to establish a Metaverse <u>Neighborhood Association</u> so that anyone in the community can participate in the Metaverse Neighborhood Association and simulate local problems to make transparent, quick, and accurate policy decisions.

<Case study> How Childcare Interrupted Women's Careers and Policy Options

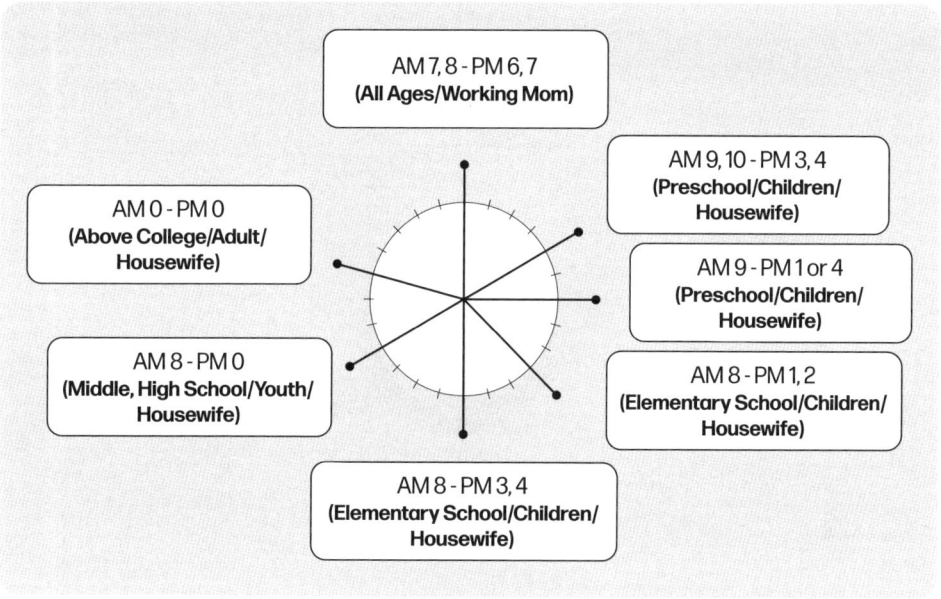

[Mom's Timetable]

- Working mothers must have childcare, school, grandparents, and aides. They must also be available to help with childcare in order to work (required).
- For full-time mothers with sole responsibility for childcare, there may be a career break for approximately 10 years when the child is in upper elementary school and caregiving is minimized (optional).
- Various employment training programs are being conducted for women with career breaks at national institutions and women's workforce development centers in local governments. However, even after completing these programs, only some high-quality jobs allow them to work a limited number of hours while raising children.
- Through the meta-government, it is necessary to consistently promote employment training programs and job linkage systems scattered within each ministry and local government as a national policy and to support the continuous development of new industries through the Metaverse to create quality jobs.

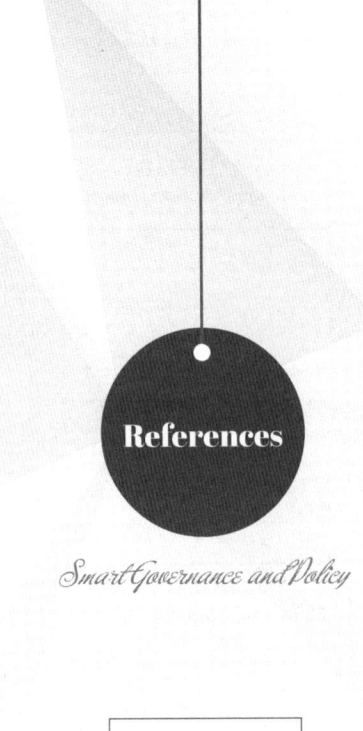

References

Smart Governance and Policy

You can download the references by scanning the QR code below.

Index

achievements of Korea's e-government and digitalization policies / 32
administrative information system / 47
AI legal framework / 196
AI policy-making / 181, 186, 188
AI public evaluation model / 195
artificial intelligence / 98, 174, 175

background of e-government / 25
background on creating an e-government strategy / 27
Barcelona / 156
blockchain / 101

changes in e-government in Korea / 34
characteristics of e-governance / 75
CIO / 160
cloud / 100
contextualized policy-Making models to overcome the limitations of rational models / 61

D7 / 125, 126
definition of e-governance / 65
Deloitte's Six-stage Evolution Model / 23
democratic government / 18
despotic government / 18
developmental stages and characteristics of e-governance / 79
digital government / 20

effective e-governance / 82
effects of e-voting / 74
efficient and responsive government / 17
e-Governance / 20
e-government development model / 23
e-government promotion flow in Korea / 28
e-government roles and Scope / 19
election principles in e-voting / 72

five technical elements of AI / 99
future applications and challenges / 218

generative or process theory / 212
goals of e-government / 37

Helsinki / 155
highlights of e-governance / 67

Industry 4.0 / 96
Internet of Things (IoT) / 103
IT ecosystems / 133

Japan / 39, 40

Korean-style e-government / 35
Korea's top-ranked e-government performance evaluation / 30

logical structure / 212
London / 153

meta-government / 230, 232
MIS / 45, 46, 47, 48, 50, 51, 52
model of the developmental stages of e-government and e-governance / 77

nature and characteristics of e-governance / 70
N-city / 161, 164, 165, 166
neoliberalism / 25
New York / 151

open data policy trends in major countries / 40
open governance / 222

PMIS / 45, 46, 47, 48, 50, 51, 52
possible changes in government organization / 87

quantum classification model / 217
quantum cognition model / 216
quantum probability (QP) theory / 214
quantum probability model / 216, 223
quantum theory (QT) / 213

ROBAMA / 185

six types of e-government / 16, 17
smart city / 141
smart city trends / 147
smart governance / 20, 133
stages of e-governance evolution / 78

success factors for e-government performance / 31
surveillance government / 18

TAM-DEF AI framework / 195
targeted tasks in e-government / 36
technical bureaucratic government / 17
the concept of e-government / 15
the evolution of e-government / 28
the rise of big data / 97
the significance of rational policy making / 54
The United Nations Five-stage Development Model / 23
transparent government to ordinary citizens / 18
types of AI / 176
types of electronic administrative services / 36
types of participation in traditional model and e-governance / 67
types of relationships between actors in e-governance / 82

U-city / 149
United Kingdom / 39, 40
United States / 38, 40

value goals for e-government / 26
vertical functions in PMIS / 52

Web 2.0 / 111
Web 3.0 / 111

About Author

Seunghwan Myeong

Seunghwan Myeong is a Department of Public Administration professor, Inha University (Incheon, Korea). He received his Ph.D. from Syracuse University in 1996. His research interests are digital government and e-governance, information management in public organizations, and information and communication policy. He served as the Korean Association for Policy Analysis and Evaluation (KAPAE) President in 2016 and the Korea Association for Policy Studies (KAPS) in 2018. He currently serves as the Center for Security Convergence and eGovernance (CSCeG) director. His work appeared in the Administration and Society, Korean Journal of Information Policy, Government Information Quarterly, Sustainability, Smart Cities, and others (shmyeong@inha.ac.kr).

Smart Governance and Policy

Korean Experience:
From E-Government to Smart Governance